T h e MASTER BOOK of
MEMES

They Are:

"Minds TOGETHER Creating Entities & Actions."

They Do:

Create Gods, Build Cities & Form NATIONS - THEN

Unleash Devils, Make WAR & DESTROY it ALL!

They Control Everyone – Everything:

They: "Harness our HATE To Destroy!

They: "Harness our LOVE to Work Wonders!

GOD Didn't Do It / Satan Didn't Do It

Ancients called them
"The Invisible Hand"--"Powers & Principalities"

Britt Minshall, D.Min.

Renaissance Institute Press

Renaissance Institute Press
2229 Pelham Ave, Baltimore MD 21213

Paperback ISBN 978-0-57859-949-6

Publisher's Contact
RIPRESS@JUNO.COM
1-844MemeLaw

Web:
www.bookofmemes.com

Editor: Daniel R. Wancowicz, Ph.D. Candidate

Table of Contents

Overview

MEMES although invisible, are the basis of EVERY human social action; social organisms which become physical, material and imbued due to their actionable component.

In 1987 as Dr. Richard Dawkins developed the Theory of MEME Group Dynamics. Simultaneously Social Science was beginning to speak of Culture and Collective Minds as being the same. We use Memes and postulate they are different then culture although both are often tied together and mistakenly taken as the same.

Culture is usually seen as the basis of human society. They mostly arise from unselected circumstances: race, ethnicity, common land and customs. While Memes often arise out of a culture's desire to change the space around it, today many Memes arise when people, perhaps unrelated, form a common bond they use to activate change. MEMES are ACTION COMPONENTS \ CULTURES are BEING COMPONENTS.

Unlike cultures which have no universal default settings (rules) but are tied together by customs, Memes are not tied together by customs or by the habits but by a cause for action adopted by the Memes founders. (chapter SIX).

MEME: A self-replicating cluster of ideas. These visions become the glue that holds Human Organisms together (Families, Religions, Businesses, and Civilizations) able to act as a unit.

Individual Meme Members, according to their depth in the Meme Organization, lose some or all of their self-will and can become a slave to the Meme. (*Howard Bloom, "The Lucifer Principal"*)

MEMES are Human Social Organisms which capture the concept of "cultural transmission of ideas spreading customs and ideas from brain to brain." (Dictionary.com)

A meme (/miːm/ *MEEM*[1][2][3]) is an idea, behavior, or style that spreads from person to person within a culture—often with the aim of conveying a particular phenomenon, theme or meaning represented by the meme.[4] A meme acts as a unit for carrying cultural ideas, symbols, or practices, that can be transmitted from one mind to another through writing, speech, gestures, rituals, or other imitable phenomena with a mimicked theme. Supporters of the concept regard memes as cultural analogues to genes in that they self-replicate, mutate, and respond to selective pressures. (Webster Dictionary)

I//: Baby Memes

STORY BOARD

Three "sweet" twelve-year-old, longtime girlfriends in a Wisconsin suburb went into the woods to play. One hour later, one has been stabbed by the other two - 19 times and is near death:

"¿ What the hell happened?"

Let's start at the bottom and climb the Meme ladder to get a complete understanding of what Memes are and how they are formed. Let's go back to the individual human mind in its infancy. From birth, the mind starts to take in, process and act out on information received as voluminous (large amounts) of data.

The brain begins to attach bits and pieces of experience and knowledge to other bits, forming what psychologists call "Mental Models" (Laurence Gonzales, <u>Everyday Survival</u>, <u>Why Smart People Do Stupid Things</u>. NY: W.W. Norton, 2008; pp 19-23).

Throughout our lives, we process and store information in two different Mental Model addresses or "boxes." (1): "**Belief Boxes**" are tied to our emotional needs. Here, ideas, feelings and hopes are handled. (2): "**Behavior Boxes**" are where dexterity, abilities to act, knowledge of how to work "IT" and needed skills are processed. While working separately, the better these two work in tandem, the more balanced and usually more content a person will be. Those who have the ability to bridge conflicts between these areas are usually the most effective in directing society.

Notes

For infants and toddlers some of these fledgling Memes form as "Belief Boxes" (information gathered anecdotally to cognitively explain this new world): "This woman, who strokes me and feeds me, must 'love' me." With that, the infant begins to develop the love "Belief Box" as the mother's milk encourages a "satisfaction and safety" Mental Model based on the meeting of nutritional needs.

Conversely, if this woman does not feed me, a "distrust" Mental Model Belief Box is generated. These formations will impact the child's behavior all its life.

The baby feels hunger and desires to kill the hunger pain, so: (1) it cries, and if no food comes, (2) it cries again, and on and on until a nipple appears from its mother. (3) The child sucks and a fluid gushes into its mouth resulting in pleasure and comfort. Soon, these occurrences are grouped and, the next thing you know, the infant doesn't have to feel hunger, but, at a certain time of day, it just cries and the series plays out.

As the years progress, this feeding action is repeated and if all goes well a Behavior Box - Mental Model is well established. Now, when the child desires to eat he/she opens this Mental Model, now automatically activated, and, without so much as a thought, goes through certain actions (toasting pop tarts, pouring milk, etc.) and the child is out the door headed for school. At the same time, the child's Belief Box structure is replenished with thoughts of safety, well-being and trust, and the child has reinforced those beliefs with action.

It must be noted here: the 25-year-old person constantly in prison, a high school dropout who has grown in to an angry and dangerous human. This is the child who cried and did not get the milk. These children go home to empty kitchens and empty houses. If no safety Belief Box is developed, a no trusting Behavior Box is opened and you get a career criminal. In this case, the body gets its needs met without the aid of trusted others, therefore the subject learns self- satisfaction with no regard for society.

As time progresses, the growing human repeats the pattern of, first, grouping actions together in Mental Models, then, attaching these together so that the mind does not need to "think out" every action. These are now attached to a person's Belief Box involving his/her concept of the world.

The person then activates Behavior Boxes to carry out needed actions, near-spontaneously.

The down-side to this is our propensity to carry-out every task in this manner.

About 10 years ago, a young man died in a truck accident in Kentucky. His young widow held a funeral and an after reception in their very tiny home, which was soon packed with friends.

The funeral director needed to have the widow sign several important papers, but there was not an inch of space where they could meet. Since necessity is the mother of invention, the two went into the small bathroom and closed the door.

She sat on the closed toilet seat (fully dressed) as the director explained the process. Next, she signed the papers and stood up and just as the man opened the door, OUT OF HABIT, she reached around and – you guessed it – she flushed the toilet.

There stood the two, facing an mouth open, silent, staring crowd. Uh-oh caught!

Last week, I asked a very nice, I'm sure bright, young lady in a McDonald's to *"NOT salt my fries."* She said "yes, of course." She then turned, the buzzer rang and she said *"I'll have your unsalted fries in just a minute."* She lifted the basket out, dumped the fries in the tray and, while seeing me out of the corner of her vision, proceeded to SALT the fries.

I didn't say a thing, but as she handed me the bag, she looked horrified and exclaimed: *"Oh my God, I put salt on them."* I took the bag and told her it was alright.

Both of these stories are examples of how our mind connects normal mundane actions into Mental Models (Behavior Boxes) so we do not have to think out each task.

Notes

Today most would refer these type of acts as "**VISCERAL**" reactions. Twenty-years ago the word meant "a bodily function that is involuntary," such as digested food being pushed through the bowls, into the colon and out the anus, requiring **NO THOUGHT**. This process is 100% involuntary and not to be altered.

But now, the word has expanded to reflect on any human function that is carried out **AUTOMATICALLY**. In the above cases they are tied to other action and then flow freely without thought.

At the end of life, these connections often begin to unravel, thus requiring the elder person to think through these formerly automated tasks and, thereby, they seem to become "befuddled." Often attributed to Alzheimer's disease, in many cases this is simply dementia, as the mind loses its connectedness and unravels.

Now, back to the child. Without these Mental Model - Behavior Boxes this would be his/her typical morning schedule requiring an immense amount of thought: (**OPEN BEHAVIOR BOX**)

1. Arise (scratch head, look out window, face new day disgust, disrobe, check mirror image)
2. Wash (turn on water, get soap, scrub)
3. Urinate (discard underwear, engage toilet, etc.)
4. Brush teeth (get brush, measure paste, add water)
5. Replace brush
6. Evacuate (at least sit on the toilet and pretend)
7. Dress (first underwear, right sock, left sock, shirt, pants)
8. Put on shoes
9. Go to the kitchen
10. Signal mom for food needs
11. Take cereal from shelf - do not replace
12. Get milk from fridge - do not replace - gulp down
13. Race to door
14. Board school bus (**CLOSE BEHAVIOR BOX**)

Even this list is abbreviated. Imagine thinking through all these steps; what a cumbersome process at 7 a.m.! The household couldn't stand the drama. So, Behavior Boxes save the day. Without a word the child learns to open the Behavior Box and acts through its steps, just like a computer loads and performs by downloading the files it needs.

Now the morning looks like this:

1. **OPEN: The "Start the Day" Behavior Box**
2. **CLOSE: That Behavior Box-done/next:**
3. **OPEN: Behavior Box "School."**

To the chagrin of parents, this **MEME-UP** thing (working in Mental Models instead of the items-list mode) does nothing for putting the milk and "stuff" back in the fridge. As a matter of fact, it makes it worse. Once the child closes the Breakfast Mental Model, any unfinished tasks (trash out, fridge closed, yesterday's outfit in basket) are gone, out of sight, out of mind – GONE!

Now you know why your 14-year-old looks at you like an idiot when your screaming: "¿Are you that dumb, to leave a whole gallon of milk out to spoil?" He doesn't have the slightest idea of what you are speaking about.

To illustrate the power of boxing gone bad, look at the tragic outcomes, as recently reported on TV, when a loving father put his two-year-old child in a rear safety seat and droves to work, forgetting to drop the child at daycare. He locks his truck with the child inside and she suffocates. This happens over fifty-times a year and most of us become furious at the parent.

In reality, in most cases the parent was only guilty of automatically closing one Mental Model (Family Behavior Box) and opening another (Work Behavior Box) and no longer had knowledge the child was there (Remember the toilet seat/French fries/milk left out).

Consequently, we have a dead child, a ruined marriage and often a long undeserved prison term.

Armed with this knowledge of Human Behavior, your help tip is: place a sign on your dashboard "**BABY IN BACK** and put a **red window sticker on the driver's side window** with BIG yellow letters **"CHILD!"**

[Fortunately, auto makers are now adding features that will not let you leave a child behind.]

Now, you see how powerful and life changing the forces of Mental Model are. It's how and why the human brain naturally develops the **Meme making process**, which is in effect as we journey through life, using a series of these Mental Models (Belief and Behavior Boxes), grouping life's activities with beliefs. It is the growing child's training and acceptance of this embryonic "Memeing-up process" (creating Behavior and Belief Boxes) that will decide where he/she fits into society.

A person not good at boxing beliefs and action will have a tough time living as an individual, but have a worse experience forming a family or growing educationally through institutional learning. This is why children missing a solid family experience are at such a disadvantage, they have little experience forming their Belief Boxes and using Behavior Boxes. With no experience at family dynamics, they lack trust, order and safety - the very FIRST step of the Memeing process.

We'll speak of it later, but persons with extreme difficulty "Memeing-up" or "in" with others who are better developed in this area often find themselves in a lower-level career or become career military people. Here they adopt the basic Behavior Box of organized military life or a disciplined "thought free" dynamic and let it become their social platform.

It should be noted that, in the United States, prisons offer the same opportunities. Many underdeveloped social personalities (remember the child going to school unfed uncared-for and angry) become attached to prison life and actually reoffend to get off the streets into the safety of the prison Meme (substitute family organism).

Now, one can see how Memes are a basic function of the brain. It becomes easy to extrapolate (think larger): just as we box our own life's personal functions, we also "box-up" (meme-up) the world around us. Just as we do not double-think the contents of our personal Belief and Behavior Boxes, **we do not second guess our lives as part of a Meme**.

In her 2016 book <u>The Gardner and The Carpenter,</u> Alison Gopnik highlights a new discovery discerning the difference between a child's brain and an adult brain. Evidently, and **THIS IS A BIGGY**, The child thinks of the world as an **EXPLORER**, the developed adult thinks like an **EXPLOITER**. First you seek and learn then you use your findings to make your way in the world.

See **DIAGRAM ONE**, below:

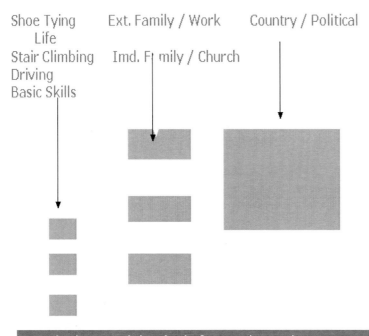

The next time you need to tie your "tie-tie," try to think it through. You can't do it; you've forgotten how to tie it by repeatedly doing it in a Behavior Box.

DO NOT TRY THIS: The next time you climb stairs, think through each step. As you do, you're liable to fall flat on your bum. When not thinking you can do it easily, but, if you "try" to do it, you stumble.

In both cases, you were thinking **OUTSIDE THE BOX**. From birth, our minds accept mental modeling (boxing): first personally, next with family, in school and in vocation. Our entire life is surrounded by Memes.

The **Forming of whole civilizations is doing the same thing** (the same Mental Modeling process), but with thousands of other people.

Our **politics and religions become sub-dominate to the cultural and national Memes** to which we belong. This "God and Country" packaging, while seen as holy, actually supplants any "think-through process" an individual would normally subscribe to.

People believing they have used their intelligence to adopt such high and lofty beliefs, is the reason people are so dedicated to their Memes (religion, country, gang) and will likely continue to believe, even in the face of proof to the contrary. This has made war and state-sponsored violence a regular way of life.

Tribal warring, like that between the Turks and the Kurds is an ancient and continuing plague upon humanity. These groups work under the same principle.

If you are reared in a Hutu family in Rwanda surrounded by anti-Tutsi religion, stories and education that teach "Tutsi's are human scum," even if you swear to yourself that you are not prejudiced, without strong personal mind intervention - you will kill on demand.

GO TO: MASTERMEMES.LIVE / CLICK: ONE

II//: Meme Structuring

STORY BOARD

Meagan Ropper was the granddaughter of the founder of the Westboro Baptist Church. She spent her entire life demonstrating at the funerals of U.S. soldiers to protest gays in America.

As she got older, she questioned why the church was we doing this.

In time, she was expelled from the church and her family ALL disowned her.

Her question: Does God hate gays?

Before any Meme is formed, it is important to remember that we begin with the Individuals who are seeking communion with other individuals. When found, this communion results in connections from which Memes spring. From this universal initiating springboard of BELIEF BOXING, all Memes are formed to fill a social need. Unlike the child's simple belief boxes, later Memes offer **a more advanced Meme Structure**.

The three stages of meme formation are:

Phantom / Informal / Formal.

Budding relationships between one person and another (see below) are not Memes.

Notes   (DIAGRAM TWO)

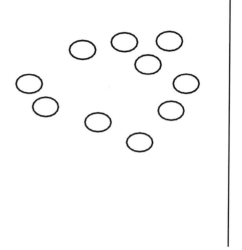

However, even in personal relationships, many of the rules that govern Meme behavior (Meme Laws) apply. The selfishness, aggressiveness and needy behaviors of individual people impact small group encounters, just as these same traits form the basis of Meme Law.

But Remember:: **MEMES are ACTION COMPONENTS \ CULTURES are BEING COMPONENTS.**

Once a common purpose is found, a **Phantom Meme** may be created, as other people are attracted. Phantom Memes have no social organism or commonly agreed markers;

(DIAGRAM THREE)

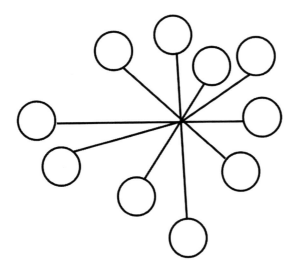

this is usually a small group gathering **in person, teleconference, public notice or on the internet.** They usually have similar interests and come from similar backgrounds, say a bunch of old Greek Americans hanging out on a corner in Greek Town in Baltimore.

Size, however, is NOT the DETERMINING FACTOR, but lack of organization is. The Hong Kong riots are unorganized, have the same basic goal and involve an estimated 150,000 people. This qualifies the group as a Phantom Meme.

If a common path is discovered, like a threat or common interest the group all recognizes, they will usually then come together in an **Informal Meme**. Say a group of men from outside Greek Town gather on the opposite corner. The Elder Greeks now prepare to stand up to these intruders. So:

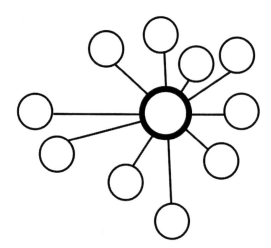

they form an informal gang called "The Old Greek Men."

By October of 2019 the demonstrators in Hong Kung had reached this stage.

If, however, the stimulus continues and is considered more serious, then they become a **Formal Meme,** choosing a name, picking a leader and setting rules, registering as a 501 (c) 3 as a Social Organization. The Old Greeks may rent a store front, get an occupancy permit and become "The Old Greek Social Club."

In the meantime, if the outsiders intend on staying, they, too, make jackets, select a name and get a headquarters.

(DIAGRAM FIVE – FORMAL MEME)

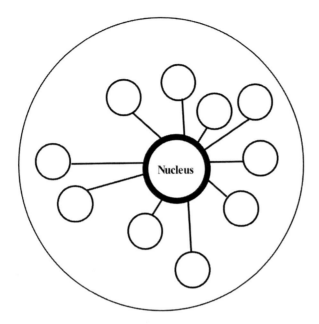

Looking to animals for primitive Meme grouping behaviors, Konrad Lorenz in his work, <u>On Aggression</u> (NY: Harcourt Brace Jovanovich, P. 1974 158 - 59), tells of ten rats, assorted sexes but of the same category, who were put in a cage together by researcher F. Steiniger in the 1940's.

After a few days of being frightened of each other, one male and one female tied the knot. This union, a mini- Meme, brought out their aggression and they terrorized and murdered all the other rats. This is a perfect example of Matriarchal and Patriarchal power in formation, the natural building blocks of a **Human Family Meme**.

Understand, however, Memes are unstable, they have no physical structure, nevertheless, they do exist and as in any other cell, organic or social, they are structured according to natural law. Additionally, never forget, Memes are mental formations (**Mental Models**) expanded to draw from many brains. Therefore, it stands to reason they would pattern themselves like all cells do.

Notes

Thinking of a Meme as a globe-shaped, three-dimensional sphere, more or less the same as any other physical cell, is helpful. A Meme would, necessarily, sport a nucleus or center, then material of lesser and lesser matter (commitment) leading to an outer shell (barrier).

Persons accepted inside this shell (Social Organism), even those near the outer fringe, such as the perpetually poor, are **"Memed-in;"** those outside are **"Memed-out."** Often this designation is made official, such as in political organisms (countries). The **"ins" are "citizens,"** the **"outs" are "refugees, immigrants, and aliens, often illegal!"**

Upon being accepted into a Meme (Memeing-in), even as an alien, one then becomes a "legal" alien, "a green card holder" and/or a visa holder. If one is not "legal," then even if one's body is living deep in the organism's borders, they are still an outsider or **"Memed-out."** At this level, these seekers have little or no rights or privileges and no say over the outcome of the meme's actions. Enough outsiders, with no method of being heard, is the major cause of revolution.

This is what happened, gradually, to the Roman Empire. Over the final 150 years of its existence, the Aristocrats (Rulers) and their Cadre of the civil government pulled away, often moving to the countryside. Simultaneously, hordes of refugees moved in, but they had no idea how to run the place. Today we talk of the "Barbarian Invasions," but in reality, they were little different than our Middle Easterners flooding into Europe today or Latin Americans migrating into the U.S.

From the outer fringe, poor or lowly status, as one interacts with the forces of the Meme, the expectation is that one will migrate ever closer to the center of the organism, depending upon the sacrifice or effort one is prepared to make and/or on the degree of acceptance the **"Meme establishment"** is prepared to offer. However, as long as the Meme is intact, those at or near the center still control the destiny of the organism as a whole and the lives of the people therein. True to their name, they are "the establishment."

Now, let's journey from the inside of a Meme to its outside, literally, from President to Peasant.

III//: Meme Characteristics

STORY BOARD

A pastor in a major American City discovered a network of "BAD" cops abusing the poor of the city: false jailing, shake-downs, and thuggeries.

He published an article, "Killer Cops in the American Police State," after which the "LONG BLUE LINE" closed around him.

Judges, lawyers, police, and city officials joined his church leaders in shoving him into retirement. His fellow pastors ran for the hills.

END RESULT: The 2015-Balt. Riots; then in 2017, 25 COPS were arrested and imprisoned; 2019-250 innocent victims released from prison.

You've never seen one, me neither. I've never touched one, you can't buy one. I, nay, WE, did not know that they existed - although they have been the basis of civilization since we began our journey thousands of years ago.

They are the **MOST POWERFUL** force on the earth!

I was first introduced to the term "Meme" by Howard Bloom, the famous author of The Lucifer Principal (NY: Atlantic Monthly Press, 1996), a book which, if you have not read it, you will have limited knowledge in understanding the basis of human existence.

Howard does the finest job ever of unbraiding human society and demythologizing the good and evil of human existence.

He defines a Meme as:

> *"A self-replicating cluster of ideas. Thanks to a handful of biological tricks these visions become the glue that holds together civilization (I add: "any social organism"), giving each culture its distinctive shape, making some intolerant of dissent and others open to diversity. They (Memes) are the tools with which we unlock the forces of nature. Our visions bestow the dream of peace, but they also turn us into killers"* (Howard Bloom. NY: Atlantic Monthly Press 1995. *P 10*).

Upon discovering the existence of Memes and their massive impact on our lives, I felt like an ignorant fool, only to find that no one else ever heard of them either. Even now, at the New York Book Expo 2017, I was approached by scores of people, all ages, asking "¿OK! What's a Meme?"

Memes have always been the very basis of the human saga, but they were never given their modern identity and explained scientifically until the 1980s by Richard Dawkins (some dispute this), the famous atheist. Actually, as in most cases, the knowledge of their existence has been with us for centuries, but as in many cases, clothed in other language, left undeveloped and considered religious superstition.

In the case of social Memes, the phenomenon was first talked about definitively in the Christian Scriptures in the Book of Romans 8:38 and again in Ephesians 3:10; 6:12; then in Colossians 1: 16; 2:5 and last in Titus 3:1. What we label as "MEMES" were then called **"Powers and Principalities."** The New Testament Greek word for "Principality" is ἀρχή (arche), as in "arch over" or "Archbishop," meaning rule over (Authority). The Semites used the word *"mu-shaw"* to indicate headship collective or dominion (Principality).

"Principalities' and 'Powers" equal "Memes."

What the ancestors have labeled "Principalities and Powers" are the invisible collective mind structures, progressed to form as viable social organisms, with outward showing "skins" that indicate the identity of the "Human Social Organisms" (family, club, the YMCA, the Democratic Republic of Congo, the Republican Party or Democrat Party, military unit or a church denomination).

Somehow, we have never thought to examine how they form and grow and adopt the rules by which they operate. These organizations are formed on Meme structures, which are invisible because they are the mind cords (telepathic brain interactions) that bond, form and connect in relationship with other minds to form unseen but powerful structures that fire the engines of Human Society.

The pioneering work of E. O. Wilson inaugurated this science of Human Social Evolution. Physical Evolution, long accepted, is now only half the equation in Human Development, Social Evolution goes hand in hand.

Some Social Psychologists have labeled these interchanges as "Emotional Contagions" and set them in a tighter more limited frame than I see here. Daniel Goleman first addressed Memes as simply "ideas that spread from mind to mind" (Daniel Goleman. *Social Intelligence, The New Science of Human Relationships.* NY: Bantam Books 2006, p 15 - 18; 45).

One can witness this "network" behavior showing up all across America, even in the twenty-first century. Today, police slaughter black people OPENLY, with near complete immunity, even though Jim Crow and the KKK of the Old South are gone. This state-ment irritates some who have police officer relatives. They say "their" COP relative would not do that. This may be true. Over 80% of police are levelheaded officers. Unfortunately, the way Meme Law works, after an incident all officers form up in "the long blue line (sub-Meme)." All meme members are required to "keep their "yap shut" and the admin-istration automatically attempts to discredit the victim. This group dynamic is discussed on pages (145-147)

Notes

ONE: Meme Law states: Memes are not sticklers for truth but, being creatures of the mind (Mental Models), actually favor myths which, when adopted by one strong Meme member, can spread like wildfire to all other members, often by force, often sparking untold madness, but sometimes, may create enormous good.

This unquestioned developing belief pattern allows Sunni neighbors to murder Shiite friends. It allowed white Floridians to massacre black neighbors (Rosebud massacre) and Christian villagers in Europe to commit genocide on Jewish fellow townsfolk. All this community-based horror was in spite of most locals claiming they personally had nothing against the community members they terrorized. This proves, again, that the Meme one belongs to supersedes one's own moral code.

But, this "Memeing-up process" can also energize other Memes such as the Salvation Army. These Formal Memes, developed Human Social Organisms, have constitutions, directors, and are accountable to the populace and may do remarkable good in the world.

Memes themselves always remain creatures of the mind that, when formed, are featureless, but have the arms, legs, mouths and cooperation of all their members. One thing that has the opportunity to muddle my thesis on "invisible mind connections," but must be acknowledged, is the fact that minds can work together (mind to mind) "telepathically" to form action and belief organizations.

Heretofore, "telepathy" has been a taboo in the world of social science. Thus, we try to ignore it and explain it away. However, I have experienced it throughout my law enforcement career, as well as my twenty-eight years in the ministry. I have experimented with it to see if it works and it does. It is powerful, universal and ubiquitous, all-be-it repudiated!

I have had a lady phone at 3 a.m. telling me her husband had just died fighting in Kosovo and another whose father had just died in Florida eighthundred miles away. **Neither had received a phone call ye**t. One couple with their son away in college knew he was in trouble across the country – they just sensed it.. In all these cases there were no circumstances of danger or sickness that forewarned of trouble. The above-mentioned boy in college had just returned to school from spring break at home and all was well. Yet all these beloved died or were in a horrible accident and their loved ones called me for prayer, but at the hour they called they had not yet received any notice of trouble.

They simply called their "pastor" in tears (not usual behavior from these people) sensing, really "knowing" a horror had happened. We can go on for decades talking about mental telepathy to no avail. I only mention it so we might all realize just how powerful the instrument between our ears really is. Individual minds connecting to form a mental model (Meme) is just as normal as breathing. Like situations or minds preconnected in common interests are especially open to this "Memeing-up" process (this explains workplace love affairs).

One encouraging note on mental telepathy: several universities have formed "epigenetic" avenues of research. Here they study, among other major topics, how the transferring of information from other than normally accepted paths, i.e. "telepathy," can be explained genetically.

Over the past forty years, telecommunications and social media have created an "electronics telepathy" of sorts. Now, rather than depend upon thought transfer, brain to brain, Memes communicate instantly with Meme members over the internet or instantly by "Twitter." Within a nano-second, an informal Meme made up of 20 people in Siberia can telecast their message to 90% of the civilized world. For this reason, discussions of telepathy have become mute, and social networking has superseded the concept.

The unfortunate result of this emphasis on Internet Memes is it has resulted in the forgetting of the original importance and extensive nature of Human Social Memes across history and society. After all, families are not raised out of internet contact, most companies are not formed online, and almost every nation on earth predated electronic data by at least a century. Most internet Memes are informal, temporary, fleeting and of no consequence.

Notes

The work of famed New York University professor Jonathan Haidt severely attacks any connection of this telepathy theory. As he would say: we are predestined by our makeup to be conditioned to accept certain positions and therefore be members of certain groups (Memes), not by encountering these mind creatures from afar off, but simply by a sort of genetic inheritance, again - epigenetics.

E. O. Wilson would ditto this aspect of Social Evolution. In his studies he talks of people being predisposed, for example, to "liberal versus conservative" by whether subjects prefer dots in a random pattern, as opposed to neat ordered patterns. One's choices in this theory can predict which type he/she will be. (Jonathan Haidt. The Righteous Mind; Why Good People are Divided by Politics and Religion. NY: Random House, 2013.)

I believe Haidt to be 100% right on, but contradicting his hypothesis there is a "ME." I, Britt Minshall, who loves things in order and loathes disorder. Yet, I come down on the side of liberal causes eight of ten times, even though I'd be considered VERY religious in the spiritual, moral sense (normally attached to Conservatives).

I have found this to be so in huge numbers of people who, like me, defy Haidt's logic. Yet I, like all other people, take into my psyche from outside my realm information that rises to emotions which should, according to Haidt's reasoning, send me running to a Tea Party rally, for example, but instead has me on the email asking the president to stop this "awful, conservative-backed program."

In the end, even one's "choice" of conservative or liberal politics is a non-choice: it depends almost entirely on the Meme community to which one belongs (family, friends, work setting or church). In America due to so-called "White Privilege" and a White wealth center, **White people are now OVERWHELMINGLY   conservative**. The reason is simple: thanks to that privileged status, Whites have accumulated more wealth and have nurtured the most power and now wish not to rock the boat and lose the same. After all, **"conservative" means CON (with or stay with) SERVATIVE (the service, from Latin *servitium*, work you are doing).**

Liberal beliefs question that "privilege" and call for a change: "It's unfair, let's do it different!" **Liberals (as in "liberate" from the current model of doing things) believe in a more "generous" sharing of society's wealth**. Therefore, they are prone to attract those that have less or wealthier people that are enlightened to the discrepancies.

One of the biggest disappointments to me as a Christian Minister, was to repeat the teachings of Jesus that model this sharing lifestyle, only to be completely rejected by congregation after congregation. They overtly chose privilege EVERY TIME.

If a person lives and works in a predominantly White world, basic peer pressure tends to make them sympathetic to conservatives. Conversely, if one lives in a more urban, multiethnic, multiracial area, and are faced with the everyday reality of inequality, they may be more pressed to stand for a change (Progressive - Liberal).

In America, a truly unusual twist has arisen. I am a perfect example. I am a White, 15th generation American, a truly pedigreed "blue blood." My Minshall family arrived in Philadelphia as Quakers with Brother William Penn in May of 1682. In March of 1854 they were one of 27 families that met in Pittsburg to form the Republican Party (anti-slavery).

My family served as State Senators and Supreme Court Justices in Ohio, Indiana and Illinois (all Republicans). Congressman William E. Minshall (1955 to Dec. 1974) was one of the longest serving representatives from Ohio in history. In 1856, William A. Minshall, his great-great-grandfather, was the first Republican elected in Pennsylvania

Yet I, being touched early on by American racism, have stood my life, along with millions of other whites and Blacks, on the side of Democrats attempting to secure civil freedom, educational equality and a fairer economic system to benefit ALL Americans.

I am further forced to the left fighting a lifelong battle against imperialism, militarism and wars of extraction, mainly perpetrated by my country.

Notes

I have chosen to live most of my life in interracial communities and urban areas in true liberal fashion, even though I do not accept the title of liberal. Rather I see myself as a Progressive - Traditionalist, kind of a Democrat – Republican centrist.

Now here is another "twist." Alternately, millions of whites, particularly Southerners (Meme titled: Dixiecrats), feeling betrayed by the Democrats for their challenge to segregation, moved their entire Meme population over to the Republicans. As a result, the right-wing American Political Meme has become almost solidly White (**I label this power force WHITE - MIGHT - RIGHT**), the left-wing American Political Meme (PROGRESSIVE - LIBERAL - MULTICULTURAL) remains mainly White, but is now joined by over 75%+ of Black people in the country, and most Latinos, Asians and Middle Easterners.

(DIAGRAM SIX)

NOTE: HOW Power Has Shifted in America over last 70 years:

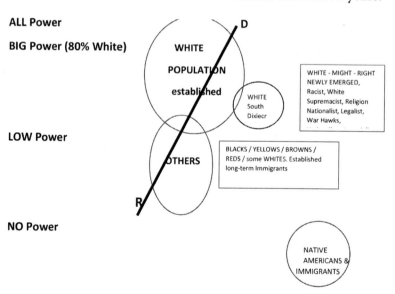

1955 Diagram of America's Ruling Power MEMEs

ALL Power

BIG Power

LOW Power

NO Power

R

White
Might
Right

WHITE (97%): Religious,
Racist, Supremacist, War
Hawks, Nationalists,
Imperialist (About 34%
Of the total White

WHITE (66% of White

population

Establishment

Other
Established

D

BLACKS / YELLOWS / BROWNS /
REDS / some WHITES. Established
long-term Immigrants

NATIVE
AMERICANS &
IMMIGRANTS

2017+ Diaaram of America's Rulina Power MEMEs

A terrific account of the development of the Right-wing Republican political power machine can be found in Nancy MacLean's new book *Democracy in Chains: The Deep History of the radical Right's Stealth Plan for America* (Pittsburg, Pa: Dorrance-Publishing, 2017).

NOTE: This is a study of social Memes and is not to be seen as a political opinion.

While I am what Jonathan Haidt would call a **"WEIRD:" W**estern, **E**ducated, **I**ndustrialized, **R**ich, **D**emocratic (Haidt page 112), YET, I walk the streets singing hymns all day, all the while warning people not to follow most religions. Actually, many think I am just NUTS, my term (Noting Universal Thoughts and Standards). Rather, I suggest, I have simply become super-aware of the Social Mental Models (Memes) that surround us and I attempt to audit every action in an attempt to: "Live with them and not through them."

The formation of Human Social Organisms by our minds' interaction and organization has been going on since the dawn of time, but we are just now beginning to define this process and identify its structure. This explains why the vast majority of speakers and

Notes

teachers have not yet grasped the concept, even though it is the basis of all human social life. Social Psychologists like Haidt and others cited in this book are at the forefront of finally understanding how we humans, really "super-thinking" monkeys, navigate our world. Robert Heinlein, a renowned science fiction writer, noted, "Man is not a rational animal, but a reasoning one" (Goleman page 17).

In his now famous book, <u>Social Intelligence, The New</u> <u>Science of Human Relationships</u> (NY: Bantam Books, 2006), Daniel Goleman acts as a pioneer in the area we are examining. He calls this interaction between brains: "The Sociable Brain," and labels the study, just now coming of age, of brain actions outside the cranium, as "Social Neuroscience." He only refers to the new word "Memes," once (Goleman p. 46), saying: "Memes may one day be understood as mirror neurons at work" (outside the cranium).

The important thing to remember is we tend to think of CULTURES which can be seen and counted as the all and end all of Human Society but there is a more advanced mental component of society which are minds gathered to accomplish a needed task.

MEMES are ACTION COMPONENTS \ CULTURES are BEING COMPONENTS.

> Just keep in mind that there is such a thing as minds gathered, which means there must be a human ability to form Mind Formations (Common Minds or Collective Minds). But, because it cannot be quantified, boxed and traded, it is usually ignored. Unfortunately, this continued ignorance, i.e. not understanding these Meme formations, is the curse of Human Society and the cause of continual repetition of even the most destructive acts (Wars, Financial Crashes, and Criminal Behaviors). We, who face the future, thanks to technology, are destined to find ourselves near drowning in Meme activity and ignorance of Meme Law will leave us as perpetual victims!

IV//: Memes Gather

STORY BOARD

Between 2000 and 2009, sales and profits shrank thirty-million dollars a quarter and the stock lost 10% of its value. During this slide, the Board increased the CEO's compensation by 245 million dollars. Business experts asked:

What happen to Rewards for success?

Memes are human minds connected, much like computers can be attached in series to form a server, supercomputer or network.

TWO: Meme Law states: The social role of a Meme is to allow the Human mind to organize society by creating and operating Human Social Organisms, where LEADERS can direct; ENFORCERS can order; the LESSER connected can function and the MARGINALS can be inspired to produce.

Later, I shall refer to these categories as Alpha (Administrators), Beta (Bullies), Gamma (Geeks), and Delta (Dunces) for simplicity.

Remembering that humans created computers, it can be easily seen that all human societies are simply a series of Memes ordered like a computer, really vice versa. Regardless of which came first, like "the chicken or the egg," the omelet has to do with both. But,

Notes

never forget that while computers have helped greatly in Meme creation, they are only a communications tool used in Meme establishment.

If you ever want to see what it looks like as a Meme gathers, go to a university science lab. Watch as lab workers makeup slides with bacterial cultures on the glass. As the minutes go by, look into the microscope and watch the culture multiply over the slide. They grow, connect and multiply. This is like Meme structures, except in the physical instead of the mental realm.

Now, in the case of the bacteria, each strain recognizes other like bacteria by chemical and biological markers allowing biofilm to form. So also, imagine minds passing in the night. While independent of each other (like how the bacteria on the starting slide are solos), their minds' thoughts and experiences look for markers to recognize in the others. Humans use race, language, facial features, smells or beliefs to draw and bind us together. If everyone present at an initial Meme gathering is a first timer in a particular setting, they are equal, so they "meme-up." This is how a new Meme is formed from scratch.

If an individual arrives in a setting where others are already established (remember this is the mental realm, not the physical, so we're not necessarily talking of a physical location, but rather, a Belief Box, or if an action is needed, a Behavior Box), then one looks for familiar markers and, when discovered, the newcomer "memes-in." This gathering-together process is defined as "aggregating" or massing-together. (Often a Meme has become closed, so as not to welcome new members and, in such a case, the newcomer is "Memed-out").

In all cases, if the newcomer does not match the marker test the meme members have set for themselves, then a "meme-out" will occur at once. The most apparent "meme-out" to recognize readily involves the snob factor. Sororities, churches and fraternities are perfect examples.

The markers used to identify a prospective Meme member are class placement, race, culture, sexual orientation, legacy and net worth. Each such group organizes themselves around "exclusivity" not "inclusivity."

I've come across churches that lock their doors, allowing only their same kind of people in. Back during Jimmy Carter's run for president, it came out that almost no Southern Baptist Churches would admit Black people. Both Mr. Carter and I left the Southern Baptist denomination at that time for that reason.

Interestingly, during the same time period, my family (White) and I, traveling on a Sunday morning, stopped to worship at a Black Baptist Church in Worthington, North Carolina. After being seated, the deacons came and escorted me, alone, to the back room, to be questioned by the pastor, who was upset that a "White man would come to my church." It took the entire hour for the congregation to accept us; no "White" person had ever visited their church in its 125-year existence. Talk about Memes being isolated from each other, the "Raleigh Observer" wrote way back in 1980: "Sunday morning is America's most segregated hour." Which all leads us to a major tenet of Meme Law:

Notes

(DIAGRAM SEVEN)

A Picture of a WAR Being Born:

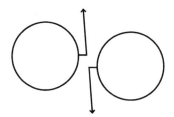

(B) Like Memes Meet
Two Families; Teams: Armies;
Gangs; Religions

THREE: Meme Law states: Like kinds of Memes repel and isolate from each other, similar to like poles of a magnetic force, which can foster combat. Unlike Memes may more easily amalgamate, cluster or cooperate.

Actually, the late M. Scott Peck talks of the fragility of Memes, although he speaks of "Community." The word "Meme" and the realization that these ubiquitous organisms work under such stringent rules, had not yet occurred to us. In his book, The Different Drum (NY: Simon and Shuster, 1987, *pp 130-147*), he notes that communities are held together, barely surviving internal, often competing forces - for example, "Inclusivity and Exclusivity."

Peck talks of **group "tension"** surrounding: "**Size, Structure, Authority, Inclusivity, Intensity, Commitment, task, Individuality, and Ritual.**" Scott writes primarily to religious and academic communities, but all Memes operate under the same structural rules and experience the same tensions.

When I inaugurated the concept of "Church for Everybody," I began a thirteen-year struggle with all kinds of interests warning me that I was upsetting the religious world's "rules" (Meme Laws). I received threats from Whites, Blacks, Muslims and even a Rabbi or two. But the most persistent rebuke came from my fellow denominational protestant pastors, who considered me a "show off." All these clergy believed churches should be "mono-cultured" and that "mixing" caused too much trouble. This "closed Meme" culture makes religion the perfect partner to any political Meme seeking to start a War. All the Ruler needs to do is enlist the priest, who will then demonize the "other religion." Then the followers will kill as ordered.

The reason is that most religious leaders, regardless of church organization, operate on a sea of distrust of other religions, which is due to endemic, visceral mistrust and fear. Religions, then, promote isolation of their group from all others. This was brought fresh to mind when the Sunnis of Iraq rebelled against the newly U.S.-placed Shiite government (2014). The Sunni clerics were screaming from their pulpits "to arms, kill the infidels." Shiite pulpits responded in like kind, both of which rang true to the same situation in Northern Ireland, just twenty years ago - Protestant versus Catholic clerics.

This reminded me of Maya Angelou's famous poem, "A Brave and Startling Truth":

> *When the Rapacious storming of the churches, the screaming racket in the temples have ceased,*
>
> *When religious ritual is not performed by the incense of burning flesh...* then the world will find peace.

(<u>Celebrations</u>. NY: Random House 2006, pp 18-19)

I wondered: "¿Where had all the clergy in these combatant faiths been, when their bunch was on top abusing some other religion?" I imagine in the same place American religious are today, as our Meme's (USA) interests are setting the world on fire for our benefit: they were HIDING!

Notes

Today we are again plagued by wars of religion. It is easy to see why Richard Dawkins and millions of others claim to be atheists.

And the root cause is people that believe their religion is more "Godly" than another and that somehow "The Creator" has chosen one religion over others.

SIDEBAR:

Humans are perpetually dogged by religious wars. My hope is every reader, especially those tied "tightly" to a particular faith (Meme), will put aside ANY notion that one religion is the "ONE!", that their religion is the one true faith delivered by God: **"It ain't so gang!"**

Religions, **ALL religions, are simply Human Social Organisms** *(MEMES), each attached to a particular cultural, race or geographic area, and are NOT connected to God in any way.*

MY PERSONAL faith is very Christian - Full Gospel, *and I feel as close to God as any person on earth. BUT, I stand back from the "organized" Meme of denominations, remembering that the Christian faiths (Organized Memes) have killed, butchered and destroyed more people than any other force in history. Everything bad Islam is doing currently, Christians invented first.*

END SIDEBAR

My most persistent adversary in the fight to end war, injustice, hatred and disregard for a person's life and property has been Churches and religions. This has led me to the conclusion that THEY are godless and the enemy of well-intentioned people everywhere. RELIGION is GODLESS, and again, it is of no connection to our Creator.

In the end it's just Meme Law:

FOUR: Meme Law states: Every Meme seeks to identify itself differently than others, seeing each separate identity as an establishing principle,

justifying each Meme's own existence and rendering it superior to others.

About ten years ago, a new convert to Christianity in an evangelical church called me on the phone. He just "knew" a pastor of a big stone denominational church could not be a "true Christian," so he set out to convert me.

After his initial invoking marker, "Praise the Lord," and he told me he "loved" me, I never met him, but a "love" greeting is deemed necessary among Christians, especially if one intends to do you harm. Among Muslims the greeting "Praise be to Allah" serves the same purpose as does "Hare Krishna" among the Hindus. He then set out to prove I was damned:

Convert: "¿Brother, do you believe in Jesus Christ as your Lord and Savior?"

Me: "Absolutely, I met Jesus March 11, 1975…."

Convert: "¿Well, have you received the Holy Spirit?"

Me: "Oh yes, the greatest gift of all, I've been sanctified and baptized in the Holy Ghost for fifteen years."

Convert: "¿But, do you have the joy of serving Jesus Christ?"

ME: "Oh yes, my brother, completely and absolutely everything I do is for Jesus, I just pray I get it right."

Convert: "But…. I ……Mean" (hangs up).

What you read in this very primitive encounter was a Meme member (new convert) who had been accepted into a Church (Social MEME) as an outsider, but who is now Memed-in.

Notes

Experiencing the inclusion of "being-in," he needed to talk to outsiders for his Meme and capture them, not unlike a pet cat who brings home a dead mouse. He saw me as a member of another Meme he presumed to be inferior, less Godly than his. In other words, the only authentic marker was "his Meme's marker." New Jehovah's Witnesses are required to find converts to ensure their meme-in; that's why the door to door desperation.

In this you see why a religious Meme should NEVER, MUST never, be allowed to play in the political world. Religious memes will never accept another religious Meme as equal. Therefore, when one religion ascends to political power in a secular society and is seen as law and authority for "everyone," many citizens would be excluded.

Most notably, in American Christianity, Pat Robertson's Dominionist movement sees an America ruled, not by a Senate and House under a constitution, but by a council of elders using Judeo-Christian traditions as its law (like ISIS and Sharia Law-same concept, different gods).

For the hope of a unified future world "under secular universal law", both Christian rule and political Islam are equally objectionable. In either case, if a religion Belief Based Meme controls a society, all other like kinds of Memes (religions) suffer badly. It must always be so - it's Meme Law:

> **FIVE: Meme Law states: Individual persons have a default setting of Communion when encountering other individuals; Memes have a default setting of Combat when encountering other like Memes. However, individual persons identified as a member of any Meme will tend to ignore, make fun of or gang up on individuals of another Meme[039]***
>
> *(*) The basis of the "default setting" concept is from Laurence Gonzales, <u>Everyday Survival; Why Smart People Do Stupid Things</u>. New York: W.W. Norton 2008.*

Here's the great irony: individuals by nature seeking "communion", need to "couple up," join in, cooperate and partner with others to achieve anything. This "individual" partnering results in a Memeing-in or up, which in turn creates new Memes who then begin "Combat" with their fellow like Memes. The point is: "You can't run far enough to escape Human Memes." My hope for society is to understand how and why Meme behaviors are so powerful and ubiquitous, thus rendering them more controllable.

The main reason people flock to a "new" social entity (church, gym or social club) is that memeing-up at a startup is less frightening and less risky than trying to "meme-in" to an established organism.

Another characteristic of a gathering Meme is to identify an "OTHER" Meme as an enemy of your Meme. This makes new joiners more compatible and more willing to swear loyalty.

So, upon meme-up and naming the organism, the first thing Memes do, naturally and seemingly without intent, is to identify or generate an enemy Meme (another like social organism) as a threat.

When the USSR was founded in 1917, it founded the Comintern (an external organization) to engage the world for communism and rid the world of "evil" capitalism.

Naturally, that caused an equal and opposite reaction, as the capitalists of the West counter-demonized the USSR. The Soviets also appointed Commissars to identify the enemy within the state (Internal Dissidents).

In the fledgling USA, the enemy was Native Americans ("Injuns, red skins"); our Meme-self pushed to get rid of "them." In Nazi Germany, it was the Jews who were victimized. Likewise, for the migrating Jews in Israel, it has been the Palestinians and of course, vice versa, all because of this natural fear of others' Memes (outsiders).

Interestingly, during the week of October 20, 2014, a high-level Israeli official remarked on an NPR news interview that "The Jews of Israel should be able to live anywhere on the West Bank they wanted." HOWEVER, when the NPR commentator asked if the Palestinians should be able to live anywhere, even returning to their ancestral homes in Israel proper, the official replied: "ABSOLUTELY NOT."

He explained that that would "dilute the solidarity of the Jewish population." He spoke these sentiments unabashedly, with no sense of guilt. After all, HIS personal conscience was now in the hands of his Meme (Israel), which saw the Palestinians as outsider enemies! You will recall that as soon as the White European power Meme took over the American continent, it was OFF to the reservation for Native Americans. Jews / Palestinians; Europeans / Native Americans; Spanish / Mesoamericans; Sunnis / Shiites - it's all just Meme Law:

> **SIX: Meme Law states: The fastest, surest way to provide a Meme with identity and member loyalty is to identify an enemy threat, either internal or external, to focus member's fears and hatreds upon.**

Since WWII, power seekers (American Empire builders) in the US Government, knowing that a nation is most profitable and powerful if it has an enemy, have acted through the Clandestine Services of the CIA (also using other government agencies to cloak its schemes), repeatedly, to set before the American people a threat we could fear.

This is not the invention of American rulers but a longstanding practice of nations since civilization began.

In recent history (1950-1990) we created a series of "enemies:" Costa Rica, Argentina, Iran, Korea, Vietnam, Indonesia, Chile and, of course, everywhere we flushed out communism, even if it was not there. (Tim Weiner. Legacy of Ashes, the History of the CIA. NY: Doubleday, 2007 *pp 1-19*). We'll cover this IMPORTANT chapter in American history later.

Beginning in 1990, seeing how successful our perceived threat program had been, and with communism on the wane, another play on "enemy" was introduced. Our rulers took the idea from Johnson's war on poverty, a good use for "war on" and carried it to a "war on drugs" and an unnamed war on immigration, both external and internal threats combined. Indeed, Memes are the easiest to enliven if a threat is presumed.

The established meme in control of the U.S. has traditionally been White and well established, while both of these new "enemies" were mainly Blacks and Latino's (War on crime etc.).

You will note, there was never a "war on" WAR (except from a few stalwarts like me and Martin Luther King Jr, who got killed, not for his civil rights work, but for his newly expressed opposition to war). **There was never a "war on" excessive profits which, along with war, are the REAL threats to all Americans**, except the power gluttons who profit from both.

As Memes gather and grow, usually early on, the earlier founders make a decision as to whether the Meme will be major and open, or minor (mini even) and closed. If the reason for gathering is social and protective, that is, gatherers seek safety (most churches, clubs, fellowships, support groups), a closed model will be adopted. In the Meme Dynamics chapter, we will discover how being an Informal Meme, as opposed to a Formal Meme, may impact this greatly. Members will welcome newcomers only as long as they are nonthreatening and match the marker test. But once the organism's needs are met, even acceptable newcomers are discouraged.

If, on the other hand, the reason for the gathering is to change the world or tackle a major problem impacting many people, an open model is adopted. Truth is, even in this "open model," many in leadership continually attempt to limit outsiders joining, thinking it is harder to control the body, the more open and sizable it is.

It needs to be said that, just because the reason for a Meme's formation is open and modeled to achieve its purpose, does not mean the gathering Meme will grow. Many times, the instigator of the process has grandiose plans, but those who attach (meme-in) are coming seeking the security of the organism. In this case, the constitution will sound lofty, but the end result will be much more limited.

An example is the World Tabernacle of God's People International, a storefront church in Baltimore, with twenty members and one part-time pastor. No matter what the pastor desires, it will never grow. She/he has big dreams and a small budget; but both the church's name and the Pastor's dream clashed with the members' desire, which is a safe place to feel wanted.

An international trading company in Chicago is a similar Meme model. In spite of the grandiose name, the chances it will ever morph into its name are nearly nil. A single ambitious proprietor, working twenty hours a day, has managed to raise a gross of $211,000 using one old truck; that's great, but usually that's it.

There is nothing inherently wrong with either small Memes or large Memes. The thing is, many people deceive themselves and those around them, envisioning an outreach to millions or promising to change the world for the better, but are continually frustrated, not realizing their Meme model won't ever let them succeed (perhaps this is your author's fate).

Memes can only grow to the capacity of the rulers' imaginations and the numbers and attitudes of the minds making up the organism, coupled with their willingness and dedication to help the Meme fly.

Likewise, when dealing with small Memes (families, small retail or family business) it's not only the vision of the Matriarch and Patriarch (usually husband and wife), but their willingness to surrender all to the Meme.

I once had a family disintegrate into divorce after 20 years of marriage. I learned in counselling that the couple loved each other, but they had given up on their Meme creation; i.e., the marriage was bad, not their personal relationship.

> **SEVEN: Meme Law states: A personal relationship fostered in and among Meme members, no matter how well grounded, does not necessarily make a good, lasting Meme relationship outside of the Meme context.**

Once divorced, this couple became the best of friends, doing all the best things a marriage is supposed to encourage.

EIGHT: Meme Law states: The destiny of an organism's size, structure and success is a combination of the founders' vision or the long-term successor leader's vision adopted in one degree or another by the followers (cadre), which then becomes much like an organizational DNA, difficult to supplant even when the originators are all gone.

In the case of an open, Formal Meme, the adjustment comes from the founders being replaced after the social organism is a fully formed "Formal Meme." Rarely will the add-ons (Meme-ins) tolerate the presence of the founding members, especially if newcomers see the potential of the organism and they picture themselves in the wheelhouse.

Usually the founders, even if beloved and well-known, are perceived as short-sighted and/or incompetent. Often, the added generation will wait for the founders to die off then change everything, but not always. Recently (2013), the iconic founder of the Men's Warehouse, George Zimmer, (you know, "You'll love what you see"), was fired by his board.

Most likely the younger board members teamed up with greedy investor types to bounce the "old" and his loyal followers out. George can take heart, however. **The day after he dies**, there will be a **six-foot statue of him** and a memory wall constructed at company headquarters, renamed: "George Zimmer Plaza." **Religions kill their prophets, then they are elevated to sainthood** also with a statue.

Pastors experience this all the time. I was warned by an elder pastor years ago: "stay twelve years, if you can, but never thirteen; the 'youngins' will want their own generation and they'll do anything to get rid of you!"

The thing to remember is: "In the end, the Social Organism's leadership is completely subject to the mass members' desire." When Tipp O'Neal (Speaker of the House) said that "all politics is local." He added "that every leader will crumble in the end no matter how highly placed, if even a small number of grass rooters pull away."

Notes   **Emperors, Popes and Presidents forget this BASIC piece of Meme Law.** Muammar Gaddafi of Libya suffered the worse fait under this rule.

Eric Cantor of Virginia, one of America's most respected and well-supported political leaders, considered a "shoe-in" in the 2014 primary in southern Virginia, was brought down by perhaps 3% of his electorate.

> **NINE: Meme Law states: Memes, even international organizations, are always the most vulnerable at their base. Meme leaders should never forget in a Meme: Power comes from the center, but power's authority comes from its mass membership.**

We are reminded almost daily that CEOs have discovered their vulnerability. In 2019, the board of WeWork Corporation fired their CEO because he nearly bankrupted the company, leaving it in shambles. But Adam Neumann, the founding Chief, had stacked the deck with the rank and file so they could not get rid of him.

As a result of his knowledge of how groups worked, he had secretly prepared for this day. So now he'll be "almost" fired, but he gets a total severance package of **one point seven billion dollars** ($1.7).

Meme Law can be a curse, but for others it ban be a blessing, some get put out – others get RICH.

V//: Memes Organized

STORY BOARD

In 1961, as the Civil Rights fight was birthing in America, Baltimore discovered it was a Southern city with big time segregation.

On a busy afternoon, three diplomats from the African Nation of Gabon entered Miller's Dept. Store and sat at the lunch counter. NO BLACK people had ever been served there before.

But now these elaborately dressed Washington dignitaries were served like royalty. It was ironic that Blacks from America were turned away routinely.

But here's the twist: the three were really reporters from the African American newspaper, headquartered in Baltimore. They were just local black people under the robes. Once ID'd and become just like other blacks, they were booted out.

Restaurant owners were horrified,
The Workers laughed!

For a few minutes the fake "diplomats" were of a different MEME!-- They were FREE!

IMPORTANT: These next two chapters deal with (V) the formal structure of an established meme and (VI) the dynamics (way of operating) of a meme structure and how every meme interacts with other memes.

THE ARENA OF IDEAS AND BELIEFS.

At a Meme's core, its nucleus, is the nerve center. It's like an anthill, and this would be the queen's chamber. (E. O. Wilson's now famous work Sociobiology, The New Synthesis (71), observing ant populations has given social scientists much data to help study human social cells as well.)

I have named this: the **"Arena of Ideas and Beliefs."** The reason for this label is to focus on the psychic or mental nature of a Meme, which is brain-centered, not brawn-based; it is an organ of thinking and cognition, rather than of reproduction.

Society legitimizes the result of a Meme formation by giving it a name, building it a headquarters, planting a flag or drawing dots on a map. But, the Meme itself will never exist physically; only its resulting Social Organism (company, army or nation) can be touched, seen and packaged.

> **TEN: Meme Law states: While Memes form the structure and platform of every Human Social Organism, which gives face and structure to the Meme's concepts and principles, the Meme itself, while the real driving force of the Social Organism, remains invisible and unlocatable.**

The USSR, one of the largest Human Social Organisms in history, existed one day, the next it didn't. Its capitol, the Kremlin, was in place; so were Moscow and the nation's power grid. Even the Republics' vital sub-Memes were in place. The military and universities were intact, but the Rulers and Power Elites at the center walked out and the Arena of Ideas and Beliefs was vacated; thus, the meme failed to operate, as Rome had done 1,600 years earlier. **DIAGRAM EIGHT:**

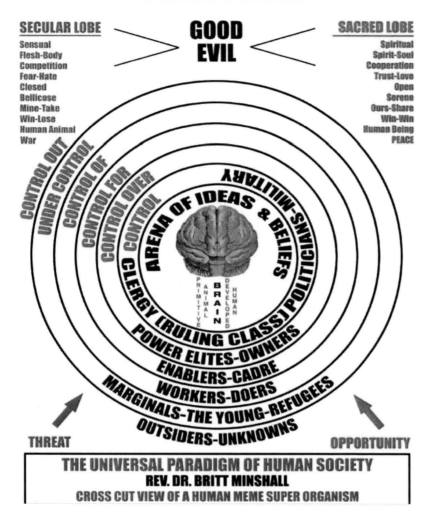

SECULAR LOBE
Sensual
Flesh-Body
Competition
Fear-Hate
Closed
Bellicose
Mine-Take
Win-Lose
Human Animal
War

GOOD
EVIL

SACRED LOBE
Spiritual
Spirit-Soul
Cooperation
Trust-Love
Open
Serene
Ours-Share
Win-Win
Human Being
PEACE

THE UNIVERSAL PARADIGM OF HUMAN SOCIETY
REV. DR. BRITT MINSHALL
CROSS CUT VIEW OF A HUMAN MEME SUPER ORGANISM

The **SACRED** lobe is driven by an ARENA focused on the **PROFESSIONAL** (shared for all), while the **SECULAR** lobe is focused on the **PROFITEERS** (on self interest).

In the cases of the Confederacy and Rome, the Meme falls into a dormant Phantom state. Soon, the USSR's Meme structure adapted by adopting a formerly abandoned organism covering the same location and population. "Russia" emerged and quite easily began operating as the Russian Federation.

Notes

After ninety years of dormancy, thanks to all the markers of the former Meme's existence still being in place: the Russian language, religion and social traditions, and thanks to this Meme being land-based (on the same landmass as the USSR), the lights were back on and the country was off and running.

In Russia's case, new titles were given to the offices of government and most of the same members of leadership simply swung over.

More or less the same thing happened from 1970 through 2013 in America.

The Confederate States of America, sitting dormant only as a memory in the social halls of Southern churches, was revived after the war and reconstruction, but now as a Phantom: "Jim Crow." For nearly a century (1880 to 1960), it blocked human status and full citizenship for Black Americans and carried out its exclusionary work (Behavior Box) using a faction of the southern Democrat Party known as "Dixiecrats" (Belief Box).

But after the Civil Rights Act of 1963, rising from the ashes of Jim Crow a coalition formed as **Ayn Rand's disciples**, known as Libertarians, joined with **Southern Evangelical Christians**, **White establishment** power groups, and the **Moral Majority** (White majority establishment religion) to form the "Christian Right." This reactive group eventually formed a political arm: the "Tea Party." These I label **White – Might – Right** which **today's Republican Party**.

Just because an Arena of Ideas and Beliefs goes dormant or becomes a dwarf organization, does not mean it's gone; it just may exist as a Phantom Meme and, as has happened in our time, we've seen that the "South has risen again!"

Due to the limitations of human societal memory, many Whites today are responding with the White Privilege advantage, saying, "Why don't the minorities get off their duffs and do what "WE" have done." These defenders are either ignorant of the past or unable to understand how human social history evolves. This is what author Rev. Jim Wallis calls "America's Original Sin" in his book of that title.

Once a society is structured, it is nearly impossible to reverse the actions made by one group over another.

THE RULING CLASS AND THE POWER ELITES:

Meme members who deed the greater part of their life energy to the Meme may receive the right to operate in the arena. These we label the "Ruling Class." In a mini Meme, like a family, this is usually Mom and Dad, but not always. It may be Mom and mother-in-law. In a dysfunctional family, it might be Dad and an outside interest, say work, leaving Mom and the kids out to form a new center, perhaps taking in a boyfriend. In some families I have worked with, the parents abdicated their parental responsibilities and passed the mantle to one of the teenage children. Whatever the arrangement, even families have a Ruling Class.

In churches and volunteer organizations, the Ruling Class, while usually a patriarch and a matriarch, are not necessarily a male and a female, nor are they always a formal couple.

Churches are NEVER ruled by a pastor. He/she is an "Intentional Outsider" within the Ruling Class, used by the rulers to exert power throughout the membership. However, in churches, the apparent elected rulers, say deacons and elders, are often not the real power either. Rather, a hidden Power Elite rules the roost, perhaps a paid secretary or the biggest giver.

This false naming stretches into government Memes as we see police as the great protector of the weak, but you'll see as you read and study in reality police are more law enforcers not guardians of the poor and oppressed. Many youth join "the force" thinking they are rescuers, only to find themselves in the roll of enforcing the powerful one's edicts of eradication, imprisonment, control and silencing the voices of the poor. The hidden controller could be a police chief, as in the case of extortion expert J. Edgar Hoover of the 1930s-60s FBI.

Notes

The "Power Elites," who control the rulers, are offstage running the show with a nod of their head or a "NO" face when addressed. In churches, the pastor's main role is to take the blame when things go bad and be fired so that the Meme can get a new start. This assuages the members' conscience and public outcries without changing a thing. Power Elites, in this case, are usually one or two longtime, well-heeled members.

It has been strongly suggested that, in the U.S., our national meme's leadership structure is such that the President has actually become a "national pastor." I can see this in that he/she is and should be an intentional outsider.

In reality, the role of U.S. President varies from year to year, depending upon the need of the **national meme.** As in a church, the "national pastor" never really runs the show. But, as we have seen in recent years, the President always takes the hit, even if he/she has nothing to do with the adverse situation.

This is equally true in most national memes. In December 2019 **Pakistan's ousted President Pervez Musharraf** was sentenced to life in prison by the very military government who formerly controlled him. Fortunately, he had fled to Dubai where the 76-year old is recovering, thus as long as he stays out of Pakistan he will escape punishment.

Nevertheless, any **Chief Executive's main task** is to bear the brunt of a national disgrace, while he/she often gets accolades for something gone well; again, even if they had nothing to do with it.

Most recently, **President Trump** has turned the political world on its head. He openly gives self-praise for everything good that happens, yet he never accepts any responsibility, even if there is no other person in the failed scheme but him.

In 2014, General Shinseki (Ruling Class) was the head of the **Veterans Administration** (sub-meme) during a huge scandal involving corruption at the very ruling center of this massively flawed organization. He certainly knew of the corrupt behavior, but was either unwilling or unable to stop it because of powerful government officials (Power Elites) who blamed the lack of congressional funding and their lack of commitment to veterans. At the same time, the inner structure of the VA (Cadre) used the same lying skullduggery to appear to "get the job done."

But in the end, the General was expected to take the hit, go down in flames if needed, and the corruption will go on unabated. What our government can't tell us is that 40 years of "War for Profit" is now backfiring on this good ol' USA Meme. Our bodies are piling up on us and our citizen investors are running from paying the piper.

Corporate life is, ironically, the same. While most CEOs do wield power (Ruling Class), "the board" is normally powerless. In most cases, one large shareholder (Power Elite) will control the entire operation using a puppet CEO as an errand runner.

As recently as October of 2019, **Boeing's CEO** found himself prostrated before Congress, being lambasted for the complete failure of the company in clearing the 737 MAX for flight. This resulted in 336 people dying and the company losing billions. The losses are scheduled to clear in 2020, but may go on indefinitely.

As in other cases cited, most likely the CEO had little to do with these decisions; lower-level managers were 100% at fault. But again, the CEO takes the fall and the real culprits take a quiet walk. By the end of 2019 Dennis Muilenburg, the CEO was OUT!

Early in 2014, the **Darden Corporation**, one of America's most successful operations, bowed to pressure from a major, normally silent shareholder, Brooklyn Capital, a hedge fund who was dissatisfied with the profits per share, per annum. They were receiving forty-seven dollars a share as opposed to their target of sixty-three dollars a share. As a result, over the objection of other shareholders (the board and the management of Darden), Brooklyn demanded Darden spin off two of its oldest and long-term profitable companies. They reformatted and reorganized the Olive Garden and the Red Lobster into leaner, meaner profit machines.

These are perfect examples of how the Ruling Class doesn't really rule and how a power-holder may be different than most people perceive. In any case, the CEO, like a pastor or a ball coach, is one loss from the front door. The journey from "beloved" to "despised"

Notes

in the Arena of Ideas and Beliefs is about as long as a train ride from New York to Washington, DC.

As shown in our diagram, in larger Memes, such as a country, there are **three main offices** that make-up the Ruling Class: the **Military**, the **Clergy** and the **Politicians** (in a municipal model this would be the police, the bureaucrats and the elected officials). Remember, these are not the real power source; that is reserved to the Power Elites, in all cases usually the wealthy.

The Ruling Class receives the most notoriety, and sometimes a permanent seat among the Power Elites, but not very often. The best treatment ever of these real world wide movers and shakers (Power Elites) can be found in David Rothkopf's book, <u>Superclass;</u> <u>The Global Power Elite</u> and <u>the World they are Making</u> (NY: Farrar, Straus and Giroux 2008).

Big cities like Newark, New Jersey (Formal Meme) are finding themselves in a severe crisis; their schools are in shambles. Hero mayors (Ruling Class) like Cory Booker (mid 2006-2013), a man of the people and enormously popular, gathered together the most powerful, goal-centered coalition in history to solve Newark's school problem once and for all.

He enlisted New Jersey's then Governor, Chris Christie (Ruling Class but of another political party), along with the power of business, receiving over a hundred million dollars, as well as onsite support from Facebook's famous founder, Mark Zuckerberg, and fellow Harvard grad, wife Priscilla. They were joined by half a dozen other VERY generous corporate leaders.

Even Oprah Winfrey and President Obama dove into the problem. So, there you have it, by far the most powerful leadership team in history: bi-partisan, citizen-backed, extremely well-funded; they were a certain win -¿right?

WRONG!!!!

¿Why? Because **the REAL Power Elites weren't on board.** Michelle Rhee, the famed author, when serving as reform School Superintendent in Washington, DC, had the entire Nation in her corner, thanks to a book and a movie about her crusade. Yet she, like Booker, went down in shambles.

In both cases, the Power Elites in the background, stopping the entire effort, were the teachers and their union. The money, the businesses, the citizens, the children and the entire nation were on one side, but sitting silently in the corner, the teachers defeated all the reform programs ("The New Yorker:" *Schooled* by Dale Russakoff. NY: May 19, 2014).

Years ago, Jack Welch, then famed CEO, who was stuck with the task of revitalizing a stagnated General Electric Corporation, ran amuck of **GE's REAL Power Elite.** In advance of his eight year adventure, he made sure the Board and all the powerful stockholders were on his side. Jack walked the factory floors in a valiant and successful effort to get the union on his side. Yet, after a two year effort of getting nowhere fast, he wrote of "**The Managers from Hell**," referring to middle-level managers in the company.

Apparently, over the years, these normally docile leaders remained loyal as Union and Management duked it out, gradually gleaning the real power to themselves. Welch joins Booker, Rhee, really good people in the religious world and righteous leaders in the political realm, in not being able to **identify the REAL Power Elites** who, in the end, ruled their worlds.

For you fans of Pope Francis' reform efforts, you'll note he has run headfirst into the Council of Bishops and the bureaucracy of the Curia who, in the end, are the REAL power in the church. Being an excellent politician, however, in his effort to see John XXIII receive sainthood (greatly deserved), he had to also nominate another Pope (less deserving) to satisfy the Power Elites. These are excellent examples of the power of Memes over individuals and Power Elites over Memes.

Just to demonstrate how the Ruling Class is not always vested with power: when a President or Chief Executive (Ruling Class) leaves office, he/she is gone. Many Presidents who leave admit going into a serious depression the very next day after their successor takes office. They realize, as Jimmy Carter said in a private meeting with me: "a former president is absolutely useless and completely without power."

Carter was almost right, and his statement is also true of former Vice Presidents, secretaries of state, attorneys general, state governors, town mayors and business managers. Ex-husbands also fit this category. Ex-wives get a reprieve thanks to motherhood; she can't be replaced as the core of the Meme.

Carter's "almost right" came from his refusal to vanish. **With NO POWER, this man has changed to world** for millions through his sweat equity at Habitat for Humanity!

This should give us all pause, realizing that these high profilers may never have had the power to begin with. They were only "loaned" the power for a fleeting moment. In Carter's case, from day scratch, Tip O'Neill - HIS OWN party's leader swore publicly "I'm sending this "peanut farmer" back to Georgia as a failure." O'Neill went on to destroy Jimmy Carter's presidency, in spit of them being both Democrats.

These Ruling Class people are, in the best sense, prisoners of their Meme, while the Power Elites control every Meme regardless of its egalitarian nature or claimed power diffusion. You will note that Adolf Hitler, Albert Speer, Joseph Goebbels and Tajo (Ruling Class) are long gone, yet the Volkswagen, Messerschmitt, BMW, Mountbatten and Mitsubishi, Power Elite families, are still going strong.

Of course, this non-vesting of power in one person is extremely good for governance and only Americans and Europeans seem to totally grasp it. Even though it's depressing for the ex-president, downright cruel, it is the reason for the greater stability in western governance.

Assad, Putin, Idi Amin, and Mao Zedong did not have the courage to face that moment of leaving voluntarily. Therefore, their nations are or were stuck with leaders who became ever more unresponsive. Most have or will have to use more and more force to retain office out of fear of being dislodged. When you witness their downfall, remember:

ELEVEN: Meme Law states: Members at the ruling power center of a Meme, many with high celebrity status, have no power of their own and are actually prisoners of the Meme, totally subject to the Meme's will as dictated by the Power Elites and the caprice of the populace.

Presidents and dictators alike surrender their entire existence to hold their office. It is natural after making such sacrifices to get and hold an office to fear giving up the chair - just as it is hard to let a child go, but it must be accomplished. In the Western democracies, with terms limited, Chief Executives actually have their lives saved. If a leader isn't forced to let go by law, the members of the Meme will often kill that leader. Julius Caesar might be alive today if he were term limited.

The **greatest gift George Washington gave** the United States was "**NOT**" staying in office. At the same time, it is worth remembering that the vast majority of those new Americans wanted to make him king. Many fear that this same phenomenon may arise from the Trump Presidency as he himself makes grandiose self statements.

This exposes a weakness in Meme structuring:

TWELVE: Meme Law states: In the human propensity to avoid personal accountability, Memes afford the opportunity to shirk responsibility and deed that obligation to others who will accept the rewards and the punishments. This is the route of authoritarian government and the reason people strain to avoid populace rule, seeking, rather, a career ruler.

THE CADRE:

Those most attached to the established Ruling Class and their Power Elites, "The Cadre," known as the "Establishment," profit from their insider place in the structure and desire that the existing structure (Status Quo) not change. Thus they also work against any alterations. Therefore, the ruler is often forced by the Power Elites and their Cadre to stay in office at the risk of his/her life and that of his/her children. Assad of Syria is currently in this position; his life and his family's lives are in grave danger.

If Assad resigns, however, his supporters (Alawites, Christians, Jews and Minorities) will most certainly be slaughtered.

Assad's coterie (Cadre), the next layer out from the ruling heart of the Meme (Ruling Class and Power Elites), is made up of career military, business executives, government contractors, upper and mid-level Clergy, the less rich, higher-placed civil servants, lesser officials and the under-rich, all the way down through local bureaucrats. **The Cadre IS the government and the established power structure. They make their living out of serving the arena, the Rulers and the Elites, while keeping the Worker-Doer populations in their place.**

In a local rural church, I am familiar with, a church secretary and the custodian gathered immense power over the years. These two became the Cadre of two and were family with the church's Power Elites. When a new pastor was assigned, he/she was told at once: "*Let's get this straight, we were here when you came, we'll be here when you leave.*" One pastor complained to the bishop and, sure enough, six months later they were there, as the pastor said: "goodbye."

In most cases, this Cadre grouping gravitates toward one racial, tribal and/or religious Meme in society. Once in charge of the Meme, they "crony-up" with each other, sponsoring each other and their children to keep tight control over the organism they dominate. This cronyism is at all levels leading to systemic "corruption."

NOTE: President Donald Trump and Pres. John Kennedy installed family members either as residents of the White House or in positions of great importance.

Look again at Syria. The "Alawites," a Shiite Muslim minority sect, slowly infiltrated the Meme's core (Syria) that had been for centuries Sunni Muslim controlled. Once inside, they Memed-up, forming a sub-Meme with other outsiders and minorities (Jews, Christians and other Muslims and secularists). This syndicate took over the government and the business community and shut the Sunnis out by "chumming" (Memeing-up) with each other, just as the Sunnis had done to them for decades.

This group stacked the deck, year after year, to hold the Assad family and their Ruling Class in the Arena of Ideas and Beliefs and they ran the nation dictatorially. The result was rebellion by the Sunni Muslims who were being disenfranchised (Memed-out), who eventually formed a separate Meme - Free Syria. These rebels received their strength and support from Saudi Arabia (Sunni) and the United States, an outside opportunist leaching Saudi oil.

> **THIRTEEN: Meme Law states: Once a particular group (tribe, family or party) takes control of a Meme, it works to Meme-in its own kind of people to operate the Meme to the exclusion of all others; thus the Cadre is in solidarity in keeping control of the Meme, eventually consolidating with the position of Power Elite.**

This is exactly what happened in Iraq after the Americans left in 2012, which has led to the Middle East blowup of 2014+. The initial conflict came as the U.S. backed, in this case, the SHIITE government of Iraq. However, the SUNNI-backed, now phantom sub-meme, called the **Sons of Iraq** (Saddam's former Army), were left disenfranchised and destitute. Here comes the rescue!

The U.S. (Obama) invited them to come and fight for us under Free Syria, this time AGAINST the Shiites, to get rid of Assad. But our effort went bad, the Syrians did not want that. So, **the sons of Iraq regrouped under the name ISIS.**

They then turned on the U.S. and began a war against their parent Meme - Iraq (now Shiite). This is DIRECTLY due to the above Meme Law being practiced from 2006 through 2015 and why people like me were led to warn of these events futuristically.

In December of 2019 this conflict broke loose again with America's assassination of Qassem Soleimani, Iran's Defense Minister. Much of the world yelled "foul" because we are not at war with Iran and because it was carried out on another country's land. While no one doubts the world is better off with this guy gone, most people are aware

Notes

this ill-staged amateurish action may cause infinite reprisals first from Iran then the US, Iran>Us, Iran>US in perpetuity!

Ironically, in all cases, it was U.S. interference that caused both countries to collapse to begin with (same game plan as Haiti, Tunisia, Libya and Egypt).

In America, White Northern and Western European migrants (Irish, English, French, Dutch, German and Scandinavians) formed our Master Meme (National Organism). Black Africans were kidnapped and dragged to America and denied any and all human rights. They were kept in slavery for 150 years (quasi-slavery for another 90 years through Jim Crow). Their sacrifices are responsible for at least a third of the White race's retained legacy, wealth and power to this day.

As later migrants, Eastern and Southern Europeans, came to America, they were allowed into the Establishment and Cadre on a limited basis, in exchange for their pledge to keep Blacks out and serve the country at the lowest levels. "**Black**" was the Meme marker for "**OUT**" anything else was barely acceptable. "**White**" was the marker for "**IN**." **Whites thereunder established and continues today as the American Cadre**. Native Americans were deliberately "genocided" from the first day. This Meme alignment remains in place, now simply referred to as "White Privilege."

Historically, as our country grew into a thriving urban culture, three things became apparent:

1. *We needed to eliminate the Native Americans ("redskin" was Memed-out) because we needed their land;*
2. *We needed tons of free slave labor (Black skin became inferior);*
3. *The poorer, darker new immigrants had to be kept under control, but were allowed a place in society.*

The newly arrived were required to keep their arms lifted and their mouths shut (the "Immigrant" marker became sub-human).

They complied. Thus the Italians began the Meme-in process by becoming the northern Europeans' enforcers.

So, we Americans had perfected the old Roman system of allowing our persecuted to persecute our targets for us. The popularity of this mindset was heard during an August 2015 talk show as a celebrity guest said with sincerity:

"¿If we deport them all, who will clean our toilets?"

> **FOURTEEN: Meme Law states: The most profitable method of enriching the established Meme members and to keep them safe from newcomers rebelling is to accept small numbers of outsiders to Meme-in and offer them a method for achieving insider status by accomplishing a series of unpopular and/or dangerous tasks.**

The best recent example of this rule playing-out is in American cities from 1960 to now. While Whites abandoned cities in groves, they maintained the urban governing power. From the beginning, bullies like Police Chief Frank Rizzo in Philadelphia stated: "there would NEVER be a Black cop in Philadelphia." So popular was his brashness among white he went on to be the city's mayor for decades.

Only reluctantly did these city armies allow a limited number of Black officers, all of whom became the harshest police to their fellow Blacks so as not to get forced out. As a side note, at 19 years of age I was a police candidate in Philadelphia when became a civil rights protester:

"Bye - bye Britt."

Just as Assad and today's dictators Meme-in certain outsiders, America's forefathers did the same thing from 1720 through America's incorporation in 1787. James Logan, an early national political leader from Pennsylvania himself Scotch-Irish, invited this practically uncivilized, homeless tribe of Europeans, known for their savagery, over to America with the promise of land.

Notes

The Scotch-Irish who answered the call were given rifles and sent to Kentucky and the West, where the established English and German settlers did not want to go. They and their guns were ordered to go west and kill off the Native Americans, so they could steal the dead natives' land (Webb, James. <u>Born Fighting, How the Scotch-Irish</u> <u>Shaped</u> <u>America.</u> NY: Broadway Books 2004).

The Scotch-Irish did a great job "genociding" Native Americans!

Now, earning the reputation as heartless killers, they were seen as extremely good at enforcing rules, even bad ones. So naturally, southern planters began to hire them as overseers, keeping the Black slaves in line - again, they did a great job.

Finally, as the Eastern cities grew, the rulers needed to get control of the street thugs, usually Irish or Scotch-Irish themselves. To wit, our newly minted Police Departments in 1800s America, ordained to keep our underlings under control, fell to this disliked and majorly underclass group , the Irish and Scotch-Irish. Again another fine job.

For these former "outsiders," this vocational move became the springboard to the developing American Cadre, becoming today's mayors, senators, bureaucrats and even presidents (JFK). Until recently, the same Meme supplied our military with the highest percentage of fighters. As a result of a new group of immigrants, the Hispanics, the Scotch-Irish have been supplanted in these pursuits.

To illustrate how slow this process is, the Scotch-Irish arrived in 1730, Andrew Jackson (1829) was their first presidential offering. The southern Irish arrived in 1840; John Kennedy was their first presidential offering in 1961. Compare this to Barack Obama, whose ancestors arrived with the first Europeans in the 17th century; yet, their first President wasn't elected until 2008. But, of course, they were not even complete citizens until 1964.

We had learned how to kill two birds with one stone. We let the former Irish street gangs Meme-up as "Police" and assigned them the task of keeping their lower-class brethren, Blacks and other undesirables, under control by beating them and other competing immigrant groups. One day you're an outlaw street thug, the next you are the NYC Police Department (Philadelphia, Boston etc.).

These police Memes remain largely Irish to this day. Hopefully, they are now completely civilized and professional, however, all evidence points to the contrary. Forty-four cities were cited by the Justice Department in 2014 for police overreach and brutality PRIMARILY OVER BLACKS!.

Hundreds of massive demonstrations across the country by multi-racial protestors, against brutal police behaviors have risen in 2014 and continue even today (2020). These have often brought the nation to a standstill.

I have written for years, trying to expose this Meme-on-Meme violent behavior ("Killer Cops in the American Police State;" For God's Sake newsletter; Renaissance Inst. May 2007 - archived at AllOneFamily.net). It is gratifying to see large, multi-generational, multi-racial actions against this social horror.

In the 2019+ era, many states are trying to correct this police overreach which has resulted in an extreme population of non-whites populating our prisons for trumped-up minor charges. This is a DIRECT result of race based genocidal exercises the Americas White power Meme has exercised over other Memes of darker skinned peoples.

You will notice, as noted above, in today's America, an inordinately large number of Latinos are entering the armed services, many not yet citizens. This is a current example of this Meme Law in action.

This process of "Cadre enlisting" is the fastest and the easiest way to create a multicultural society. The only problem is, when you need to change things, these now established insiders will almost never give up their new advantage, reacting as any Cadre in any established organism.

When the Egyptian revolution took Mubarak out, Egyptian friends of mine were cheering and partying. I warned them that Mubarak did not run Egypt, it was the cadre-military sub-meme who held the real power; neither Mubarak nor the rebels had any.

Additionally, because the general public and the rebels, were ignorant of Meme Law, they did not realize they had to stand up and take responsibility in order to earn that power and continue the revolution. Because Mubarak was only the symbol of the Ruling Class, a sub-meme member who, like all leaders, was made to be sacrificed once gone the Elites reestablished their power. The revolution was for naught.

A most unique treatment of the revolution in the words of people on the street in the thick of things, can be had in Denis Campbell's book Egypt Unsh@ckled where he monitors social media as an insider but from Wales. The entire book is a candid conversation with the rioting public.

Workers - Doers:

I label the next group out from the center, the "Worker - Doers." My graph is deceiving in size, as this group should show as 90% of the population (Diagram #8).

Here are **the "rank and file" citizens,** known from Plato to modern day theorists as the "**Producers, Peasants, Workers and the Proletariat.**" Most of the people reading this book are of this group.

These are the obedient ones, the slumbering masses akin to Pope Francis' "slumbering churches." They send their children to war, their taxes to the government and they obey the law. These are the real stuff of history.

The negative side shows that this group is often misused and abused. It is from this group where most of the causalities of war occur. This is the group that loses almost everything when the economy takes a dive. Memes need these people as their energy source, the heart of Meme strength, more than any other group. Yet, rulers despise and disregard them nearly as much as the Marginals and Outsiders who, according to the system, hold no value in the scheme of things.

The next down Marginal-Outsiders are only seen when assigned the role of internal enemy. They are attacked first by the the Workers-Doers because the W-Ds are only one step closer to the center; they fear the Marginals will rise up and the Rulers will make a deal with them for the Workers-Doers place.

Conversely, the Rulers bait the Worker-Doers with fear of the Marginals, hoping to spark the established ones to fight to keep their place. Often this fear causes people-killing riots but are tolerated because they producers profit bonanzas.

Many, from C. S. Lewis to yours truly, have spent a large portion of our lives in order to enlighten the working class (W-D). Lewis, addressing the average church member (who represents the Worker-Doers), said: "If only the Christian Church and its members would stand against war and injustice, the world would see peace and abundance forever" - alas, he was right.

Enlightenment Christian leaders and academics, responsible for founding modern society, saw the education of leaders and the education of the masses as an antidote to social interclass intolerance and injustice. That's why the Enlightenment Churches founded many institutions of higher learning such as Swarthmore College, Harvard University, Princeton, Boston University and the University of Chicago.

America's continual problem is that this large group of "the people," enabled by their Enlightenment educations, are still afraid to challenge the rulers of their own Memes out of **FEAR** of **LOSING THEIR PLACE in the MEME**.

Likewise, the Ruling Class and their Power Elites get to their levels because they have conquered their own fears. They understand that to keep control they can use fear of loss in others to accomplish the task. They realized they needed to move forward, no matter what the challenge to their plans and threats may be. But, just as fearless as rulers seem to be, the average person, part of the working class, is fear-filled.

That is why: the workers' children die in wars and the rulers' kids live to go to Congress. It's not a conspiracy; it's understanding MEME Law.

Notes

The Workers-Doers FEAR losing their jobs, lives, and **their children's well-being,** and justifiably so. Rulers at all levels have, since the beginning of time, raped, terrorized, tortured and murdered both their own subjects and those of any other Memes counted as an obstacle.

In 2014, women in India were gang-raped on orders of a local court. Torture and mass rape were inflicted on masses of people under Pinochet's rule in Chile. BOTH happened with a wink and a nod from the U.S. Ruling Class (Pinochet was our boy in Chile; India our staunch ally). American politicians allow a foreign country great latitude as long as it is in "the interest of the United States."

With their rich benefactor's approval, that of the U.S. Power Elites, Pinochet and many right-wing Latin American dictators were encouraged in these behaviors, seeing themselves as invisible and unaccountable. In later years (2019), this same behavior has led to Turkey's strongman Erdogan crossing into Syria and expelling our closest ally, the Kurds. Again, another good old U.S. President abandoning our friends.

Milton Friedman, famous economist of the Chicago School, was sent to Latin America to teach "**OBJECTIVISM,**" a radical brand of capitalism. He and his U.S. government sponsors have left a vestige of death and destruction, resulting in dictators and criminal gangs.

During this period (1970-2000), alternatively, communism seemed like a step toward putting the working class in charge of their local social organism (developing country).

It did not work; it CANNOT work because, as a POPULIST Memes-up to form a national organism, it ALWAYS follows the structure I portray here, that of MEME LAW.

Even a "perfect" or perfecting "just" state will eventually succumb to Meme Law which, **NOT EVEN KNOWING its precepts,** and no matter how egalitarian the leaders, will result in class structures. In **every Communist Society** established during the 20th Century, a **SUPERCLASS** of insiders formed up to take dictatorial control. This happened as their Meme evolved and naturally divided the population into the layers of Meme life from the Ruling Class out through the Marginals.

Average citizens like most of us are even more ignorant of Meme Law than the rulers who ply it against us!

Unfortunately, a mass gathering will usually turn into a mob without a ruling center. So no matter what Social Theory states, mass rule without structure can't work because groups of any makeup require a hierarchical structure. Remember any representation of a developed Meme is really, spherical, like DNA cells with the so called "top" as the "core". see DIAGRAM # 8

Once established, **this hierarchy becomes the Ruling Class and the Power Elites,** followed by an administrative **Cadre,** a **Worker-Doer** class, and will soon sport **Marginals and Outsiders** waiting to be Memed-out or in. ¿Why?

Because it's Meme Law - The alternative is ANARCHY.

SIDEBAR:

After the 2016 elections, a term: "DEEP STATE", surfaced. This term is nothing more than a developed interacting Meme Structure. Our National MEME is integrated with all parts working together = DEEP STATE. This deleterious word change arises out of the opposition's desire to destroy the existing process.

END SIDEBAR

MARGINALS - OUTSIDERS:

This brings us to an area our species needs to work on, but which most societies haven't ever addressed: the most outside group, the "**Marginals**" (the unconnected young of our Meme) and the new migrants, the "**Outsiders.**" **How do we handle those outside the Establishment,** who are attempting to "¿Meme-in?" In today's world, as throughout history, this Memeing-in operation is an out-and-out crisis.

Notes

SIDEBAR:

The Syrian refugee crisis continues to tear Europe apart (Brexit), the Turkish planned genocide of the Kurds, but closer to home in 2019 we discovered that MOST former foster children in the U.S. graduate to a life of crime and drugs. These mostly Black youth are fine until they age-out of the system and are simply DUMPED on the street at 18 or 21 – NO family, NO help. Next stop JAIL!

END SIDEBAR

Our own Meme's children we handle differently than outsiders'. As individually we struggle to ensure our kids a solid entry into the larger society. Yet even as we do this, there are those in government (Betsy Devos the right's Sec. of Ed.) who attempt to "Meme-out" even our "own" children and, even more so, the children of the lower socio-economic class. She was directed, being part of an administration that wants the Federal involvement in Health, Education and Welfare of the public to end!

Meanwhile, many insiders work diligently to exclude new arrivals' kids. "Education," is being used bombastically to re- segregate America.

Children of the lesser-positioned, usually of a color or language marker, are isolated to underfunded schools, while the "in" crowd (establishment) is complaining that they should not be "their brother's keeper." White establishment school districts across the country spend an average of $5,000 a year more, per pupil, than minority, more urban (Black-Latino-immigrant) districts. Even college is severely divided. Legacy universities, especially the University of Chicago, Harvard, and Yale, are gathering places for the **International Ruling Class and children of the Power Elites**. Even the world's upper-level Cadre send their children to these famous schools for a sure shot at owning the world.

Marginals' children and lower-middle class youth are off to community college to learn to operate the machinery that the rulers supply. This includes the current heavy call for technical and computer skills education, which is great but temporary. This field constantly changes, leaving these lesser-educated youth constantly caught up in an "in-out/in-out" scenario.

There would be nothing wrong with this if, after the sheep skin, only skill and knowledge counted as it should be, but that's NOT the criteria for social success. The diploma from an International Ivy League or a select state university allows one the **networking credentials** to attempt entry to the upper levels of social strata.

Conversely, a terminal community college degree closes those doors automatically to upper level ascendency. Then of course there is **the value of the "network."** Only grads from the top twenty can be assured to have the ear of social elites. **This is what REALLY determines "who is a big shot and who will end up as a little spark." Education** has become just another **Meme Marker** along with **language and race**.

To America's credit, major players of both political parties are putting forth stellar efforts to open the doors of societal leadership to the children of lower socio-economic families. The Ivy Leagues, such as my Alma Mater, Boston University, along with Columbia, Johns Hopkins and Princeton, are giving scholar-ships to millions of gifted young Marginals who could not afford such an opportunity just ten years ago. Being a big fan of community colleges, I am thrilled with the recognition these excellent schools are finally receiving. **"Go America GO!!!!"**

GO TO: MASTERMEMES.LIVE / CLICK: TWO

VI//: MEME DYNAMICS

STORY BOARD

A young man from a good family grew up attending a small rural church. He was the "peace-loving,' 'good son," a choir member who "wouldn't hurt anyone." With no local jobs, he joined the Armed Forces. Fifty-four weeks later, he had deliberately killed an eighty-year-old, his two granddaughters and their two infant sons, for no apparent reason, in Al Fallujah, Iraq. His stunned family asks:

"How could this happen?"

Now that we have covered Meme Structuring and its layers of stakeholders, we can tackle the role of each member in these various layers.

The handicap most of us have, as we "stumble" our way through life, is our tendency to deny or avoid the pressure of the structures with which we deal.

Most people live and die unaware that we're NOT dealing with Joe, Mr. Jones, Mom or Sergeant Smith; we are actually dealing with the Memes they and we are engaged in, respectively: school, neighborhood, family, Marine Corp, etc. In most cases, the individuals who seemingly give us so much grief are not isolated persons but are officials in/of a Meme. Literally, they are no longer themselves but are now role players.

In Diagram #8 we have identified the six layers out from the core or the center in the Arena of Ideas and Beliefs, where all major decisions and principles of the Meme are formed. These again are:

1. The Ruling Class (clergy, military, politicians)
2. The Power Elites (The real stakeholders)
3. The Cadre (enablers)
4. The Workers and Doers (producers)
5. The Marginals (the young, aliens outsiders)

We now need to discover the primary function of persons within their respective social layer.

Understand, at any one time, most of us are attached to several Memes and hold different positions in each. A Professor of mine at Boston University had been the Pastor of the Cathedral of the Midwest, a United Methodist Church, which in its "heyday" was one of America's richest churches. The membership, some 5,000 strong, was made-up of all kinds of people, from all levels of society. But in true Meme fashion, those members who were the more powerful in business and community also were chosen as leaders in the church's highest levels (volunteers).

At one time, the board boasted the CEOs of two of the biggest car companies, serving along with two department store magnates including S.S. Kresge (Kmart), a mayor, and several state and national senators. You get the picture. However, it soon became apparent that these big-time leaders were, in this church setting, extremely docile and completely uninspired. If they found interest in a project, they'd simply write a check and then retire from the scene. There was no personal involvement of the giver nor of the Spirit.

Contrast this to another setting down the street. A high school janitor was head trustee of this MUCH less prestigious church, where he spearheaded a drive and supervised the building of a million-dollar facility. His personal check was for $870, a year, but he

Notes

labored for five years crying when things went badly. But due to his perseverance – HE GOT HIS NEW CHURCH!

We each exhibit different personalities, depending upon the Meme and our place in it. The rich and powerful kept the ball rolling but the dedicated servant built God's house!

¿Remember your cousin Robert who enlisted and became Corporal Robert? He was no longer your cousin if you crossed his path in basic training. Your wife or husband, devoted and true, is no longer the same person if you both become upwardly mobile in the same department. Now, she is your competitor and a Meme loyalist. To win the title of the CFO, the person you thought was a devoted mate will disown you in a second and have you fired, if necessary. Don't feel bad ladies, men have done it for eons. Look at Henry VIII and his poor eight wives.

But, for our female readers we have a note: don't forget that Isabella, queen to Edward II, had her husband tortured to death in an unspeakable fashion. So much for the myth of eternal family bliss. **Meme Law trumps love at every turn.**

When joining a corporate Meme, ambitious people on their way to the top, will shred a good friend's heart. Likewise, Clergy within a denomination and military players will live to support each other until the Bishop's chair or a pair of "birds" become available. Memes foster competition as their main tool for selecting leaders and insiders. Again, sometimes it's for good, sometimes for bad!

Reviewing the "Memeing-in" and personal process, let's begin, this time not on the insider level, but at the "outsider" level, where many start their journey. Here they start in the role of "invader or intruder" or as the "tolerated," if needed by the rulers.

MARGINALS - OUTSIDERS:

In a larger setting such as a nation, say America in the twenty-first century, we all know these Outsiders as the "illegals" crossing our boarders. Once inside the physical boundaries of the Social Organism (USA), they, whether legal or illegal, are still "invaders." As long as they are Outsiders, they will be caste as nearly subhuman and dangerous "intruders." Our recent presidential election (2016+) argues this point almost extensively, with certain candidates vying for the meanest anti-immigrant policy! In this instance the most outrageously vindictive champion won!

Those of us who are already "Memed-in," as well as the young of the Meme's own (Marginals) and other previously arrived migrants, look at these invaders as a double threat - a danger to "us" and "ours." We mark them as such by name: "wetbacks, Chicanos,' and 'rag heads." We also describe their clothing, their eyes, their odors (usually spices they cook with) as other identifiers, to keep them "**different, excluded and inferior to us**."

We not only label them, but we snarl with disgust, saying words about them to further dehumanize them.

Juxtapose these indictments to the friendly - smiling greeting we offer our own young Marginals: "greenhorn' or 'tender foot" or the 'new kid."

Fresh up from slavery in America, Blacks were treated as outsiders, even though they'd been in the U.S. from day one; just as long as the Whites. They had been permitted to maintain a physical presence like an insider, but received all the disgust of a freshly arrived immigrant from elsewhere.

Unfortunately for some, race and color are markers that drag on forever. Many noted when President Trump visited Porto Rico after the hurricane in 2017, he interacted with the people with scorn and disrespect, even tossing out paper towel rolls. To him they were not "his people," even though he is their leader, they were Outsiders.

Before the Civil War, the U.S. Constitution counted slaves as 3/5th human beings each. Many Whites don't realize it, but many continue this mindset even today. Worse yet, many Black people have come to believe the rule as fact.

Notes

After emancipation (1865), former slaves were given a special pass of "resident outsiders," as long as they obeyed the godless contract terms we Whites offered them. These are: **(A)** Receive lower than legal wages; **(B)** Do only menial jobs that will be assigned by Whites; **(C)** Look down and never address a White person face to face; **(D)** Live only in restricted areas, and **(E)** Accept whatever the Whites hand down and expect no more.

In an **ADDENDUM**, after the Civil Rights Act of 1963 had done away with the above, we added a new condition: **Surrender your males to decades in prison for microscopic or non-existing crimes, in order to keep Black men and families childless and penniless.**

The election to the White House of a Black president has awakened this White racist monster as never was expected at this time in our national maturity. The popularity of the conservative political movement in America is basically a reaction to people of color rising up into the formerly all-White Meme that constitutes the United States of America (98% plus of both Tea Partiers and TRUMPERS are White, mostly militants, angry at the government, and have joined to form the **WHITE – MIGHT - RIGHT**.

Many other long-term established "Memers" (Connected Insiders) in the Workers - Doers group do not take to newcomers either. They are threatened by the newcomers seeking jobs particular Latinos, to them "spicks," Asians are seen as "slant eyes," and the list goes on. In my observations as a cop, counselor and chaplain-pastor dealing with all kinds of folks for 60 years, I have found **FEAR to be the common emotion creating this "xenophobia"** (fear of outsiders). This fear probably comes from a sense of their own vulnerability and shaky place in the structure, pushing them to fear and hate the new competitors out of fear of displacement.

By happenstance and social engineering, America and Western Europe feature an "establishment power base" that is 90%+ White European or pan-European. Most immigrants, including the 2015 influx, are made up of Middle Easterners and Central Asians. A XENOPHOBIC catastrophe, which is forcing Britain out of the E.U. (BREXIT)!

Any competition-based society (USA and the west) will see more of this than others. Natural Law supporters will tell you that the animal kingdom is fraught with this compete-or-die competition based on a "survival of the fittest" theme. The age-old question remains: "¿Do we want to base human society on animal behaviors?" However, unlike the "old days," when religious superstition ruled (you remember "the devil made me do it"), NOW we must, in this age of science, identify our individual animal traits and their effects on our Meme structures.

> **FIFTEEN: Meme Law states: Competition, as a method of expanding productivity among workers and selecting candidates for Meme leadership, even though it fosters interpersonal disputes as the populace battle each other for supremacy, does create wealth which, unfortunately, is almost completely driven to the center (top) of the organism for the benefit of Rulers and Power Elites, who foster competition and combat in their continuing quest for wealth acquisition.**

Often, hate groups, which are establishment-based, use these fears to ignite pogroms and campaigns against outsiders. Most of these groups are funded by a rich person or small group of Elites to benefit their own particular psychopathologies or, more often, their own bottom line. Interestingly, fear among minorities and outsiders used by unscrupulous businesspeople and politicians to enrich their own interests, is often employed by those supposedly representing migrants and poor minorities as well.

These especially evil people use the plight of their charges to enhance their own wealth and power, all the while scaring already fearful established Whites to death to keep the fear burning. In the 1970s, unscrupulous real estate dealers, wanting to "churn" the market, would place a Black family in the middle of a White neighborhood. Then they would infiltrate churches synagogues and neighborhood gatherings with warnings of race riots.

The result was Whites listing their homes by the millions - cheap - and rebuying in the suburbs, while home-seeking Blacks bought the abandoned "White flight" homes by the millions for big bucks. I do not know if a formal price tag was ever established for

Notes

this greatest of American business frauds, but it has to be in the double-digit billions. It almost single-handedly destroyed America's fine cities (1970- 1995) and created a legacy of hate on BOTH sides of the issue that stalks us today.

This same tactic was introduced by the White House during the spring of 2019. With no evidence other than a possible outlook, the President began to presage of "hordes" of mega-thousands of people massing to begin a giant "caravan" to march and overcome the United States.

Actually, at that moment there was literally no "horde" at the border only a few stragglers; the majority of troubled people were still suffering back in their home villages.

The rumor was designed to muster fear to help Trump get the funds for his border wall, but the rumor he started resulted in a large group heeding his call and the oppressed headed for our border.

IMPORTANT AUTHOR'S NOTE:

During the flooding-in of immigrants, mainly children and youth in 2006-8, I guested regularly on national TV shows and on NPR as the original **BUILD a WALL GUY**.

I called no one names and admire Latin American's greatly.

My argument was: (1) In a system of national borders YOU CANNOT have open unregulated borders, **(2)** We must seal our borders even if requires a border wall in some places (I specifically called for **Canadian** as well as **Mexican** sealed borders, **(3)** BUT we must simultaneously provide EXTENSIVE hands-on help to rid Latin America of the FLOOD of gangs and rid them of the dictator thugs which ruin their countries. The gangs came from the USA.

AMERICA MUST ACCEPT THE BLAME FOR THIS HORRID SITUATION – the gangs are ours and WE created many of the dictators and the resulting poverty!

MY POSITION: Close the borders –

accept RESPONSIBILITY

Throughout history, revolutionaries are usually Meme insiders who turn on their "own" kind and have reached out through the layers to enlist or gather together outsiders, seen to the rest of the Master Meme as intruders. These "**intelligentsia**" occasionally offer them a place at the table in exchange for them acting as insurrectionists against the establishment.

Lenin and his Bolsheviks were good examples, as was the entire Russian revolution (1915-18). The revolt's leaders were all from the landed aristocracy (sons and daughters of the rich) and the children of upper-level Czarist families.

Notes

They promised newly arrived outsiders to the cities and very lowly placed Marginals a new deal at the expense of their own families the landed aristocracy and Czarist establishment. The French revolution was a kindred effort. Only the American and Haitian Revolutions (1776 and 1805) were not between economic classes in the country.

This brings us to move closer into the layer of the Marginals, seen by the establishment as "Interlopers; their own kind - yes, but outsiders not wanted, who are pushing their way in." You'll note on the Meme chart this includes legal refugees and legally welcomed aliens, who are outsiders, allowed just a foothold into the Meme. They are allowed to do chores no one who is "Memed-in" wants to do. In America today it is Central Americans who are permitted to cook and do dishes, cut grass and do formally well-paid construction work for a fraction of pre-1996 pay levels.

These persons receive very limited perks and give little problems, as long as they accept the lowliness of their state. American Blacks have been supplanted in this group by Asians and Hispanics, leaving the Blacks, still Memed-out by the color marker, completely unattached.

Europe is facing the same dilemma as the United States, having allowed Turks, Middle Easterners and Islanders from the Americas in as legal immigrants. Now, many native Whites want them gone and want to take those formerly unwanted jobs back, but they are hard pressed to do it. This "interloper (intruder) status" is always kept alive among Memers so that these unwanted ones can be asked to leave. Actually, once "in," they won't go willingly.

One major example of a turnabout on this gave birth to one of the most awful massacres in history. In the 800s A.D., after the Angles and the Saxons were invited to the British Isles by the establishment Brits to be workers, they joined with the newly arrived "Red Shanks" (same as the Russians in the east - migrants from Sweden) and butchered their hosts wholesale. Next, the few remaining Brits joined the Angles and butchered the Saxons. Evidently, Meme Law is centuries old!

SIXTEEN: Meme Law states: Newcomers to Meme membership are both applauded and exploited by Meme leaders, while the Meme's individual members resent the new arrivals; nonetheless, they take advantage of their newness as well.

Most long-term Memed-in members (say citizens of a nation) only experience this phenomenon as a new employee or when a new member joins the family.

¿Remember back to your first few visits to your in-law's house? If you were differently raced, of a different religion or under-educated, you had no doubt, no matter who was saying; "Momsie and Popsie will love you," that, you were not accepted.

If you've ever joined a three or four-person office staff like Ann Hathaway did in the movie "The Devil Wears Prada", you've experienced being a Marginal, barely in, but viewed as an interloper in deference to your "beloved predecessor."

You'll note, I've placed the young of the Meme in this category. Most would not do that, but the vast majority of the young in a society, even those of long-term members, especially the lower levels of the Worker-Doers, are nevertheless treated as intruders, albeit with MUCH LESS cruelty than are outsiders.

I have pastored several churches that were peopled by the post-World War II generation. As their own children came up (1960-80) and tried to take "their" place in the family church, their parents gave them a fit. The result, especially among mainline Christians, was the expelling of their own progeny. These churchless young people either gave up attending church or they began and grew the new so- called "charismatic" and evangelical revivals (1970-2004), founding thousands of new churches.

My grandmother (beloved as she was) stood in her kitchen in Boothwyn, PA, some fifty years back (1957), complaining, "¿Why should I pay for a new high school to educate 'their' kids?" She could not fathom that someone before her had paid to educate "her child." In this next generation, as new children of the former outsiders, now the newly "established," come up, there is a good chance they will have less difficulty because each generation and their children are better Memed-in with more connections.

Notes

But, let's never forget the 2012+ effort by the American establishment to deport children brought here as infants (DREAMERS), themselves never having understood they were illegal aliens. All the while, "youngins" who are the offspring of the power-established, the Ruling Class or Power Elites and their close Cadre, are accepted easily.

SEVENTEEN: Meme Law states: Memes always favor the acceptance of and provide for their established members and their offspring (Marginals), while they discriminate completely against Outsiders and their offspring.

STORY BOARD

Lights In The Distance

In June of 2018, stories of trapped passengers, kept on rescue ships for weeks after being rescued from little rubber boats. The rescue ships went from European port to port seeking to land. Despite seeing the onshore lights were turned away. Finally, out of food with many sick, Spain let the refugees land. The same story has played out in Mexico (America blocks) Greece (Europe blocks) and in India (tribal – religious block)

(D. Trilling / London Review of Books)

Blood IS indeed thicker than water

it's Meme Law.

WORKER - DOERS:

Now to the vast majority of any population: "the Workers

- Doers." They exist as the "Under Controlled" ones, the most valuable to the Ruling Class. They are kept ignorant of what's happening around them (the Rulers are quick to praise their work, while demonizing those one step down). They are usually extremely cooperative in their assigned role, often acting nearly slave-like. In the United States and Western Europe, this group is better off than in almost any other country. But even here in America among this group, which represents nearly 86% of the population, they have only 18% of the wealth.

Contrast this with a pure oligarchy like Haiti, where this group represents 96% of the population but has less than 2% of the wealth. In Haiti, as elsewhere, there is almost no middle class to hold their share, so the Workers and Doers are compensated as Outsiders and treated as Marginals in their own country. What most do not realize is that Haiti's poor are all pan-Africans, native to Haiti since the French imported them as slaves. But the 2% of oligarchs who rule Haiti are Lebanese, Middle Easterners who came to the Island and took over all the assets in 1921.

Ignorance, one of the biggest contributors to Worker-Doers as the "controlled," is the same old furnace firing the rest of societal "fear." As I've said before, "**Those who know how to use this fear factor rule the roost.**" A perfect example of this manipulated fear at work is found in the fight for the "Affordable Health Care Act in America."

We are told in surveys that 60% of Americans don't want this law. That's because 60% of Americans already have or could easily get health insurance. They are being convinced by the would-be profiteers on healthcare and the politicians that represent them that if "everyone gets healthcare, you'll not be able to afford yours." This group of near criminals base all their fear factors on pure lies told with a straight face and false facts.

Also, playing into this **class insider vs. outsider fear** is the same fear of exclusion that haunts those more Memed-in persons who resist and repress any effort from the Marginals and Outsiders to break into their lifestyle; it's another case of: "If everyone gets a good lifestyle, then I lose my superior advantage over "THEM" (the excluded ones).

Notes

Any seeker of the truth needs to be aware that even America's religions, which claim to advocate for the Marginals and Outsiders of society, actually support the "Doer" population and everyone in society who are already vested with the best health care regimens available.

This explains why "the church" did not open its mouth to support this law, even though it fits squarely into all religious theology. They ignore the precept that the Creator is no "respecter of persons" (sees all as equal with respect to basic needs that everyone has the right to receive, regardless of one's status in life). ¿If this is such a basic tenet of all faiths, then where was the church during the fight for this basic human need?

Among religious this is APOSTASY - Shame Again!

To this day (2020) religions have not come forth to fully support Universal Health Care.

I should explain: virtually "all clergy" (Christian, Jewish, Muslim etc.) in America receive health care through their denominational group insurance. Also, the vast majority of "churched" people are better off than the bottom third of society, thus they are more heavily insured than poorer people who may need the most help in getting heath care.

Being a follower of Jesus, I can say without reservation that the teachings of scriptures and the established theology of the Christian Church have been violated by the American church in ALL settings. As usual, religion has allied itself, NOT WITH PEOPLE'S NEEDS, but along with INSIDERS in society in not supporting "Health Care for All."

Interestingly, the true faithful were elated when the Affordable Care Plan was passed into law, only to see churches support a new president who, in addition to being morally flawed, promises to get rid of "healthcare for all" (both godless pursuits). ¿Could it be that racial Memes are at war as we witness White Memes (White church) seek to expunge any trace of a Black president?

The biggest violation to Christian and other prophetic teachings came from those "already taken care of" who **supported their church's or synagogue's effort to deny those "neighbors" less blest than they**. As to the "fearmongering" politicians supported by so many of these "fine establishment types," they're doing their job, carrying out the wishes of the 60% who desired the status quo.

For clarification: I joined the Health Care For All movement, not when Obama picked it up, but way back in 1976, when President Obama was twelve years old. My 45-year active membership had nothing to do with partisan politics and EVERYTHING to do with Christian Holiness. (During many of those years I voted majority GOP.)

It shouldn't surprise us, remembering back to prior ages of the American Meme, that when virtually EVERY stakeholder in U.S. society was an active church or synagogue member; and in an era when most of the people of Earth decided they wanted to live together in peace (1946 +), **not a single American religion actively supported the formation of United Nations**. As a point of history, for decades many have continued to vilify this world organization at every turn.

CONTRAST: Most of the Earth's religions actively promote war at one point or another, as an everyday part of their religious message. The Old Testament openly promotes genocide and mass murder.

The Workers-Doers, with all their power in numbers, simply cowl-down as the grim reapers (the rulers of most societies) roam their streets, terrorizing them, stealing their children for war, robbing them blind and profiting from their misfortune. They huddle in fear and often empower their tormentors, if not personally, then always through the Religious and Cultural Memes to which they belong.

Too often we fail to give the German people and their churches proper recognition for their near blind support for the Nazis of Hitler's era. We ignore the fact that Hitler was a "big-time" hero of the German people and that all but 40 local churches (the confessing church) out of 5,000 supported him right to the 1945 end. As Humans, we are hard-pressed to realize that it's not the Hitler's of this world that ruin it for all, but it is "us," the Workers-Doers, the common people, that support these Rulers that instigate such evil. We give them our blessing by our silent obedience (even when we KNOW, darn well, that our country's actions are wrong).

> **EIGHTEEN: Meme Law states: Meme members are inordinately loyal to their Meme. Once they are Memed-in or up, they tend not to leave from external pressures, but only from internal forces, and will defend their Meme to the death, even if they know their Meme's position is incorrect.**

CADRE - ENABLERS:

We now move even closer to the center of our diagram and enter the territory of the "Cadre" or administrators of the Meme. These are the "interpreters" of the edicts of the implementers, the directions of the most powerful people in a society. They are employed by the Ruling Class to carry out the laws and instructions of the Power Elites and the Ruling Class, and in such a role, many times they have great discretion in their enforcement.

This discretion is the heart of "corruption." It is those with the greatest number of options who usually have the opportunity to be the most corrupt and the most dangerous. **Throughout most of the underdeveloped world**, order is kept by a separated class of police, a quasi-military class, usually named "Security Forces (Cadre)." Most are drastically underpaid and are encouraged to get their needs met by extortion and torture of the population under their "protection."

Unfortunately in **America, thanks to establishment FEAR, police have adopted a third world MO.** Police personnel can choose between "fair and professional" treatment of citizens or acting out, as is happening in many American cities, as "thugs and warriors." The lower on the socio-economic ladder one finds oneself, the more easily you will be terrorized by government officials wanting to relieve you of all you have, balancing their budgets with your blood (Ex: Ferguson, MO).

In some places like China, there is an unwritten code that allows police and private guards to lock someone away, often in public view, until the victim gives in or gives up. In China, as in America, police are conditioned to treat the wealthy and the establishment one way, while encouraging a hired "goon" status to their behaviors with poorer classes of people.

The Cadre is a broad term that, at its outermost levels, hosts dogcatchers, street cleaners and clerks. These folks aren't usually impactful, except for their part in a network of workers who support and communicate with each other. This group is infamous for blocking those more outside than themselves from contact with higher officials.

For example, in Haiti until 1992, there was a shadow secret police force, the "Tonton Macoute" (the good uncle). This small band of SS-type citizens were part of Papa and Baby Doc's (dictators) goon squad. It was their task to neutralize anyone who questioned the government. They received most of their "tips" from informants who were part of the Cadre's lower-level government supporters: pastors, sanitation people and local cops who, hoping to gain approval and move up, would turn on their neighbors, their own children and their "best friends." This is a perfect example of people being Memed-up, losing all sense of a personal life; the more Memed-up one is, the more sold out to the organism one will be.

The same was true in the Shah's Iran, Mubarak's Egypt and is true in every other not fully democratic nation on Earth to this day. But, before we Americans get our hind quarters too high in the air with false pride; growing up during the McCarthy era, I personally witnessed all kinds of local people "ratting" on family and friends, identifying them as "reds." Then, after the accused failed from social banishment, others gathered around to take their houses cheap or get a government job more easily.

It's hard to imagine that, just 60 years ago, this inner-Meme tendency to pit one player against another could have been so strong that thousands of GOOD citizens lost their professions and a few their lives, at the hands of one rogue "Catholic-Republican, alcoholic politician" who discovered he could manipulate the entire population of the United

States with scare tactics. McCarthy like tyrants everywhere understood Meme Law and used it effectively.

> **NINETEEN: Meme Law states: Rulers often pit one Meme member or sub-Meme against another, with no rules of fairness or sense of right or wrong; the goal being the ruler's receiving enhanced loyalty from the winners and enrichment from the defeated one's losses. When invoked by the rulers, this process trumps all personal and family loyalties.**

In a recent Rwanda war trial in The Hague, a Hutu man testified that when the tribal war (Meme vs. Meme) broke out, his best friends were a Tutsi family. As the war erupted, sponsored by Hutu Rulers and Cadre, he went next door and killed his best friend, his wife and all their children. He "macheted" them to death, willingly. The greatest horror was that he was the godfather to all the dead children.

So far, we have focused on lower-level Cadre. But as we gravitate to the center of a Meme, we discover devoted members with higher rank and more influence.

In a Family Meme, the elevated level of Cadre is probably the two daughters-in-law married to the two inheriting sons. In a corporation, we find this group with keys to the "executive men's/ladies' room" in upper mid-level management. In the military, you would be addressing full-bird colonels up to Major Generals, and in the church, Vicars General, Bishops and State Superintendents fill these slots. In the American political governance system, these may be elected, such as newer House members or appointed officials, such as CIA Bureau Chiefs, Cabinet Secretaries or agency chiefs like J. Edgar Hoover, who had immense power even over presidents.

When these people get the word from the Ruling Class (Arena of Ideas and Beliefs) or directly from the Power Elites, they attempt to institute the ruling to satisfy the hierarchy as best as possible, although they very often disagree. A case in point would be the Catholic Church's prohibition of birth control. I know many Catholic priests and some Bishops who believe this tenet of the faith is ill-advised, but being part of the Cadre, they don't dare utter a word. Many secretly confide that, "When I make it higher up, I'm going to speak out."

You can guess the outcome. Once they receive their dream job and a big-time title, they become more, not less of a dupe to the system. We think that the higher (closer in) we get, the more easily we can change things, but in reality, regardless of Meme type (business, religious, military, political), the closer we get to the center (top), the more obedient we become to the status quo, that's why so little ever changes. **The system of rewards keeps reinforcing the rising stars**, who are more reticent to offer meaningful changes. Interestingly, Pope Francis led others to speak openly, indicating certain doctrines were in question. But as the days progress, no one uttered a note of dissent and he himself backed off many sought changes.

When still a Senator, John Kerry was a power to be reckoned with and a bit of a radical. As his time in the Senate progressed, his establishment-self grew over the years. Upon becoming Secretary of State, out of necessity, he became tied to the administration, even if he disagrees with his historical self.

The Syrian Crisis proved that Kerry, generally cautious when it comes to war behaviors, challenged Syria and quickly threatened an attack. Any psychologist could see by his nonverbals (face, actions, tone) that he was insincere in his own threats, but he was dutiful to the Meme rulers. At this high level (Meme center), everyone in the Meme obeys to the letter. If you do not, it's out with you. Using Syria as a model, President Assad personally is seen by the United States as THE problem. Yet he, like all other rulers, is really a slave to his ruling National Meme. **The closer to the power center of any Meme one gets, the less of one's self remains**. As previously stated: This is why Assad can't step down. His very life and that of his wife and family depends on his staying.

We have covered this point before, but it cannot be stressed enough: the ruler is the most ruled by his/her Meme, without which, even a former ruler disappears, becoming a non-entity - a persona non grata. That's why most **rulers, whose authority goes bad, would rather fight to the death than leave and live**. They cannot envision themselves living a life separate from rulership at the center of the Meme. Again, it's much

Notes

like the queen ant in the center of the colony. She cannot just pick up and leave. Her enforcers would sting her to death; the ruler is the major prisoner of any Meme. Robert O'Connell in his book: <u>Ride of the Second Horseman, The Birth and Death of WAR</u>; suggests the human act of war comes directly from inherited ant behaviors within the Human psyche

After WW II, General Smedley Butler, the most decorated U.S. Marine in history wrote a paper denouncing the cabal of wealth at the top of the U.S. Power Elites, who staged the war to enrich themselves and their Ruling Class. Millions died from 1914-1918, but billions of dollars were made. Butler was slated to be Commandant of the Marine Corp., but despite two Congressional Medals of Honor and a twenty-year unblemished career, he was out. He was virtually unremembered until a courageous historian, Bill Huff of Maryland, lead a decade-long crusade to retell Butler's story. The Meme (U.S. Military) to which he belonged at the high end of the Cadre had tried, with near success, to obliterate him, until this one motivated man stood up for the truth.

> **TWENTY: Meme Law states: Meme members can never achieve high enough leadership, even the ultimate office, to successfully challenge the Meme's Operating Philosophy as sanctioned by the power center, without suffering consequences from others in the Meme's leadership and severe reprisals from the Meme's members.**

Remember that both School Superintendent Michelle Rhee and her champion Mayor Adrian Fenty, both well-qualified and sincere leaders, were ousted by Washington's powerful Teachers Union while the citizens (lesser in Meme status) of the city stood idly by to watch their schools brought back down.

If you feel **major change is necessary**, you will face your only options: **(1)** self-exile, prophesying from the outside, in which case you may make it happen and leave the organism intact, but you'll lose your place inside, or **(2)** begin a mini-Meme to challenge the Operating Philosophy within the master Meme, in which case you will end up losing much of the original Meme members. In either case, you may personally land up criminally charged, demonized and/or dis-fellowshipped, and may end up with an enemy Phantom Meme in your bed.

When attempting to face up to evil, Jonathan Haidt in his famous book, <u>The Righteous Mind</u> (NY: Random House 2012, *p 220*), cautions us to realize: "We the people care more about looking good than truly being good. We lie, cheat and cut ethical corners … then we use our moral thinking to manage our moral reputations to justify ourselves to others." He goes on to speak of our Genes being selfish. Then the product of those Genes go on to create like-organisms ("Memes" - he did not use the word).

In other words, if one attempts to stand for righteousness against any organization, it will cut the advocate to ribbons, then dawn a smiley face as the champion goes through the grinder. You can take comfort to know, as in St. Francis' and Abraham Lincoln's case, when dead, the righteous champion may be glorified. A similar force plays out in the American custom of **naming places for its defeated victims: Pontiac, MI; Cheyanne, WY; Red Skins Stadium; Broken Arrow, OK and Indiana State.**

At the beginning of the Obama administration, a promise was made to allow a more open dialog with government employees discovering corruption or illegal activity to speak out and be safe. At the close of that administration, despite the "Whistleblower Law," these employees are being terrorized by their government, arrested and ruined. This has been a major failure in the American Meme, seeing that even its own civil and criminal laws can't overcome basic Meme Law.

During President Obama's term in office, his abandonment of his word, while serving to associate himself to the Rulers, has lost him much of his credibility with his supporters, while he put many of his adversaries at ease. We see here an example of a Meme's hold. The power of the collective usually prevails (trumps) the individual leader's wishes. Remember Bush senior: "**read my lips – NO MORE TAXES.**" Then guess what happened?

Obama's successor has openly called for the Whistleblower Law to be ignored after all Trump is a loose cannon. In the case of the law, he likes to defy that "collective interaction" and go it alone.

> **NOTE:** Throughout this work I will juxtapose the mentality and methodology of **Obama vs. Trump.** This is **NOT a political statement,** but simply an exercise in comparing two polar opposite leadership styles. Evidently the public first choose far LEFT, then became afraid and reversed, going far RIGHT.

Elijah and Jeremiah of the Hebrew Scriptures, General Butler, Edward Snowden, Jesus and thousands of other "change agents" lived this drama and the story is far from concluded.

Members of the Cadre (all levels) find themselves in this most difficult of positions all the time. Each one at one time or another are faced with a personal choice: be a **(1)** Corrupted Coward or become a **(2)** Public Prophet.

We have witnessed this situation playout during the 2019+ impeachment hearings. Many GOOD people, part of the governments' Cadre, have either chosen to be corrupted and thrown away their chance at being "honorable" or chosen the Public Prophetic route by coming forth to testify as to what happened be hind closed doors.

Keep in mind, whatever information they share carries HUGE penalties or rewards, for them and for society!

THE POWER ELITES AND RULING CLASS

Now, onto the role of rulers, who are made up of two separate, but totally intertwined groups. First are the Power Elites, and second is their legates, the Ruling Class. The Power Elites are the "Instigators" in any society. It is their spoken or implied interests that the Ruling Class attempts to satisfy. Power Elites such as is Warren Buffet, David Koch, and Bill Gates may be well known or completely in the shadows, calling the shots nearly anonymously. In America and everywhere on Earth, these are the folks with the means; they control the jobs, natural resources and wealth of a society.

These positions (Power Elites and Ruling Class) look different, yet are codependent in every organism of society. Let's look at a church I pastored. The **Ruling Class** was made up of a Deacon and a powerful trustee. They ruled the church with an iron hand, but the **Power Elite** ruler, was a quiet, behind the scenes local businessman. He insisted I have lunch with him each month, the day of the church board meeting. He wanted to make sure I knew how he "wanted things to go." He had already touched base with his other two ruling chums, who never crossed him, but always did his bidding.

Every church in the country, congregational or not, is operated much the same way, as are corporate boards. In that setting, the CEO and the Board are the Ruling Class, but large institutional stockholders are the real Power Elites. These unseen ones dictate the Board's every move, often revealed at a private lunch meeting with the CEO or head person.

In a National Meme (Political/Social), the Power Elites spread their influence by where they place their money. They send their children to a small network of schools. Often, they just spread their mind's opinion, which is their right. But, more often, like David (Died August 2019) and Charles Koch, they simply make money available from the sideline to groups like the Tea Party who carry out their wishes.

The highest placed Power Elites of the **Right** support the **American Legislative Executive Council**, a lobbying group that supports only Republican Legislators at state and national levels and nearly assures their election given their vast wealth. If a legislator disagrees with them, they can guarantee his/her ouster. **ALEC is a virtual dictatorship** by the American Right's Power Elite over its Ruling Class. Through this mechanism, often nameless Power Elites engineer the greatest "democracy" to ignore the needs of people who need and enact laws that benefit only the rich and the powerful.

The **Lef**t has a similar hammer in America's unions, who almost always support Democrat causes as does George Soros and his Open Society Institute. The concern here comes from observers who see the Left's support dwindling due to decreased union membership and a new attitude among Americans that reveres their own personal wealth. **The outcome is the ever growing right-wing rule and a decreasing influence of the general populations welfare in America's civil life.**

It is hard to separate the Power Elites from their siblings, the Ruling Class, but in the interest of scrupulous honesty, we must try.

On TV we see the Ruling Class at work (West Wing, House of Cards, etc.), however we only catch a glimpse of the Power Elites in the shadows, where they work with NO accountability, often at a secret lunch or secret meeting on a secluded mountaintop.

Most Power Elites are from wealth; many of the Ruling Class, like Bill Clinton, John Boehner and Harry Reed, are not. Many of the Power Elites are legacy holders, that is, they inherited their wealth and privileges. Yet, some from this inheriting group rebel against their legacy and adopt programs for the people - the Roosevelt's, Warren Buffet and Michael Bloomberg for example. This reminds us that while Power Elites are almost all wealth – they are NOT all Republicans. There is lots of Porsche driving Dems in "them thar hills!"

The Power Elites lean Republican because they favor business legislation but most successful of players can adapt and turn on a dime, that's why their so wealthy.

It may seem weird, but growing up among this American aristocracy, From a very young age I witnessed "old money" being far more eclectic, open, progressive and sympathetic to peoples' needs than "new" money. Through my growing years (1953-1960), this was a major conversation around the table at the DuPont Country Club in Wilmington, DE.

So, just being labeled the Power Elite does not make you of a particular political ilk. Often, the newest fortunes are the most self-centered, excluding others from their shared background from attaining insider status. The older fortunes (The DuPont's, Weinberg's,

Sterling's and the Pew family, along with a thousand others) are the most liberal in sharing their advantage.

The Power Elites sponsor those rising to the Ruling Class, which usually reflects the spread of the Power Elite's ideologies. The result is a Ruling Class being chosen by varying ideologies. Some will champion the people (Left), while others will champion limited interests, usually connected with business and wealth (Right). In today's America (early 21st century), young industries and a glut of new fortunes are temporarily favoring the right-wing power block; while old money is playing a more hidden role in social endeavors.

> **TWENTY-ONE: Meme Law states: No matter how widespread the violence of the parties in contention in an inner-Meme conflict, it is always either focused on or sponsored by those in the center of the Meme in the Arena of Ideas and Beliefs, with the outer Meme members suffering the greatest consequences.**

Always keeping before us **Meme Structure, at the center is the Ruling Class,** forming the **Arena of Ideas and Beliefs**, which is made up of three distinct groups: The **Politicians** (in America elected, except judiciary are appointed, but all are political), the **Military** (in America subject to civil authority) and the **Clergy**. Here, Clergy means the rulers of the varying denominations and should not include the lowest parish ministers or the religious prophets who, even today, often stand against church and civil rulers, trying to expose the subjugation of the people.

The establishment clergy (all Religions) are usually assigned the societal role of silencing these Social Correctors (Prophetic Speakers), as the "Temple Prophets" (ruler-appointed insiders) did in the case of Elijah, Amos and Jeremiah (Outside Correctors). Very often, as in the case of Jesus, John the Baptist and Bishop Romero of San Salvador, hierarchical religious leaders murder them.

The **Ruling Class has the duty of being the "implementers,"** that is, to inaugurate programs and institutionalize the will of the Power Elites (some populace centered, some wealth/power centered). In this process, America has done a fairly good job throughout the twentieth century of balancing moneyed interest with social interest, even though our system tends to act like a pendulum (right - left - right – left).

This process ruins many individuals along the way, usually those in the lower third of society. These "outsiders" have little inside information, especially of social swings and Meme Law, therefore they are the last to be warned of a pendulum swing, which means they get "**SLAMMED**" because of a late bailout. In the political or corporate setting, those people **IN THE LOOP** receive the profits, while the lone **OUT OF THE LOOP** people get the prison time.

A big problem America and the rest of our national Memes is suffering from at the time of the writing of this book is that all of our sub-Memes (self interest modules) are no longer seeking compromise or common ground. Rather, one, usually a mini-Meme of the Right (White Nationalist in the U.S., tribal nationalist elsewhere) is working deliberately to disrupt the Master Meme (country) to get its own way. And even though they claim to be part of the "Right," right-wingers themselves are fearful of them. This hard, radical, Right mini-Meme acts out punitively against their own party members. They are not willing to enact "**implementation**," as is their duty, but rather to create "**insurrection!**" Other nations, including Great Britain, are beginning to deal with this same paradigm.

Like a dam in a river, they have disrupted the flow of the Meme force and made the Meme structure vulnerable to collapse. In the end, however, this hullabaloo may do America some good. We had become lazy, just approving compromise after compromise, often not tracking outcomes.

But, traveling through this storm will remake our Meme to some degree or another. Also, seeing much of the world going through a similar political upheaval, we can appreciate the blessing of a Meme which allows its members to make any complaint they want, even to disparage our leaders. It works like a boiling tea pot, where even the Tea Party can blow off steam instead of revolting.

Discovering the White racist makeup of this right-wing group, ignited by our having an African-American president, has actually led to their being discredited by America's rank and file, who did not realize the entire thing was a racial hoax. The good thing is America is FINALLY looking at its own racist self with honest introspection and shame.

For at least the past fifty years, I saw the U.S. as "the Great Pretender." We faked our racial inclusiveness. These ugly secrets about us, in emerging, have done our National Meme a world of good.

The BAD thing is that in the confusion (the freedom coalition, the united America society and other groups sporting false names are now deceiving people. Truth is more Whites have gravitated to the side of bigotry and elected racist-White supremacists to responsible positions. Fortunately, by 2019 this really bad movement is reversing itself.

> **TWENTY-TWO: Meme Law states: The stated purpose or label given a Meme may often mask another purpose entirely.**

This principle also explains the phenomenon of "frienemies," people who act much like your personal friend, but are mean and often destructive to you. I have had this kind of encounter, as have both men and women friends of mine. What's happening is that the would-be friend is acting out subordinate to you in attempting to form a Meme relationship, but is at the same time battling you for superiority. Meme Law principles apply here, even though your arrangement isn't even a Phantom Meme (this is common with employers and business associates).

This also explains why husbands and wives have difficulty engaging the same friends. The would-be friends come into the foursome as a separate Meme and each Meme of two can take in another member (individual) but not another like Meme (couple).

No matter what takes place in these inner-Meme conflicts, in the end, America, just like every Meme, will settle back into the Meme structure that every Meme in the world shares. Who gets Memed-in or Memed-out will change, but the process of Meme-making never changes.

Notes

TWENTY-THREE: Meme Law states: Regardless of the degree of "inner" Meme disputes, in the end the Meme must achieve Homeostasis (Balance) in order to continue to exist, otherwise it will rupture, splinter or disintegrate.

This explains our ever-evolving landscape of social organisms. Religious denominations are a perfect example as every denomination is a break off of at least one other. In small towns you'll notice the First Baptist Church, then the Second Baptist, and so on up to Fourth or Fifth Baptist.

In St. Augustine, Florida, there is a famous seafood breading invented in Osteen's Restaurant seventy-years ago. Through the years employees have left and started Barnacle Bills, the Sea House and others. Each new restaurant is a brand-new Meme, but all serve the same great breading.

Companies split and re-split; at one time Republicans were Whigs and Southerners were Democrats and, of course, many of us were married two or three times. Meme Law forms up, creates and often destroys, but, then, recreates a new organism to take the old one's place: same Meme laws, "same great breading."

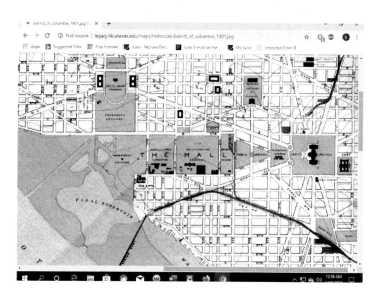

A CITY BUILT FOR A MEME: Washington, DC was planned to reflect the MEME seated there. Note the central bisecting lines (North Capitol and South Capitol Sts.) cross in the center at the home of CONGRESS. The Supreme Court is just to the right and The Presidents Mansion is 16 blocks west (in 1800 out in the country. The founders intended the House and the Senate to be the CENTER of the new republic.

LOOK FAMILIAR?

Meme Law effects groups but, ¿ how about entire nations?

SPECIAL INSIGHTS:

"Nine Hills To Nambonkaha," one of the best book ever written (Sarah Erdman. NY: Henry Holt and Company 2003), recounts the author's "Two Years in an African Village" with the Peace Corps. One thing she discovered was the villages were of a **native culture** complete with dress. customs, music and community rules. At the same time she discovered the **state government of Cote d'Ivoire**, a modern-western type formalized nation-state, with national borders (truly a modern day invention). It was

Notes

represented in this far flung village by a Government Agent, living with his wife and children as nearly a foreigner, isolated from the others..

Here the "country" was of NO significance. the local genetic culture was everything!

In this one can see the explicit difference between a **CULTURE and a MEME**.

A CULTURE is just there, it requires NO planning, it is akin to cultures on a microscope slide growing spontaneously, usually based on the sameness of the organisms present – in Sarah's case the tribe of indigenous people.

But, according to Barbara Tversky (Mind in Motion, How Action Shapes Thought. NY: Basic Books 2019) the main task of "cultures" are to be an action force which changes the space around the organism transferring the cultures design to the world. Barbara uses the term culture over Memes.(Her model: Actions > Thought > Action > Thought).

In reality, cultures alter the space around them but remember they are spontaneous NOT PLANNED – NO DIRECTION..

Now back to Africa: all over the continent there are scores of "villages" many unmapped, boasting 8-10-12 MILLION people, tribes persons all, who definitely form a culture and, yes, they change their surrounding with their dumped waste, water run-off, air pollution and miles long traffic jams due to lack of proper roads. There is usually NO government.

Compare this to a western city (Chicago, Miami, London or Moscow with proper sewage, paved roads, air purification and well-equipped hospitals. In Africa the daily death count is so large and with no systems in place, the real figures are unknown.

THE ONLY difference between these two societies is **CULTURES** exist in much of Africa and are the ultimate change agent, but in modern societies, many multicultural, **MEMES** arise from deliberate, planed groupings of human minds, often UNRELATED, joining to design the space where they are to deliver and improved their space. **OUT OF MEMES** come the roads, sewage, medical care, schools – **ALL PLANED** by TEAMS of people, not arising from spontaneity but through planned action.

CULTURE Directed OR MEME Directed

States & Super States (98% Meme 2% Culture)

Corporations & Nations (70% Culture 30% Meme)

Tribes (91% Culture 9% Meme)

Packs / Clans (99% Culture 1% Meme)

Individuals & Families (100% Culture)

GO TO: MASTERMEMES.LIVE CLICK: THREE

VII//: Meme Operating Platforms

THE EMBRYONIC MEME

720 million B.C. bivalve mind begins to develop **MEMORY**. Researchers at Cold Spring Harbor Lab discovered that by 200 million B.C. **a gene DCREB2** enabled rapid storage of data. Richard Dawkins followed the evolution of this skill as discovered in early humans, soon expanding to **MEME Creation** which permitted a habit, a technique, a twist of feelings, a sense of things to **FLIP** from **BRAIN to BRAIN**.

Memes could carry their message via the swift intangibles of scent, sight and sound. The result would trigger a **KNOWLEDGE EXPLOSION** of data webs with a whole new style. The key to this revolution is the early learning of a child – **the medium in which Memes THRIVE**.

Bloom, Howard, *Global Brain, The Evolution of the Mass Mind*,
p.30 John Wiley & Sons, 2000

Now we answer the questions: Exactly how Memes function; What forces make them go; "¿ Does the ideological basis of a Meme (purpose) alter the dynamic or change Meme Law governing its operation?" and " ¿Are there different sets of laws for each type of Operating Platform?"

Let's examine the types of Meme Operating Platforms:

1. **Blood** – Family, Kin, Tribe
2. **Belief** – Religion/Politics
3. **Boldness** - Cause/Crusade/Movements
4. **Badness** - Criminal Enterprises/National Cleptocracies/Thuggeries/Invaders
5. **Business** - Profit Producing Functionary/Commercial Enterprise
6. **Beulah** - Culture Centered /Tied to a specific Land- Location

By determining the main Platform upon which a particular Human Social Organism is built, you can more easily understand the dynamics (forces) that fire the Meme; even though all Memes work on the same principles (Meme Laws), there are still fine nuances. The paths taken in forming-up and performance criteria are different, depending upon the Platform used to classify the Meme.

While some simple Memes are single Platform, that is, they are of one type and operate on one platform, most Memes are somewhat more complex, and many are extremely involved. The problem is made worse when two of these more complex organisms collide and both are impacted by their own dogmas and conflicted by the others.

Further confounding the situation is the widespread practice of the **DELIBERATE DECEPTION** in naming a Memed-up organization. For example, a few years ago a group calling itself The Children's Rescue Center was found to be a recruiting home for children, with the express purpose of distributing the kids to child slavers (sadly a woman ran the place). The Sudanese Liberation Army existed ONLY to enslave and terrorize the population. The most popular name of all is The People's Party of _____ (location doesn't matter, these groups are NEVER for or of the PEOPLE).

For example, take the **Palestine / Israel conflict**. Simple-minded people like to make it a Religious issue, seeing only two separate faiths in conflict. Evangelical Christians, who support the conflict, believing it to be a way to bring Jesus back, see only the Judeo-Christian Bible accounts of the ancient scenario and that's it. They say, "Right or wrong,

Notes

Israel is our guy." Their end goal, however, is open warfare to inaugurate "The Rapture" and force the "Second Coming" (BAD BEHAVIOR).

Conversely, Muslims the world over see Islam being attacked, so they exclaim: "Destroy Israel!" thus playing into the plans of the Christian fundamentalist hope for all-out warfare (BAD BEHAVIOR #2).

The "simple thinkers" would say, "There are two Religious Memes (**BELIEF**) involved." But there are also two "**BEULAH**" Memes involved (each side's god married to the same land). Both groups are thus "married" to the same land, that's the ancient meaning of "Beulah." Each claims that "our" god married this land and both groups believe that, and that's it!

Next, they are both "**BUSINESS**" Memes, both needing one another, but competing. For example, the Israeli boycott of Palestinian goods is allegedly to protect Israel's safety (bombs etc.). But the ban extends, mysteriously, to the flower dealers of Palestine, who are no danger to Israel, but who do sell flowers at half the price of the Israeli farmers. The result is: Israel bans the flower sellers, who in return dig tunnels to bring in their flowers, Israel turns a blind eye, until a provocation occurs and then Israel can come down hard on the tunnels.

Next, this is a "**BLOOD**" Meme-based conflict, because these two groups come from differing tribal groupings that were originally the same peoples. However, 2,000 years of journeying has driven them apart.

Finally, there is present a "**BADNESS**" Meme. Muslim groups in Iran call for Israel's annihilation, while U.S. World Scripters (imperialist) see Israel as a wedge power to divide the Muslim world in half (Africa from Middle East).

Of course, as in any war setting, Badness Memes, such as criminal enterprises and weapons dealers masquerading as legitimate enterprises, complicate the conflict even more.

Many national governments are Badness type memes, little more than "**Cleptocracies**." These countries are deeply involved in corruption and terrorizing their national populations, shoving wealth into the treasuries of their oligarchs. Somalia under the war lords was a good example:

Rulers rake in the cash, the People spill the blood!

So, you have just ONE MEME CONFLICT involving **Belief + Business + Blood + Beulah and Badness** and the whole thing is backed up by people around the world, thus introducing a **Boldness** meme. This is to say, the conflict is now a **cause or crusade to win**, a curse to people the world over.

> **TWENTY-FOUR: Meme Law states: The more Platforms (types) a Meme can claim, the more diverse its support and the greater power it can wield. Conversely, the more Platforms involved, the greater the possibility of long-term unresolvable conflict.**

Here is where we should explain that every Meme is impacted by two basic forces: (1) **Internal** and (2) **External**. These can be for the benefit of the Meme or to its detriment.

Since a Meme is a mental structure (cognitively formed) rather than a physical one, its internal forces are generated by the thinking processes of its members and supporters (some clandestine). Memes rarely react to stimuli from minds or attitude from outside their inner circle. Often, the membership actually thrives on the deleterious thoughts of outsiders towards actions being perpetrated inside the organism.

Belief-based Memes are the most intransigent - religion, for example. But also, wherever you see the suffix "ism," you have encountered a Belief-based Meme, religious or not; **Capital "ISM"** vs. **Commune "ISM" and Democrat** Party **"ISM"** vs. **Republican** Party **"ISM"** are two current hot examples.

In these cases, reason and factual arguments will usually hold little sway on their course, as they emanate from the emotional brain rather than encountering the rational brain (frontal cortex).

Notes

Religion, a pure **Belief-based** organism, is strengthened by external beliefs about it and these Memes actually appear stronger under societal fire. Take the early Christians, for example. After the death of Jesus, first Jews and then Romans persecuted the sect. For two hundred years the Meme became stronger and more cohesive due to the persecution.

The same is true today, as fact-based Americans see the horrible behavior of Donald Trump. No matter how many stats and videos are revealed proving the president is out of order, it just impacts his believers to stand firmer. The reason: his **followers have converted him into an ISM**, (Belief-based) like a religion. His followers are NOT Republican they a simply "Trumpers" and that is an "ISM" and a sub-Meme therein.

As we have said before, the most famous example in history was the seemingly insane devotion to Herr Hitler by the German people, even as the bombs destroyed the German nation.

In the fledging Christian sect case, when the sect became Rome's state religion, external threat gone and receiving thousands of new members, it actually ruined that faith, from which it never completely recovered. Every 60 years since, new "bottom up," very internal forces break from the faith, starting reform movements.

The Master Meme is demonized during the revolt, but most of these upstarts are in time absorbed back into the Master Meme, which then regains homeostasis. Religious Orders (Benedictines, Jesuits, etc.) came from this process, as do Protestant denominations. Both are leftovers from past internal Meme conflicts.

One can see this same obliviousness to outside opinion in today's Middle East conflict. Islam is ripping itself to shreds as the entire world looks on. The Sunni sect and the Shiite sect hack each other to death with nary a word from inside that structure, while international groups speak out, only to receive disdain from inside the faith from both antagonists.

Even normally docile organizations, like the Egyptian Muslim Brotherhood, are changing into militant machines, seemingly, from a mysterious outside force, which we now understand to be smaller supporting Memes or self-serving larger Memes looking to profit from the warring. The result is that the region and the major sub memes are now joined at the hip in battle (Shadi Hamid. <u>Temptations of Power</u>. NY: Oxford University Press 2014: *pp. 19-30*).

An unsettled inner Meme conflict is found in the U.S. with our struggle with capital punishment. The rest of the Western civilized world has long abandoned this practice, so much so that other civilized countries will not sell our country the chemicals to kill our own in protest of us. Normally, Memes care little what other groups think of them, because they react only to their own internal forces.

In spite of this international condemnation, we stagger ahead blithely looking for other ways of carrying out this primitive practice, even to the extent of rebirthing electrocution rather than repenting and changing. Emotions also enter into the tide of support. I myself stand in front of the TV at news time screaming "kill the bas_____" when hearing of gangs of three or four teens, beating people to death and the latest atrocity: setting old people on fire so you can rob them.

We had the same conflict deciding on slavery, keeping and defending the practice 40 years after it was outlawed everywhere else (1830-1860).

> **TWENTY-FIVE: Meme Law states: External pressure from other like-kinds of Memes elicits a combative defensive response from the targeted Meme, which usually requires a punitive response from the correcting Memes to achieve changes in the target Meme's behavior. This principle of other-Meme interference, if pushed to the extreme, can be the primary lead-up to war.**

Since these external forces are always present in the form of conflict with other like-Memes, it is vital to the understanding of the human condition to be ever aware of the type of Memes with which you are dealing.

Business-based organisms are always aware of competition, creating the need to adapt and readapt to market forces. **Blood-based** Memes (Families), that is,

Notes

matriarch-and-patriarch centered units, are often assaulted many times in their partnership by would-be suitors desiring to steal away one or the other.

A perfect example of the Meme Law above comes when dealing with a Family Meme (Blood) working with Memes outside the family (schools, family services, etc.). One can often run into severe resistance when attempting to achieve a corrective action to save a family's children. I have been threatened with violence if my church and I didn't "butt out!" In any Meme, conflicted outsiders are in danger of being "**triangled**" (third party in a conflict) into becoming "the Beating Boy".

The police and the courts receive the same resistance to outside intervention. The children that I was blocked trying to help went on to become criminals and/or suffered early deaths.

In India, an entire government (National meme) finds itself at risk, finally forced **from outside criticism** to call for the end to routine rape, often ordered by local government officials. The above should help us see that, just because your Meme leaders call you to fight against an "external threat," it may NOT be a threat at all, regardless of the ranting of your leaders calling any objections TREASON!

SIDEBAR: Beginning in 2017 President Trump began to use this CRIMINAL rhetoric MORE THAN any other leader in our history. Twenty-four (24) times in two years he referred to Democrats, other world leaders, civil servants and news media as TREASONOUS. This is a record! Most chief executives have NEVER uttered the word. Remember "LOCK HER UP" (another first)

RI is Not POLITICAL, We are a Group Dynamic Inst..

Keep in mind: external threats almost never destroy a Meme. The competitor may assault, the lover may woo, or the other religion may proselytize the believer, but Meme challengers will not secure victory until some "internal force" pushes the targeted Meme into troubled waters.

In EVERY Meme structure, especially a BUSINESS model, the focus of the culture is usually determined by those in charge of the **Arena of Ideas and Beliefs** (lead Clergy, Politicians and Military at the behest of the Power Elites.

This CULTURAL FOCUS is either **PROFESSIONAL** (Professing the highest of ethics and an effort for the good of all) or **PROFITEERING** (Profit as the motive for those in charge).

Remember this headline:

Two BOEING 747 Max CRASH – 346 DEAD!

Most people believe this happened in October of 2018 and March of 2019, but that's only a half truth.

The events that made these plains go down began in 1997 with the buyout of Boeing (a company famous for it engineering PROFESSIONALISM) by McDonnell Douglas (a company known for its high profit margins, a lean-mean machine focused on PROFITEERING).

From the first day lifelong professional systems engineer Cynthia Cole said the new company was "appalling" emphasizing cutting cost and pushing for speed.

Prof. Leon Grunberg (author of <u>Emerging from Turbulence</u>, the story of the takeover of Boeing) says "the bean-counters, the finance guys became the dominant people," the engineers and PROFESSIONALS were out and the PROFITEERS were in.

This fast emerging management style change is ruining American business top to bottom. Even our chief commercial adversary Russia and its leader Vladimir Putin warned in a NYT article that this change from excellence in product to profiteering would destroy American business

The crashes happened in 2018-19, but those 346 people were already doomed years before.

A real internal threat to a family may be more along the lines of a job calling one member of the Meme, say the wife, to another job in a foreign city. Another may be vocational advancement of one member to a level where the spouse cannot find a way in.

Nevertheless, just as "no one is an island," no Meme can last unless it interacts with the world around it. In unhealthy Memes, that may mean total withdrawal from the world. Interaction among healthy Memes brings changes in their Operating Philosophies and each adapts or adopts if necessary. In unhealthy Memes, this interaction is blocked, which will eventually destroy an unhealthy Social Organism. Isolation from the world causes stagnation and if nothing else, the isolated organism will die from lack of fresh bodies (attrition).

To would-be dictators this "WE are superior and need no other nation" attitude is a necessity in segregating his/her population so the ruler can invoke total control.

The American Amish community is a perfect example of this scenario in a Religious Meme (Belief). An exclusive "Club" in center city Wilmington, Delaware, an elite body accepting very limited entry, is another self-exiled group. They have even removed the sign on their building and avoid seeking new members. Once extremely influential in the area's affairs, they are now seen as irrelevant.

> **TWENTY-SIX: Meme Law states: Closed Memes, more often "Belief – Blood - and - Beulah located," seek to restrict membership, which often brings an end to the Meme through attrition. Open Memes, most often "Badness – Business – and - Boldness located," depend upon large numbers of people to achieve their goal, so they willingly expand membership accordingly.**

America's "Charismatic" churches are the best at Memeing-up or Memeing-in usually disparate types of members to make a big successful Master Meme. Often, these normally limited Belief-based religious memes will also include a crusade theology to go out and convert the world (Boldness). Then they will operate TV and radio stations, bookstores and even theme parks, or work with cruise lines, thus adding a profit Business-based Meme. This accounts for the abundance of their churches which often boast 10,000 to 50,000 members.

It should be noted here it is NOT the theology which creates the "evangelistic" imperative, the Landmark Forum, an out-growth of Est, has no God call in their doctrine, yet they capitalizes on their participants to contact EVERYONE they know to "bring them in."

Business-based Memes are by nature, open, and have it the easiest in facing change and accepting new people. It is simple: "You change and adapt, or you're gone." External forces, are here mostly seen as good. Not all businesses stay true to form and the results are disastrous.

Recently a family in Baltimore bought a famous old, but many-years-abandoned restaurant. They spent hundreds of thousands on the renovations. They assumed the long-ago fame would bring them business, so they waited inside for the public to come. They had shut themselves off from the outside community insuring that no one would come and they failed.

Political and Religious Memes (countries and churches), which are a combination of Belief and Beulah-based Platforms, "seem" not to understand that, while it is human nature not to trust other humans, and especially others from other Memes, this mistrust hurts the isolationist Meme the most.

In all cases, since like-Memes tend towards combat with each other, so also, people that belong to opposing Memes are so identified. This non-trust facilitates combative relationships which have been harvested by political leaders throughout history and are employed by rulers to muster their populations off to war (external threat). But also, the individual component is used to conduct pogroms against "foreign" people within one's own society (internal threat).

Notes

In his famous book <u>Awash in a Sea of Faith,</u> (Cambridge, MA. Harvard Univ. Press, 1990), Jon Butler reminds readers that the American Rebellion against Britain was at a dead standstill and nearing failure when the leaders began enlisting the churches in support of the fight. Without this allegiance, America would be a British Colony today. **Without a "god" factor, there can NEVER be a WAR.** That's worth repeating:

POLITICAL MEMES REQUIRE A RELIGIOUS MEME TO CREATE A WAR!!!!!!!

IBM shot itself in the foot back in the 1970s by allowing a sub-dominant but powerful sub-meme, its Main Frame Division, to use this xenophobic fear to engineer an inter-departmental fight (internal threat) to persecute and force the closing of its fledging Personal Computer and Software Operations. Prior to the closing of the new PC Division, IBM was the world's leader in the computer industry. Bill Gates, HP and Dell would be unknown today if it were not for this internal sub-Meme dispute as part of a successful Business Meme. IBM nearly went under from this "monstrous" BOOBOO. This goes to demonstrate how just two or three people, using Meme Law, can derail a major enterprise with an **Internal Threat**.

> **TWENTY-SEVEN: Meme Law states: When a subordinate-Meme forms inside a Master Meme, it must be quietly expelled or accommodated, if not, great harm or dissolution will be experienced inside the Master Meme.**

Countries and corporations are little different from street gangs. They never allow a like kind of meme (another country or company) to draw near, seeing them as an invader or as a competitor to be squashed (xenophobic response). So it is that we live on a planet where we are infected by continual "wars and rumors of wars."

REMINDER: *At all levels, Memes meeting other like- Memes have a default setting of combat (ML Five).* This is the Meme Law that has kept Europe divided and at war with itself for 2,000 years. It is also the principle that keeps Europeans shunning and combating against Russians (migrated Swedes) for 1,264 of those years. Currently BREXIT (ML 5) may spell doom for the E. U.

TWENTY-EIGHT: Meme Law states: Memes desiring to merge with other Memes, which they would normally repel or conquer, in order to survive and thrive, require strong internal leadership to overcome the will of individual members, who normally reject such transplanting of Meme loyalties. This rejection is entirely visceral, caused by organizational DNA, just as our physical bodies reject transplanted organs.

European tribes (countries) used this internal leadership change agent for centuries to attempt to bring the continent to peace. The ruling families were cross-bred and inter-married to accomplish this goal. A German family was brought to England, where they still rule. One of them, Queen Elizabeth's husband's mother, Grace, was married off to a German, who was then called to be the king of Greece.

External forces that affect a Meme may be social standards set by a larger more powerful Meme to which the lesser belongs. Look at the Mormons. Upon founding, one of their most deeply held theological beliefs was polygamy (GOD said: one husband, many wives). When seeking statehood for their homeland in Utah, this **subdominant meme** faced a condition set by the American community (**Master Meme**), which was that their denomination had to surrender to this outside external force and give up polygamy.

SO – God changed God's mind and forbad polygamy.

Interestingly, polygamy among the Mormons rarely existed until their leader was "forced" in midlife, to accept it, if he wished to continue as the leader. His new bride was a 16 year-old. The first and much older Ms. Young never forgave him, but old Brigham soon liked it a lot, wonder why? (*)

(*) **DISCLAIMER:** The above attempt at cheap burlesque humor is a perfect example of **how we make fun of the tragedies in another Meme.** I am reminded of the horrible gas stove jokes after WWII targeting Jews! **My inconsiderate attempt at comedy mocked the plight of women and inadvertently gave a wink to girls who suffer through pedophilia - BOTH of which I appall. I deeply apologize,** but instead of doing a simple correction, I leave my insensitivity as a teaching-tool showing **a Meme member (ME:**

non-Mormon, male) ignoring the cries from another Meme (THEM: (Mormon, female) and making fun of their situation (ML: 5; 37; 38; 41; 45; 50)

Here's a current interesting observation on Mormon Meme beliefs. In June of 2014, the church excommunicated a woman who began an organization to see women ordained to the priesthood. She was soundly rejected, as was this cause in EVERY other religion throughout history. Now that she is booted out, according to Mormon Law her marriage bond is also dissolved, and she can't go to heaven - little do religious lawyers know!

¿Have you ever noticed that almost all these religious cases of severe dissent involve women? This universality means the "sexist" thing is both an external threat and an internal one.

I personally believe this massive rejection of the female by the religious Memes is because the religious Meme is itself a Female Meme, that is, a Meme dedicated to handling issues of feelings and emotions relating to the female persona (child rearing, family, morality and the sacred).

Males lean toward Memes that deal with the profane, operations, production and the secular. So, in this case, the female gendered Meme rejects and controls OUT its own gender.

> **TWENTY-NINE: Meme Law states: Memes may have a tendency to support a gender identity, i.e., MALE or FEMALE, usually determined by the operations of the Meme being gender specific.**

The Mormons more easily gave up their probation of Black members after the Civil Rights Act (external threat). Yet, there was another external force also involved in this decision, resulting in the Mormons changing their belief structure. In the past, only 144,000 of them could go to heaven. The addition of their one millionth member called for adjustments to be made. It would appear, **nothing is sacred to a Meme needing to survive**, regardless of what god (?) has spoken for centuries! Poor god (?)!

Let's look at the **Internal forces** that impact a Human Social Organism. In order to understand these social cells, though abstract in nature, and these mysterious internal forces, we need to be aware that all social cells are impacted by the same natural forces that affect physical ones.

> **THIRTY: Meme Law states: Memes are just as subject to universal scientific principles and physical laws as the rest of the universe.**

By way of example:

> **FIRST**: *"For every action there is an opposite and equal reaction."*

> **SECOND**: *Human social cells (Memes), like physical cells, have the tendency to divide.*

Both of these very basic UNIVERSAL truths work, both with and against each other, to fire the furnace of every Meme on earth, from the smallest family to the largest state. Know these truths and you can predict future events and understand the world's most intricate developments.

Rulers, throughout all history, have kept these principles before them as they create the paths of history. Ancient Prophets, understanding these basics of human society, were able to predict outcomes with astonishing accuracy.

All through my life, I have witnessed a seemingly mysterious epidemic of war invade the human species. This pathological behavior has kept the West in a killing posture for the past 100 years plus and the East fighting against it for the same period. Armed with this knowledge of the internal Meme forces listed above, those ruling us are able to profit enormously for themselves, even if thousands of us die in the process.

Knowing the External and the Internal Principles of Human Social Organisms has allowed the Western oligarchs (**corporations and capitalists**), beginning in the early 1800s, to continually **control the peoples of Africa and Asia mostly to the benefit of Europe and America.**

Notes

We began extracting their natural resources (oil and base metals) by setting them at odds with each other, while Western power elites plundered their lands. All the while millions, on all sides died in the struggle.

As we touched on before, Tim Weiner, in his famous book <u>Legacy of Ashes,</u> tells the tale of a war-weary America and Europe (1945) sitting down to end this Meme combat model of running the world. They began a United Nations to inaugurate a world peace model based on collaboration and universal respect and prosperity. Their goal was to end war once and for all, an idea that would have halted the U.S. Power Elites' plan to dominate the future world.

Unfortunately, natural law reared its ugly head as an "equal and opposite" reaction to this effort was started in a small group of WWII intelligence leaders and ambitious American Imperialists. The anticommunist John Birch Society joined Ruling Class would-bes, led by Secretary of State John Foster Dulles (America's corporate big boy) and his brother Allan (CIA) to lead the reactive fight.

Their dream was that the U.S. would prosper into an Empire, taking the seat of the then defunct European Empires, if we followed some simple Meme Laws. This group of future international "terrorists" met at a home in Georgetown on Sunday evenings (1946-47) to plan programs to **counter the spirit of the United Nations** by keeping **combat and competition and WAR alive** in search of their goal of world domination.

Their knowledge of Meme Law (remember they never heard the word Meme) led them to form the **Central Intelligence Agency's Clandestine Division**.

> **CIA PLAYBOOK:** *"The United States will use the CIA-CLD to irritate other nations to discourage and manipulate them, inflaming them to WAR or civil conflict, creating competition and conflict worldwide to the benefit of capitalism and American advantage.*

Understanding that **like-Memes will combat each other as a natural process (ML: 3;25;31;33), the CIA operatives circled the globe fomenting unrest**, while other agents backed by establishment, wealthy Americans, fostered the cry: **"Get us out of the UN!"** Many Christian churches in America (subordinate Memes to the establishment, and members of the Ruling Class) either remained silent or most often joined in the anti-UN, anti-Internationalist crusade.

Virtually every time shots were fired or some group from the Third World rebelled at the yoke Western powers had placed on them, the American establishment and their political-religious arm blamed the United Nations, the Communists and "Evil Empires." While all the time, it was **U.S. cloak and daggers creating the havoc** and exploiting the former European colonial's dissatisfaction.

This group of fledgling American rulers, although by nature anti-Semitic, backed the planting of Israel smack-dab in the center of the Middle East with the deliberate goal of dividing the Islamic power Meme, remnants leftover from the then defunct Ottoman Empire, in half. Understanding Meme Law, they full well knew that resettling hundreds of thousands of "foreigners" (European Jews) and taking millions of acres of land from longtime residents (Palestinians) who had occupied it for 2,000 years, would set the Middle East on fire. It still burns today!

At a conference on anti-Semitism in Washington (2015), many of the panelists were ready to acknowledge the many people who try to establish evenhandedness in the world's relationships with Israel (this writer and President Obama included).

Critics are NOT Israel's enemies. The panel worked to lift the name "Anti-Jewish" or "Anti-Semitism" from those who seek parity between Israel and Palestine. People who have pointed to the unfairness of the West's dealing with the Palestinian people continue to be sidelined and labeled as "troublemakers." While former U.S. leaders fell short President Trump has done much to reignite this conflict.

One major publisher refuses to publish anything the slightest bit critical of Israel. I have been caught up in that dragnet with this book.

Notes

Within the first ten years, the CIA clandestine group had indeed set the world on fire, destroying the governments of El Salvador, Venezuela, Iran, Argentina, Indonesia and the entire Middle East. All they had to know was basic Meme Law, introduce certain enablers to the mix, and "voila" nature takes its course!

In her earth shaking book, <u>The Shock Doctrine</u> (NY: Henry Holt and Company 2007), Naomi Klein actually mirrors Meme Law when putting forth that: the rulers of the West have made the most of this scientific principle of "opposite and equal reactions" to control history.

IMPORTANT – WORLD RULE PRINCIPLE

When a **Power Center** of a Meme understands the principle of "Action vs. Reaction," they can **orchestrate events** to elicit an **opposite negative reaction** to a **staged event**. Then, by making sure their **money** is where it is badly **needed** and very **profitable to lend**, the **manipulators make a fortune**, no matter what the outcome.

RESULT: We *Americans live well /others starve!*

The UN was nearly destroyed, and the American finance, manufacturing and military complex made billions cleaning up Western-staged disasters.

President Eisenhower (R) witnessing these events warned of their "future shock" impact, but he was unable to stop them. As a result of his exposures, he fell into the disfavor of his own party by warning of the coming danger from this growing **sub-meme**, which he labeled: "**the military –industrial complex.**"

We have all seen these type of scenarios play out in our own communities. In my high school (1958-60), a little twit of a kid used to run back and forth between two street corners a half block apart. One was where the Black guys hung out, the other was the roost of the White guys. This kid would run up telling a Black guy, "That White guy over there says you stink." He would then run to the Whites telling them, "That big Black kid said: "F-c- all you Whites." You can imagine, within two more trips a gang fight would erupt and the "tattle tale instigator" would steal all the best bagged lunches and be gone.

This is what Klein correctly purports the U.S. did for twenty years after WWII. I remind us all, "a leopard does not change its spots," and this same U.S. behavior continues to this very day.

> **THIRTY-ONE: Meme Law states: Memes seeking to disrupt the world at peace will work to accentuate the Meme markers of two opposing Memes (race, language, religion), resulting in a xenophobic backlash and a "Dogfight" of spontaneous combative relationship.**

Another of these Universal basics is that human social cells, like physical ones, keep dividing. This helps explain why Memes are bipolar, just as all people are bipolar to at least a small degree. This bit of Meme Law is a factor responsible for the dynamic, often unpredictable movement within a Meme.

We tend to think that only a small portion of us who are classified as "clinically depressed" suffer this malady. But, it's not so! We all struggle with the internal opposition (the other "me"). It's just that some people have a weaker pendulum than others and show more symptoms of vacillation than others.

This division in personality has much to do with the dividing cells idea and it is enhanced by the principle that every action has an equal and opposite action. Even in the beginning of a human's life, we are both male and female. As we develop, we are at the same instant a selfish grabber and a lovely sharer. As my mother used to say of me (age 9), "You are a street saint and a house devil" (Mom was a manic depressive).

Also, by understanding the basic law of the ever-dividing Meme combined with the axiom: "for every action there is an equal and opposite reaction," we can understand why, when a Meme is formed, immediately, there will form an opposition to the ruling philosophy and its rulers within the life of the Meme. As a result, we can safely say:

Notes

THIRTY-TWO: Meme Law states: ALL Memes are bipolar and subject to being ignited by certain triggers, the most usual of which are fear (paranoia), greed and self-interest, any or all of which can trigger schizophrenia (internal opposition) and render a Meme unstable and dangerous.

When Memeing-up takes place and a new Human Social Organism is created, even though everyone believes it to be homogenous and in solidarity, splits begin to occur. In other cases, when two opposing forces attempt to Meme-up to defeat a common foe, once that foe is gone, the newly unified partner Memes will turn on each other and often the resulting civil war is worse than the first condition.

A case in point would be Nicaragua and the iron fists of its dictator, Somoza (1936-74).

Both rich businesspeople and poor farmers opposed him, but neither could dislodge him because United States interests, the United Fruit Company (there's our John Foster [Sec. of State] and Allan Dulles [CIA] brothers), were behind him. President Franklin Roosevelt said of the dictator, "He may be a son-of-a-bitch, but he's our son-of- a-bitch" (Penny Lernoux, <u>Cry of the People</u>. NY: Penguin Books 1980 p. 81).

As a result, the poor (Sandinistas) and the business class (Contras) joined forces and they won in a matter of months. However, the blood was not dry on the sidewalks when these two bedfellows began killing each other. Backed by the United States, the Contras were given guns, paid for by the CIA's sale of drugs on the streets of the United States, in exchange for even cheaper fruit for our markets (see the motion picture "To Kill the Messenger," 2014).

The USSR helped the Sandinistas when the U.S. refused to provide weapons to protect the common people in this fight with their former "friends." Both the USSR and the U.S. were completely responsible for the civil war that followed.

The initial pole of the bipolar Meme occurred when a Master Meme (Nicaragua) had its center taken by dictator Samosa, who then enslaved his people with the help of an external force (The United States). This external force could then acquire cheap produce.

A second pole (internal), made up of ALL the Meme's lower class population, formed a sub-Meme and warred against its own center. That is "revolution."

Upon winning that revolt, the sub-Meme (now the new Master Meme) formed two opposing poles (Contras – Sandinistas) and civil war broke out. As always, external forces, again the United States and, later the USSR each backed one of the combatants. Thousands died!

Finally, the Meme fell into peace when the population gave up their struggle and the externals backed away. The fact that the USSR was soon to collapse had an impact on the de-escalation. A political change in the U.S. served the same purpose.

In Nicaragua in the 1980s, Syria in 2012, and in Ukraine in 2014+, it is the externals that enrage and expand inner- Meme violence by pulling the two poles apart and fortifying the opposing forces. The U.S. is a major player in these efforts and responsible for most of the bloodshed in Central America in the 1965-92 era, much like the High school twit that cried: "Fight," and then stole the lunches.

Ironically, all this skullduggery involves the principle of "**Quid pro quo** – if you'll do this, we'll do that." This principle of inter-Meme extortion was unearthed in the fall of 2019, wielded by the U.S. President in illegally withholding a congressional grant to Ukraine until he received a PERSONAL favor.

Powerful people are manipulating Meme Law again. I say, "again," because Great Britain, the Dutch, France and Portugal employed this same "divide and conquer" strategy with tribal Memes in India, Rwanda, Indochina, Burma and the Asian Pacific for two hundred years before the U.S. started playing.

Rome invented this "imperious" method 2,000 years prior (Timothy Parsons, The Rules of Empire. NY: Oxford University Press 2010).

THIRTY-THREE: Meme Law states: The most effective way to extend control over another Meme is to allow Meme Laws to divide its population into its subdominant parts, then set each at odds with the

Notes

others and conquer the target Meme, using its own polar opposites to effect its downfall.

One very recent example of a people trying to undo Western nations' interference leading up to their colonial takeover is in Burma (Myanmar). During that postcolonial era and especially over the past ten years, on U.S. and European news we have heard how these bad guys in Myanmar (the West EMPHATICALLY calls the country by it's colonial name "Burma") need to be replaced.

What you weren't told is that a hundred years ago, wishing to control this area, Britain chose one of the four tribes populating this area, the Burmese. They armed them, gave them authority and money, and told them to subdue the other three tribes.

Once done, the Burmese tribe built their new capital at Rangoon and the members of their tribe became wealthy and powerful, while the other three tribes were allowed the honor of being poor and destitute.

For decades, the Burmese tribe subjugated the other three tribes, funneling their indigenous wealth off to London. Burma was "good" to their benefactor Great Britain."

After independence from Britain the people as a whole, wanted to better express what the area meant to all the four tribes, so they used their native word for "The Land" (Myanmar), meaning all of the people, instead of the Brits-imposed name for one tribe.

However, when Hillary Clinton, the "White Westerner," visited Myanmar, she verbalized, "Burma," and not Myanmar. By the nature of her office in the Western Meme, desiring to restore homeostasis to the Western model and to keep the peace with our buddies, had to endorse the Brits' title once again. I'm sure she was unaware of the fact that she betrayed her own call for fair justice, but that's Meme Law.

As in most other cases of Meme Law, this "divide and conquer" also applies to fledgling Memes just as it does in personal relationship building. ¿Have you noticed that among three or four friends, one or more are always attempting to drive wedges between the relationships? Usually, that is due to the activist person desiring to control the relationship by isolating the others in the group, one from another. This phenomenon infects smaller Memes, especially Families, Churches, Garden Clubs and the like.

It can become acute as it did in our earlier Storyboard highlighting the three girls going into the woods (chapter 1). It becomes world-changing when nations isolate other nations from a rival nation (Russia vs. the United States).

Now, to the most prevalent internal force governing Meme dynamics: **the natural flow of its members' energies is toward the center** (usually referred to as the "top," but we avoid "pie slicing" our diagram). Just as natural as high and low pressure areas impact our globe, this inward force is always present and an important dynamic, no matter what kind of Meme we are investigating.

Looking once again at the Paradigm of Human Society (Diagram #8), you'll note that there is a ubiquitous pressure from the outside to gain admittance. Also, just inside the Meme there is like pressure exerted by those most outside the security of the center to push their way into better places ("in" or, more popularly, "up").

So now, we have outsiders, aliens and/or migrants pushing to get in, while just one step inside, others (the young and refugees) are the poor pushing to get accepted at the table. This pressures the largest group, the Worker and Doers, usually thought to be oblivious of such forces, to animate their own efforts. First they must keep the new arrivals out, then climb closer to the center themselves (more money, job promotions, children to better education). As all these forces converge toward the center, they push the cadre, the first inner circle, interpreters of the society, to respond to this perceived threat.

All members will fight to keep their preferred place by putting down the newcomers and by conniving to see themselves promoted to a more inside (privileged) position.

In this process, the Power Elites and Ruling Classes are protecting their positions by promoting their allies among the Cadre to more powerful positions. Simultaneously, these elites harvest the energy produced by the struggle of those lower than themselves.

Notes

These powerholders push the flow of energy back at the people using their own productivity, now placed into the ruler's own coffers, creating ever greater wealth for themselves (this is the very basis of corruption).

The World Bank, under its President Jim Yong Kim (whom I've met with on three occasions), estimates that this upper level corruption in corporations and governments is a 35% reducer in the world's gross wealth index. That means that everyone's earnings from legitimate labor are reduced by a third, thanks to this "skimming" or "syphoning-off" the top.

> **THIRTY-FOUR: Meme Law states: The more powerful a Meme member becomes, the greater the opportunity and tendency to retain Meme wealth that passes his/her way for personal use. This is a consequence of a leader's requirement to completely surrender to the Meme, therefore, there is a tendency to view the organism's wealth as their personal largess.**

The final step in closing the loop of this dynamic happens when the Ruling Class enacts laws, sets rules or changes moral standards (religious controls). In this way, the wealthy and their handpicked rulers profit from this "inward-upward" flow of the economic energies and then they can use the rule of law to push the producers back down and out.

Once the playing field is altered and the smoke clears, the outsiders are still out, the poor and Marginals are just as poor as before, the Workers are decidedly worse off than before, lower level cadre are in jail or on the street and the major champions of reform are in prison. All the while, a few very clever players make deals and fly into the inner sanctum, the Arena of Ideas and Beliefs (see "House of Cards" TV series on Netflix for an excellent, albeit fictitious, portrayal of this continuing phenomenon).

> **THIRTY-FIVE: Meme Law states: The "Arena of Ideas and Beliefs" (Ruling Class) is represented in each society by the three major groups needed to control any organism. In America and most modern states,**

the POLITICIANS make the rules, the CLERGY assuage the masses and assure them that the Deity has sanctioned the Meme's authority, and then the MILITARY (including Police) force dissenters into compliance.

It should be noted here that throughout the modern era, the Academy (educators) have been, to one degree or another, associated with the Clergy among the Ruling Class. Actually, they were relegated to a Cadre function, nearly at the lowest level. This was because the Renaissance in educational rebirth (1400s) came from religions who spawned the first universities.

Interestingly, they were simultaneously attempting a defense of superstitious taboos that are the stock-in-trade of religion. Society is well on its way to disassociating pastors from professors and already thinks of the two in completely different ways. But we still see the academic process as a "salvation" of the world mechanism. This transition must be accomplished to produce a more authentic social model.

In my opinion, the Academy has formed up in the Arena of Ideas and Beliefs as a fourth power module, which is not sustainable. It seems natural to predict that the academy will supersede the Clergy, taking their place in the equation, which may save religion by pushing it back among the people. Science is now in the process of replacing the superstitions linked to religion and should always be part of the academy.

We need to caution, as even now, Corporate America is attempting to usurp science with grants and big cash gifts, just as they are going to do with civil governance, all in the hunt for patent rights and never-ending royalties.

In the worst cases, this power process involves war-based Power Elites and a Ruling class advocating for combat events, some as foreign wars (Korea, Vietnam, Iraq and Afghanistan), some as uprisings (Egypt, Syria, Tunisia and Arab Maghreb) internal to the nations involved.

To all this, other harms done in this "war-violence based model," we must add hundreds of thousands of deaths, dismemberments and ruined generations. And, while this is natural law (survival of the fittest) and normal Meme force flow (Meme dynamics), it is not the dynamic itself that causes the killings. Rather, it's the knowledge of Meme Law and its dynamics (how Memes work) manipulated by unscrupulous, ambitious players (Sociopaths), combined with public apathy and/or ignorance of Meme Law, by the general population that allows us all to join in on the slaughter!

One can find numerous social experiments from professional journals, like "Social Research: An International Quarterly" (The New School, published by Johns Hopkins Press) each of which use different definitions, explanations and titles. They all agree, however, that whenever humans Meme-up (gather-up), they will invariably need Leaders and Enforcers to make "it" happen, Nerds to smooth the interaction and Dupes or Jokers to bite the bullet, laugh away the tears and carry out the duties.

BEGIN SIDEBAR:

This model is ubiquitous across human society. Experiments conducted in a myriad of venues by many researchers, beginning with Richard Savin-Williams, found that Meme-up behaviors are nearly "preordained," like "blueprints" in EVERY situation (Howard Bloom. The Lucifer Principle *pp* 91-93).

In one series of experiments, campers, both male and female, chosen at random and unknown to each other, upon meeting, would spend a few minutes getting acquainted. Then, they would appoint Meme-up) one as a LEADER (*Alpha- Authority*), one as a BULLY (*Beta-Enforcer*), one as a NERD (*Gamma-Geek*) and a fourth as a JOKER (*Delta-Dunce*). *Titles in Italics are mine from my seminars,* all caps are Bloom's. Knowing these "gather up" norms, one can easily see how Memes are organized and structured without plan, but out of need as normal human group behaviors.

At the center of a Meme, cascading outwardly, we find three of these positions: *Alpha* LEADERS=Politicians; *Beta* BULLIES=Military & Police; *Gamma* NERDS=Cadre, Clergy and WORKERS-DOERS which are 80% of the population. Last is the *Delta* JOKERS=the party guys, the avoid responsibility bunch, also the social dropouts.

END SIDEBAR.

VIII//: Meme Madness

STORY BOARD

It was the fall of 1864. Two solders approached a small stream in Virginia from different directions. One was Confederate, one a Union. They drew down on each other immediately!.

Then realizing no one from their Memes (army) was watching, they decided to make a fire and share their rations. They laughed and talked.

As time went on their opposing armies were closing in on their stream, but these two isolated ones became friends realizing they had so much in common (same dreams, same everything).

But, after several hours of fellowship, with their respective armies only feet away: they both stood, picked up their rifles and killed each other.

War memes are humans' worst failing!

One of the world's great philosophers wrote a book (1852) entitled: <u>Extraordinary Popular Delusions and Madness of Crowds</u>. While Charles Mackay had never heard the word Meme, had never studied group dynamics and even sociology was an unknown discipline, he managed to discuss the mysterious mad behaviors of otherwise rational people within a group or social setting. He never knew it, but he wrote the first book on "Meme Madness."

He highlights three major incidents when seemingly rational individuals acted like crazed animals in pursuit of riches.

First, he tells of the "South Seas Incident of 1711," as investors literally shoved millions of pounds (dollars) at those running the trading companies working to establish trade among these newly discovered islands. For nine years, shares grew by 1700 % (percent) until a single share would buy a house in London. All of a sudden, the bubble burst as realists discovered that while there was wealth to be had, the price of buying in had been inflated beyond any possible return. Within days, thousands of people lost their entire fortune, homes, businesses and titles.

Later in France, the exact same thing happened, as Scotsman John Law (credited as the real founder of what we call capitalism) sold and resold French citizens on investing in France's new territories in the "Membership Scheme of 1717." Year after year, there were duels fought over the right to buy stock. At one point, the entire issue was worth about what it would likely be in the 1940s, two hundred years in the future. If only the investors could have waited.

Unfortunately, they couldn't, and soon that bubble also burst and investments worth about $3,000 in today's dollars were worth less than $8 dollars.

The irony, as Mackay reported it, was that these incidents happened after a similar one in 1634 Holland. Here, a run on tulip bulbs drove the price of a single bulb from about ten cents to $10,000 in a matter of weeks. People were borrowing on their houses to buy one bulb.

Again, when the correction came, "Tulip Mania" was over in a single weekend. In debt for half a million dollars, people were left with a dozen bulbs worth ninety-nine cents each.

Before we start pontificating over "their" stupidity, let's not forget America circa 1929, when the stock shares in corporations became inflated, not because the corporations were worth more, but because the shares themselves were in demand. People paid 3% to 25% to even 500% over value for stocks, until on a single Tuesday, the market crashed and many stocks worth $1.00, but not their listing of $500.00, sold again for the proper price of $1.00. Another edition of "millions ruined."

As for our generation, let's never forget 1983: Enron, Tyco, World Com and the "Dot Com" bust. Then came the real-estate-based crash of 2008. Many readers lost everything in pursuit of a home as a "secure" investment, while some of us became homeless. **That too was "Meme Madness!"**

Understanding how the human mind works within social Memes, in this last case, my own society, I watched as people begged, borrowed and stole to get cash to buy homes, that, in 1999, were worth $80,000, as they sold for "150 thousand dollars, oops I mean 300 thousand dollars, oh no, there it goes again for 450 thousand dollars!" That's how fast the frenzy was escalating.

I reacted as a pastor, going from house to house, writing articles of warning and inserted "greed" into my sermons, warning people: "**Don't do this!**" But it was **to no avail. The Meme we call "American Society," including my church and my friends, were struck with "Meme Madness."**

As a PS/ to all this, we are at a spot AGAIN (2020) as folks are borrowing and buying every house in sight. The dream is the same appreciation will make us rich. In the mean time this buying frenzy is "skyrocketing" the price of real-estate and almost every one is a loser, the exception is the trainers who loan you money to get started. When the market collapses they'll take the house, all your equity, sell the house and you will be on the hook for the unpaid loan.

A good lesson in Meme Madness: when a Meme gets in trouble (Workers and Marginals) there is always another group (sub-Meme) say loaners, who will profit immensely.

In private, people would agree with me, they were sensible as individuals. But, when involved in interactions with friends and family Memes, they "bit the bullet." People, who a month before could not pay their electric bill, were borrowing three, four and five hundred thousand dollars to buy homes that were worth $50,000 just a year prior.

Next, investors were lined up to offer another mortgage on the same property, so the formerly impoverished couples could purchase a "Condo in Paradise" with no money down. "What luck!" they said, "We went from near homeless to dual property landowners in ten days, with no money down."

Guess what: As in the tulips three hundred years earlier, in 2008 and soon in 2021(+ or -) we (will) also imploded! **Meme Madness came home to roost again.** In 2010 those $300,000 homes were worth $149,000 and the loans came due. It will repeat next year!

In 2011 Bank of America stock crashed from $23.00 to $7.70 in one week. The party was over. Unfortunately, the goofy pastor who was told to stick to "God stuff" had been right, again. **The truth is ALWAYS God's stuff even in finances!**

Shockingly, it was later revealed by **Allen Greenspan**, Board Chair of the Federal Reserve at the time of the meltdown, himself a lifelong member of the powerful, political-economic Meme and **Ayn Rand's Objectivist Economics cult**, that he: "Never saw it coming" ("*Foreign Affairs,*" *Nov/ Dec 2013*). In the article, he admitted that the crash of 2008 took him "totally by surprise"

Following this revelation, Ben Bernanke, his assistant in 2008, later Board Chair himself, said the exact same thing in 2013 interviews. They both admitted, time after time, that this big mistake was shared by most of the "big time economists" of the day. Naturally, most of whom were also part of the "Chicago School of Economics," named for the University of Chicago. This **faculty was completely sold out to Rand's teachings**. I have named this "**Empire Philosophy**," they call it "**Objectivism**." The acknowledgement of "Empire" simply adds a cultural, even theological, component to objectivism (God has chosen US to RULE the others).

Here is an excellent case of a "Hidden Meme," not openly participating in, not openly touted, but in near total control of an entire nation's economic system.

This is also a perfect example of how even "experts" can be blinded by a "religious-type" Meme (Belief-Based Meme) to which most of the faculty (Chicago School) and Rand's followers belong. This Informal Meme, "Empire Philosophy" or doctrine, is not formalized as such anywhere, but it is the backbone of the "Chicago School of Economics" and now the American republic including at Boeing, in the get rich real-estate game and most American corporations..

Then and now, this **Ayn Rand-powered hidden Informal Meme** rides just below the radar, controlling Western economics and reflecting Rand's "theory" of objectivism, which was evangelized worldwide by Milton Friedman (University of Chicago Economist) and other Rand disciples. Many of these labeled non-religious followers, like other religious-type people, name their children after their iconic leader Ayn Rand (Rand Paul).

The thing is, a scientific belief or ideas, especially in economics, must be proven by mathematical proofs and detailed research. But, in economics, the math is "subjective" and can be manipulated by the practitioners' belief structure. The **Chicago School's Meme teaches the principles: 1)** strength over weakness; that: **2)** "profit justifies anything," and that **3)** "humans have NO duty toward one another's wellbeing and are 4) objects to be commodified."

It is then natural that two of that Meme's chief disciples, Greenspan and Bernanke, just as in any other religions, had their perceptions, successful as they were, blinded to the facts and evidence, just as most religious people do (snake over science). Their faith in their Meme was guiding them to avoid reason, which would have been gained by examining all the facts.

I have a close friend who is well attached to the Hare Krishna movement. I thought this well-informed "gentle" man and I were on the same page concerning the lunacy of war. Come to discover, we are not. He sees war as a necessary part of life, supported by his god.

In his Holy Book, the very first teaching involves a good peaceful young man being scolded by Krishna (a Hindu Christ-like being), telling him he should "get up and pick a side in the war and go fight and kill to the best of his ability."

Notes

Because my friend can't challenge his faith community (Meme) and hold up war as immoral, he must accept war as a godly thing, even though he knows it is evil as hell (pun intended).

¿WHY? The HOLY book says...!

NOTE: *To Judeo-Christians:*

The **Old Testament** is clear: God (?) wants his followers to support war and slaughter of **EVERY MAN**, most **WOMEN**, except those chosen to be concubines [private prostitutes] - that's **RAPE**, and enslave **BOYS, "SHOWING NO MERCY!"** It's in the HOLY book! –

The Hindu prescription for doing war continues down through history, trumping the teachings of the founders of each faith. The first Christians (33 - 400 A.D.) held out as long as any. But, once their religion became a state church, even they gave up their antiwar dogma.

> **THIRTY-SIX: Meme Law states: In order to carry out any act of high destruction and violence, such as war, the Arena of Ideas and Beliefs must be in total accord - The Political, The Military and The Clergy in complete agreement.**

Some may say this is much of what Shankar Vedantam refers to in his 2010 book, <u>The Hidden Brain,</u> *How our* <u>*Unconscious Minds Elect Presidents, Control Markets, Wage Wars and Save Our Lives.*</u> (NY: Spiegel & Grau).

While he never refers to the concept of Memes, he does say that the decisions we make are mostly predetermined by beliefs and standards we unconsciously hold, forcing us to make decisions we think little about.

He is 100% right. I simply add that "these Hidden Brain decisions" are grouped in our minds by the Meme process and many are manipulated by the needs of a Meme, rather than for the individual's benefit.

The "God and Country" process inherited by most of us from our birth community is fostered, DELIBERATELY, in every nation's war room, Kinder-care and in Sunday School. So as you sit in your church pew singing and praying for peace, you are actually being primed for war.

Most likely, the greatest volume of these auto-actions (nearly visceral) arise out of family. In a recent case, a 78-year-old father, a good and noble man, found himself in business failure. Rather than just packing it in and retiring, he inadvertently encouraged his entire family and their Family Meme to keep the failing business together. Instead of releasing his kin, who were on the brink of personal failure and bankruptcy themselves, he continued to accept their sacrifice. Remember, this was one of the least selfish people I have ever known. He and his family had no idea the Meme (business) had so taken over their lives.

Who we marry usually depends on who our father was if we are female. If we are a male, our mother becomes the model - even if you hated your parents. How you handle money is usually the direct result of what you witnessed growing up in your family's environs.

SIDEBAR

Many families have **two polar opposite Memes** coming together. One, say the **father's family**, are frugal and deliberate in making decisions. The other, the **mother's people,** are carefree spendthrifts who decide on the fly. In this case, **one child** will mimic the dad, **the other** the mom. Interestingly, the **third child** just opts out and is demonized by the first two.

END SIDEBAR

Notes

Currently (2020) this drama is playing out on international TV as Diana's grown children, Prince William (like the royal family) and his brother Prince Harry (like his mother) have splintered and like Diana Harry has receded from Royal life. Each now resides in an entirely different Meme.

On and on, Vedantam's "Hidden Brain" is really the edicts of the Memes we all serve.

During the 2008 madness, some of us saw differently than the Rand Empire model. We witnessed the same circumstances, but not being part of the Rand Meme, we could conclude a disaster was about to occur. We tried to warn of the madness, but the population had faith in Rand's teachings through their leaders, so they chose to follow her and soon we had madness again.

So, ¿how come people, gathered together in a Meme, lose their intellect and act out as they, as individuals, would never do? One answer is:

> **THIRTY-SEVEN: Meme Law states: When a person "Memes-up" or "in" to a Human Social Organism, they lose their sense of self, safety and faith in empirical data and become a different, often unrecognizable person, depending on the degree to which they surrender their life to the Meme.**

This can be witnessed most easily and is socially seen as good, when young people graduate to one of the most powerful Memes anywhere, their nation's military.

We expect a youngster to join, to follow strict discipline and obey orders. We rarely say it, but the military's main task is to fight and kill. Please know: "It does not have to be so." I feel it should not be so, but for now, it is.

Personal Note: *I, like General Eisenhower, am pro-military, but antiwar. With a world full of floods, storms, civil unrest, massive wildfires, earthquakes, plagues and International Law Enforcement needs –*

¿WHO NEEDS WARS to fight?

So, let's follow Jack and Jill (a parable). This boy and girl duo come from Perfectville, USA. They are both religious: Jack - Jewish; Jill - Christian. Both kids have been active churchgoers, good students and according to their families, "wonderful, gentle, loving children."

According to the Pastor Jones, Jill "would NEVER hurt a soul," Rabbi Smith says the same about Jack.

Yet in 1969, twenty weeks after high school graduation and fifteen weeks after leaving "Perfectville," Jack and Jill found themselves in Southeast Asia. Jack has fired shots at close range at a family of two women, three children and one very old man. ¿Even though four of the six died, would we say Jack is a murderer? Of course not. His Meme directed him to do it.

Meanwhile, Jill has fired her first rocket Napalm salvo from her chopper, burning to death three families as they picked rice in a field. The women carried at least four babies in back sacks.

¿Does the fact that we now know **Viet Nam was a contrived war** by the United States, Jill's Master Meme, lead us to label Jill a murderer? No, of course not. Military rank and file are the victims of war, just like the oppositions. Jill has already suffered, risking her life for that which she thought to be godly; her Meme called her a hero.

Unfortunately, decades later, **Jack, Jill and hundreds of thousands of their brothers and sisters carry the memories of the people they killed and the horrors they participated in, causing them years of mental anguish (drugs, drink and suicide).**

TELL ME: " ¿Was Viet Nam worth even one person's life?' My answer is a **RESOUNDING "NO!!"**

(*The above story is true but all the names and places are changed to create a well lived-out parable.*)

Notes

DISCLAIMER: I am NOT "picking on the U.S. Every other nation on earth has done likewise **BUT I live here!**

When we join a Meme, these are predictable requirements for Memeing-in, and the average person tends toward doing most anything out of fear of punishment, including exclusion or expulsion.

As time progresses, the inductee realizes the low guy on the pole is expected to do the ugly work in order to obtain status as a "good member." Later, as Meme leader, luxury living becomes the reward and one leaves other newcomers behind to do the violent and the ugly.

Back during the Viet Nam War, before America fell in love with being a warrior state, we anti-war types suggested the draft age be raised to 50 years-old. We believed, if "old men" had to go off to war, war would end at once. We were correct. We postulated that only the young and the new will gladly give up their lives and souls for the Meme; the older ones can then live comfortably off their blood. NOTE: This applies to EVERY nation on earth!

> **THIRTY-EIGHT: Meme Law states: Sacrifices and unpleasant tasks needed by a Meme are assigned to the newcomers and the young members, even to risking their lives; while safe and comfortable duties are carried out by older, more established members.**

This is an excellent time to revisit the stages of a Meme's development. Let's recall the three stages:

Development Stage One: *Phantom Meme.* These confront us constantly. A permanent Meme does not exist but on occasion, two or more people find themselves in agreement on an issue. If Memeing-up does not occur, those joined by a common idea will simply separate and remember that one time, in one place, when two, three or however many were together in harmony on an issue or occasion.

If no action is taken and each goes his/her separate way, a Phantom Meme is left in place, dormant. Never having actuated, it will soon dissolve. Phantom Memes are not necessarily "Hidden Memes," but often are. Sometimes, those involved continue to activate the precepts of the Meme without being aware of the powerful memory. Once out in the open, the hiddenness disappears, but if not at all organized, it may still be a phantom in waiting - a flash mob event, for example.

However, if the common issue that drew their minds together is acted upon and a common agreement is held on that action, the phantom grows into:

NOTE: A **Phantom Meme** can also occur at the end of a Memes lifespan. Having achieved Formal Meme status and being abandoned, the organism lives on in memories and often in hidden status impacting its society as a Hidden Meme, e.g. *the Confederacy became Jim Crow, the Rexall Company, their symbol RX now survives representing all pharmaceuticals.*

Development Stage Two: *Informal Meme.* As an example, a few years ago a story appeared that a girl was gang raped in a poolroom attached to a bar in Boston. The gathering of the men and their common desire to have sex with the female instigated the forming of a Stage One Phantom Meme, the lusting, the looks and the shared desire.

An Informal Meme was formed when the males began to collaborate with each other on how they could force sex on the girl. Once agreement is reached, if some males object and/or leave, the Meme would be abandoned and that would be the end of the process. If, however, the group agrees and just one male acts out on the plan, an Informal Meme would be activated.

This action, although newsworthy, even to international media, although accountable, is still a temporary organism. Often, these Informal Memes will still have wide-ranging effects. Most things we label "Meme Madness" are of this ilk; even though an organization, like the Tulip Growers Guild of Holland (Formal Meme), may be used to foster the activity, the rushing crowd is still an Informal Meme. In Boston, the madness and the Informal Meme ended as the members went to prison. In Holland, when the market crashed and all were broke, the madness and the Informal Meme then died.

This process of **"Meme Madness," can occur in seconds**, so I encourage each of us to be ever aware, least we are driven into an informal Meme ready to ensnare its occupiers into collective actions. Some of which can, while not intended, be deadly.

This is what happened in all the manias we discussed. The forces of greed and the specter of getting rich (being satisfied) were brought together. Just as with the sex desire of seven young men, who met one young woman, both the sex and the greed became the catalyst to destroy everyone's life.

Holland's population of investors lusting with greed could have walked away from the madness. But, just as the young men in Boston, they didn't. Instead, as more minds Memed-in, a sort of synergy raised the fervor exponentially.

When those uninvolved had encountered the stimulus and formed the Phantom Memes (greed and schemes), the second they wrote their checks or planned steps to do the rape they enter into an Informal Meme - "no rules - no regs." They did not know it, but together, they became the victims of this synergy and being Memed-in, it was now hard to pull away.

> *The strength of inner-Meme pressure (crowd influence on those gathered) outweighs reason and common sense, making Meme Force the strongest in human existence, the parent of mob violence, police brutality, gang rapes, mass murder and its best friend - WAR!*

Here's where some groups, relatively few, move into "Formal Memes:"

Development Stage Three: *Formal Meme.* If the actions seeking to be carried out in the Informal Meme are deemed worthy of longevity and the labor to organize is present, then we have on our hands the forming of a **Human Social Organism** bound together in an action. But this time they are to be carried out under those missing "rules and regulations." In this case, groups are incorporated, officers selected and operating philosophies written. Thus:

We have achieved ACCOUNTABILITY.

A Formal Meme is more exempt from Meme Madness, unless the Meme is self-destructing or becomes infected by a human social virus, say apathy, corruption or violence. Formal Memes do madness all the time, but, as in the case of war, it is justified by planning and strategy and endorsed by the National "deity" through the religious establishment.

Remember, Jack and Jill were NOT held accountable – their Formal Meme, our government, was (or more properly should have been).

Memes are just gathered minds (Phantom Memes) who act out to create Informal Memes, who then organize to act. The resulting Formal Meme, then, is a progression from an Informal Meme that goes on to take on a visible structure. It becomes named and legitimized by society, with order and layers of structure. This Formal Meme manifests itself as a Human Social Organism (Free Masonry, General Motors, Republic of Uganda or the Lions Club of Burbank, CA).

A good example of this process would be the revivals in the Appalachian Mountains in the early 1800s. A camp meeting would more or less spring up along the Red River in Kentucky (Phantom Meme). Frontier people, living isolated and primitive, were hungry for collective activity. Civil order and organized society were completely missing from their lives.

As an antidote to loneliness and isolation, they spontaneously flocked to these weeklong camp meetings by the thousands and, instantaneously, an Informal Meme was formed (no order or structure). As the days progressed, experiencing hours of "protracted" preaching, people began to gather collectively into "God-fearing families" (Belief-Based) of fellow believers and Informal Memes became more formalized (just like cultures forming on a microscope slide).

Notes

By the end of the week, people located near each other "back home" agreed to meet jointly to work in Formal Memes by creating local churches. Upon arriving home, they did just that, choosing elders, selecting names, locating a building and becoming Human Social Organisms.

Many joined with other formalized Memes (meetings), becoming groupings of these independent organisms, forming denominations (Super Memes): the New Light Baptist, the Christian Church and the Cumberland Presbyterian. (*Jon Butler. Awash in a Sea of Faith. Cambridge MA: Harvard University Press 1990*).

The reverse can happen. After the Civil War, Southern society was in ruin. The only things left were Phantom Memes like families, political domains, churches and plantations, all left de-funded as former Social Organisms (Formal Memes). Now abandoned, they became phantoms. In the 1865 South, these abandoned remnants of Southern churches, plantations and a dormant economic system based solely on slavery, seemed as dead as any in history.

> **THIRTY-NINE: Meme Law states: Formal Memes are forever. Their structures and outward identifiers (Social Organisms) may disappear, but their force field lies in a phantom state, continuing dormant, awaiting a group with like-minds and needs to reinvigorate and rebirth the dormant organism usually with a new name.**

As the Civil War phantoms were repopulated, the "South" (Confederacy) chose to reinvigorate their failed slave state, but now as "Jim Crow." Their Phantom Memes (family, church and government), simply reconstituted the former Memes of Southern society (cities, counties and states), and rejoined the Union, and continued operating, nearly as before, with anti-Black laws in control, minus the word "slavery."

See the STORY BOARD in chapter IX for the gravity of this little-known Meme Law.

Interestingly, in true Meme survival fashion, the economic need for Southern cotton led the North to stop "Reconstruction" in its path, leaving Southern Blacks, again, to suffer abuse. This abandoning of Reconstruction also ignored the fact that nearly 620,000

Union soldiers had died to end this oppression. Little did these heroic soldiers know we would "coward" them out for cotton money!

This is an unpleasant truth about our American society:

FORTY: Meme Law states: Memes are capricious and opportunistic. A Meme will sell out its faithful, break its contracts and perpetrate mass fraud in order to protect and enrich itself and its members in power.

Southern neo-slave society, throughout, has been built and rebuilt on the phantoms of the South's churches (CLERGY); the South's plantation system worked through local governments, police and courts (POLITICAL), and an armed forces unit, Gen. Nathan Forest's Ku Klux Klan - its own militia (MILITARY). At ALL-times, the old phantom was really in charge.

Even after the Civil Rights Movement (1956-70) supposedly crushed this race-based cabal, today's radical Right (same Southern entities), joining Rand's "anything-for-profit" politicians, still impacts American society. Not understanding that "Memes never die," but may lay dormant for centuries, makes us vulnerable to continual repetition of sick behaviors. We are discovering, reborn Memes can still create "Meme Madness."

GO TO: mastermemes.live CLICK: FOUR

IX//: My Meme And Me

STORYBOARD

Moderator Heather Conley, Director and Senior Fellow at CSIS (Center for Strategic and International Studies), a brilliant, well-educated, experienced expert on International Affairs and extremely knowledgeable on nations and their actions, delivered the closing question.

She addressed her guest: "There is something that has plagued me for years:

"How come organizations and movements disappear and are gone, I mean really gone, for decades, and then, mysteriously, reappear and come back to life?"

The expert Zbigniew Brzezinski (D: 12/2017), answered:

"I haven't the slightest idea but have wondered the same thing!"

I was in the back row figuratively jumping up and down: *"I know; I have the answer."*

IT'S MEME LAW!

In the 2007 movie, "The Interpreter," when Nicole Kidman returns to the UN to kill the visiting President from her nation, Edmund Zuwanee (fictional), who has become a vicious dictator-tyrant, she says, "¿How could someone so good do such evil?"

¿How could a poor Austrian paperhanger kill over 20 million people? By now, you may be able to answer this question: he didn't! So, then, let's ask: "¿How could over 69 million, normally "nice, kind" German people, considered in 1939 to be the best educated, most theologically informed people on earth (there were more churches and seminaries, per population, in Germany than in any other country on earth), support the killing of millions of people?

Does that not beg the question: "¿How could a twenty-one-year-old former choirboy turned U.S. Marine kill five-plus noncombatant, innocent, unarmed people, including infants?"

The answer is the same as the rest, the choirboy was joined in his murders by 180 million usually "good" Americans, just as 69 million "good" Germans (1936) joined Adolf in every atrocity. We've asked these questions before and the answer always remains the same: "**Once a person joins a Meme**, the more of an insider he/she desires to be, the more that person believes in and desires to be part of the Meme, (ML: 37) the more that person is the property of the Meme, he/she will act out as expected."

The thing is, **WE ARE THE MEME!** "They" didn't do it; **WE,** as in "**I - ME - YOU**" did it! Until we grasp this concept, that: Boom > Bust / Peace > War / Abundance > Poverty / Fear become Dread which then becomes Violence is our destiny. Our future, **will be to continually DRUDGE our way through life, destroying the earth and ourselves!!**

The universal problem among humans is that we are cowards; I mean, we are real "scaredy-cats!" We are like Spider Monkeys, stealing bananas and running to avoid capture. As Haidt put it in his book, "We are selfish cheaters who only act righteous to look better to society." By the same token, we are terrified to stick our head out of the hole for fear of getting it cut off and Memes let us get away with all that unaccountability, thus amplifying the threats. As in military lingo, "Never volunteer for anything;" in corporate vernacular, "Keep you yap shut;" to a politician, "that is a horrible situation that I was not aware of," in theological circles, we are warned, "it's best to leave these things to God's will." After all you may step on someone's toes.

Notes

It's all the same ethic common to all people: "Keep a low profile" and you (personal "I") may survive. Let somebody else save the day or stand for the victim.

> **WWII LAMENT**: *"We (I) saw* **THEM** *come for the Jews, but I wasn't a Jew, so I said nothing; they came for the Catholics, but I was Protestant, so I said nothing; they came for the homosexuals, but I was straight, so I said nothing. BUT* **then they came for ME and there was nobody left to protest!"**

This **MASS COWARDICE** is the best definition of the human collective condition: Meme-enabled and encouraged! It's important to remember that the "they," above, was not Hitler; it was the entire German Nation, who were the killers. The "I" who did nothing to stop the injustice was just another scared monkey (who, incidentally, got killed in the end anyway).

Today, we've gone a step further. Social media and its complete envelopment of people as they sit, walk and work, allows a person to "zombie" their way through life. Now, we no longer have to ignore a human travesty; we just "Face Book" it away.

But Meme Law has produced an antidote to this super-apathy:

FORTY-ONE: Meme Law states: As the populace ignores or cowards-out of its responsibility to the whole of humankind, Celebrities or Prophets, who are powerless, will be generated by the organism to engage the people into the world from which they hide. Rarely, some become leaders, most will be discarded, but, hopefully, some of their corrective efforts survive.

In addition to unusual hairdos and galleries of tattoos, celebs who sit in the Today Show's hotseat are all extremely involved in various causes. Some, like Brad Pitt and Angelina Jolie, work to a sacrificial level. This makes up for a huge portion of us who are shirking our responsibility to the whole of society in favor of self-satisfaction. *Their divorce shattered me!*

> **FORTY-TWO: Meme Law states: Memes are amoral. A Meme knows nothing of right or wrong, it only knows survival and victory over other like- Memes and control of its environment. It does whatever it needs to in order to achieve its purpose and that purpose is not seen as good or bad, but "achieved" or "failed" - win or lose.**

If the organism achieves success, it will celebrate those who ushered it in and will act gratefully to its members. With this promise in front of the members, many will throw their all into the cause of the Meme, even if not asked.

Memes are forgetful and their gratitude wanes rapidly. Persons serving Memes for thirty to forty to fifty years, once retired, are gone and forgotten in days.

> **FORTY-THREE: Meme Law states: Memes have short memories of members' contributions. Once a Meme member retires or is removed from participation, they will soon be forgotten.**

A few years ago, I had occasion to call the Baltimore Board of Elections Office. I asked to talk to a lady I had known for some time. She had worked in that office for twenty years. Even though there were only fifteen people in that office, no one remembered her. She had retired the year before. Like so many others, "it was out with the old and in with the new," an age-old and well-known Meme behavior.

About eight years ago, a thirty-five plus professional career nurse at a major Maryland Hospital asked me to lunch. The second we sat down she began to cry. She informed me that she had been Head Nurse for ten years. She had poured her heart into her job and her three-hundred staffers. She threw a big annual party at her large home and got personally involved when personal troubles came to one of "her" nurses. She was even the godmother to many of their children. In professional circles, she was regarded as "the best" in Maryland.

Nevertheless, a new administrator came to the hospital, "who wanted his own head nurse," so my friend was out. She was broken-hearted, but even more so, when, after a few short weeks, her old friends (staffers) did not return her calls and ignored her completely. She was FORGOTTEN!

She had discovered a basic fact of living in and serving a Meme: when you're out, you're gone. When one is fired or retired from a Human Social Organism, you are quickly past history.

> **FORTY-FOUR: Meme Law states: A Meme is a here and now, an all-usurping organization that will abandon any and all agreements and solidarity with its members for the benefit of the Meme itself.**

Soldiers in America's Revolutionary War were promised a pension. The war ended in 1783. As of 1820, that is forty-two years later, not one penny had been paid to these heroes. During this same postwar period the Washington family, the family's of Ben Franklins and Thomas Jefferson became enormously wealthy.

The United States government repeated this action after WWI, when the "dough-boys" were literally cheated out of their pensions. When these veterans Memed-up in Washington to demonstrate, the government sent in bulldozers and tanks, and with shots firing, they expelled the vets from Washington. **Memes easily and regularly forget relationships and promises to their members.**

It appears the Veterans Administration is up to this same old behavior, as the 2014 scandals arose concerning fraudulent reports and veterans dying from lack of treatment, all so a handful of executives could collect a bonus.

America's largest corporations made promises to workers all through 1960 to 2000 and beyond during the great prosperity years, only to renege on their promised pensions and healthcare in 2008 when the economy tanked. Now elderly workers were left flat and destitute. We all stood-by and let it happen because our Meme in the "here and now" was in trouble and it was easiest to dump the now outsiders and the underdog.

When attending college and graduate school, I worked as a janitor for a large Jacksonville Baptist church. Fortunately for writers, janitors see and hear everything.

One evening, just before a church dinner, an elderly lady, Ms. Lee, came to the dining hall. She was anxious to see everyone as she had been in a convalescent home for five months. She sat by the front door, where over 150 people filed in, each making a fuss over her: "Aw, Miss Lee, we missed you so much, so glad you're back!" They all repeated many variations of the same sentiment.

When everyone was inside, she whispered to the janitor standing silently by (me): "¿If they missed me so much, why the hell didn't they come see me?" Sorry Miss Lee, Memes remember no one unless it aids their bottom line. Yet, the Meme wants all of its members' loyalty!

> **FORTY-FIVE: Meme Law states: Within any Meme, the greatest accolades are reserved for those at the Meme's center, past and present, usually ignoring those at the outer levels of Meme life.**

Truth is, Meme organisms of any kind are slow to remember workers and volunteers at the lower end of the scale. Interestingly, CEOs and their cohorts, usually the ones who gut the treasury, receive the company's eternal gratitude. The Meme called "**American Capitalism,**" has little regard for its biggest contributors (workers). Trophies and headlines go mostly to its Power Elites and Ruling Class players.

> **FORTY-SIX: Meme Law states: Memes are insanely jealous and, while having little regard for their members' welfare, Memes demand every measure of their members' being.**

Even casual witnessing of the six o'clock TV news brings hundreds of stories from small towns to large cites of couples and families (Memes all) committing domestic violence right down to and including mass murder, rather than allowing a member, husband or wife or perhaps a child, to experience life as an outsider.

Notes

Often in such cases, not only the culprit but the offended member (victim) is also cheating on the side, but the Meme members have no mercy. Once the members discover a defector, the Meme becomes a vengeful unswerving master, its members a lynch mob. Criminal enterprises such as gangs and patriarchal Mid-Eastern religious families are well known for these vengeful behaviors.

The same is true of nations. While every nation recruits people to do espionage and spy on other nations, at the same time, these target nations (Memes) are spying on the first. In spite of the first nation carrying out an identical program, if the opposing nation's spies are caught, it's off to the gallows. As Meme members celebrate the deaths of these "awful people," they are simultaneously "praying" for the return of their own "beloved" spies (say 007).

For example, Mr. Phelps (Mission Impossible): "If you or any of your team are caught, the United States will disavow any knowledge of you." Yes, it's true, if you are an American spy and you get home safely it's a "miracle." Conversely, if you are caught, the USA will not know you. That's Meme Law and it proves true in any country, any vocation.

The astonishing factor to me is that we humans are devoted to our Memes, knowing full well that most relationships with a Meme will end seeing us cast off and forgotten. Yet, when asked to give up all of everything, most of us will comply in order to be fully accepted in Meme life. Memes demand everything of their members and most of us respond (**this is the enabling principle behind war - mass obedience**). This is why "nice" Americans, Germans, Japanese and Arabs have, and will, "kill on command or be killed."

It took me decades inside the church to realize that I was not ever going to be accepted as a "clergy" among clergy and denominational leaders. Being a pragmatist, I have always viewed my call as one from God to serve people, and I worked at it with joy for twenty-eight years. I never regretted the years, some with no pay, and I never surrendered my integrity or my promises for a high office or promotion. I should warn: "If you are an idealist and a righteous person, this path will almost certainly lead to personal integrity, BUT also, the rebuke of your peers."

This is not exclusive to Clergy; they're just another power Meme inside a Meme, and total obedience is what is expected of its insiders. Since I did not fit the mold, I was assigned a role as outsider. My Bishop labeled me a "character." Among the clergy class, as in any other profession or political work venue, it's everyone for themselves, but we stroke each other's backs in facing outsiders. Therefore, I was kept at a distance, as are lay people.

Humorous but sad is the night my first bishop stopped me in the hall, announcing to my face: "I know why you're such a pain in the ass.

¿You're a man of God ain't you?" my answer was "I hope so sir." To which he replied "Who the hell needs a man of God in his conference." He walked off discussed.

In business, the workers are separated from the executives, and among politicians, the pros are separated from the electorate.

The same is mostly true across all types of Memes. Those wanting to get the best seats or the center slots must play the game or its life on the streets. Many honest people love life on the street and hate using the "executive" washroom.

Another thing one must expect from his/her Meme is avoidance.

Baltimore, Maryland had a great Mayor, Sheila Dixon. She did a foolish thing, not really illegal, more irregular; I hope out of ignorance. Big time building contractors give all the politicians gift cards "in bulk," usually $10.00 or so (Baltimore is home to many mega-million-dollar building projects at any one time). The assumption (but not the obligation) is that politicians will hand them out as he/she visits the neighborhoods. It's important to note that these cards are not listed or reported as campaign gifts, just public relations tokens.

While this process should never have been allowed, for years it was accepted. Most politicians before her had used the cards openly without account.

Evidently Ms. Dixon, had a small bunch of these gift cards about to expire, left over in her home, so she used some for her own purchases, before they expired, to buy a

$630.00 worth of merchandise - just the kind of thing the opposing party drools over, even though it was not thought to be illegal.

She was charged and convicted by an ambitious new prosecutor (from an opposing Meme) on one count of failure to report. She resigned. But that's not our whole story.

During her year-long ordeal, all of her former "friends," fellow party members and people close to her, turned away and did not know her. Now, nationally famous people, including Martin O'Malley, avoided Sheila like the plague, following a major tenet of Meme Law. (*Ironically five years later another mayor, Cathern Pugh, was also put from office for misreporting money and has been abandoned by her "friends" as well*)

> **FORTY-SEVEN: Meme Law states: More powerful Meme members always abandon one of their own in times of trouble, especially one of a lower rank. Lower level members, conversely, tend to blindly support one of their own in trouble, except if the leaders order that person abandoned.**

In The Jesus Book I labeled churches as "households of cowards." As individuals the people were fine, but the church was a place they go to hide from their faith responsibility to "faceup to and expose evil in society." The problem is Memes avoid risk, pain or harm to themselves. They will expel members who try to push the organism to standup for goodness or to expose evil. This, especially when it is committed against less powerful insiders and/or outsiders, if it is carried out for the benefit of the Meme.

A good example of group cowardice took place recently in Precinct 81, New York City. The New York Police Department was pursuing a policy of "stop and frisk" and arresting any person they came across in this poorer interethnic area. The idea was to get criminals before they did a crime.

At one time, one out of every four male citizens of this neighborhood was in jail or in the legal system. Most people hauled in were innocent and the officers knew it, but they were pushed by Mayor Bloomberg and their supervisors to "nab" as many people as possible. An unfortunate side effect of the program was, even though most people were released in 24 hours, it soon was obvious that people living in this area could not keep a job because they were repeatedly incarcerated.

One young man, age 31, had been busted 24 times in three years for walking down the street. The good thing was that it reduced crime; the bad was that it alienated good citizens from the police.

In 2019, as former Mayor Bloomberg is running for the Presidency, he has need to apologize and repent of his support for stop and frisk. Now he is no longer part of the NYC Meme, so now he must disavow his former Meme and become part of the National Meme in order to have a chance at election.

For those witnessing the Baltimore riots in the spring of 2015, it was this exact condition, out-of-control policing, which caused the entire problem.

In the midst of this nationwide charade, one officer, Adrian Schoolcraft, started complaining to superiors. He was concerned about being forced to arrest people for non-existing crimes: "We don't care if a crime was done, we just arrest everyone," was the commander's response. When Adrian refused to go along, he was threatened by fellow officers with beatings and fled the precinct for fear of his life. The police, including fellow officers and "friends," took chase and busted into his home at gunpoint.

Another famous police "whistleblower" of the 1960s, Frank Scorpio, is aiding Schoolcraft in his current federal suit against the NYPD. Former Mayor Bloomberg, the author of "stop and frisk," forgot one of the great principles of Meme Law:

> **FORTY-EIGHT: Meme Law states: Meme members who are given authority to use force on others will do so exponentially and with little reserve. Having received approval from the Ruling Class, the target could be a close friend or family member, but in this case, they are just victims.**

This is a valuable lesson in Meme Law for everyone expecting their workmates to come to their aid at a time of need.

Notes

A second principle is equally true, as Mayor Dixon, Officer Schoolcraft, our fired head nurse, pastors being challenged, and millions of terminated employees and government "whistleblowers" have learned:

FORTY-NINE: Meme Law states: No one in any Meme, including churches, clubs, military and corporations - in ALL Memes, at all levels, is a true friend to any other member. The Meme authority reserves the right to encourage or disallow relations between its members, most of whom will obey the order.

Looking at religion, again, we find a perfect example. Some fundamental faiths will order a family not to speak or have relations with a disobedient member. In these cases, wives and children are not permitted to have anything to do with their father. This practice of "shunning" is kept under lock-and-key and a big dark secret of the churches practicing it. This brings us to another widespread practice in Meme life:

> **FIFTY: Meme Law states: The inner workings, failures and disputes within a Meme are seen as "our dirty laundry" and internal secrets, never to be discussed with those outside the Meme.**

This principle is widely known among families and small groups, especially not-for-profit gatherings. As a Pastor, I have run headfirst into this misguided "circle the wagons" ideology for years. It seems that Meme members feel their Meme is the only one (family, church, club or small town) that has suffered an embarrassing happening. The real truth is most social organisms have had EXACTLY the same kind of dysfunctions.

At one time, I hosted a gathering called "Prayer and Share." No explanation should be needed, given the title, but the idea was to provide a safe atmosphere for people to "let it all hang out" (the famed John Wesley invented the concept nearly 300 years ago; it became Methodism). Getting people to share their fears and concerns was like pulling teeth.

Then, one night, a very young Black man told of a brother about to be released from the federal penitentiary. He shared of his concern over the release.

At once, a very proper middle-aged White lady stood to confess that her husband was about to be released from the same Federal Penitentiary; a shock since the church did not know she was ever married. Given the spirit of sharing, an elderly White lady stood to confess to the church that 30 years prior, when the church was told her son was in the Army, he had also spent six years in the same Federal Prison.

Just imagine all those months and years of holding that stuff in one's soul. Indeed, Memes are places of big secrets. I used to tell people: "**The best thing you can do for the devil (Secular: to make matters worse) is keep your mouth shut;** it allows the problem to grow and multiply, causing more damage than it should."

Larger organisms, like governments and businesses, have more difficulty keeping the lid on bad stuff, simply because there are more people involved, giving a greater chance for a whistleblower to come forward. But, never forget, a very large Meme once built an "Iron Curtain" to hide its laundry from the rest of us!

In recent years, another major and world changing exercise in this secrecy statute of Meme Laws played out.

After 911, Pres. Bush, Dick Chaney and my friend, retired Gen. Michael Hayden (NSA and CIA), came together and decided in lieu of this extraordinary circumstance, to suspend all the rules concerning electronic surveillance on individuals. It became the biggest violation of civil privacy laws in history. But as before, that's not really our story.

I personally see nothing wrong with what they did. Most of my acquaintances, even inside the Washington setting, had thought it had been going on, in a limited setting, before. Now, it was thought to be really necessary.

But, here's the troubling story. Six government employees at many different levels, in discovering these "secret" surveillances and knowing them to be illegal, carried their concerns to their bosses - that's what they are supposed to do.

Notes

Instead of reacting in a sensible mature way, the employers they reported to within their respective Memes (Departments) began to harass these honest employees, good American citizens all. Over the next five years they and their families were terrorized by the FBI, illegally arrested and persecuted in a massive police thuggery, much like Officer Schoolcraft (NYPD) had suffered.

Soon, the entire charade came to light, severely damaging the FBI, police officials, President Obama (who inherited but did not stop it) and the entire United States of America.

This is the primary reason that, when Edward Snowden discovered all the illegal things the government was doing (thousands of violations), even to allies and innocent civilians, he was forced to travel to another country. If he had tried to make things right while remaining here, it is certain he would have disappeared forever or popped up dead some Sunday morning. He was still forced to be locked inside of a foreign embassy in London to escape severe persecution.

This tragedy has caused many like me to lose faith in our government, including Barack Obama's ability to get our rulers under some kind of moral posture. This failure is not exclusively his, since a majority of America's White population rejects his leadership over the color of his skin anyway, but rather an ongoing operating philosophy of our government.

Here's the real irony: at a Washington meeting (summer 2013), I was sitting next to Gen. Keith Alexander (NSA Chief) when the Snowden case first blew open. He spoke of the WikiLeaks by saying, "We should have just disclosed these programs years ago." Again Meme Law is NEVER wrong!

Most observers have acknowledged that the vast majority of Americans would have approved of the programs after 911." The look on his face was totally sincere and he was 100% correct.

¿Why couldn't they have just told the truth? Here's why:

FIFTY-ONE: Meme Law states: Meme leaders tend to elevate themselves and their decisions, thinking them to be sacrosanct and above other Meme members' understanding, which, in turn, adds to their sense of elitism and superiority. As a result, leaders make secret their rulings leading to social rupture, illegal actions and often, unnecessary internal violence.

Once a member stands up against a bad Meme practice and attempts to correct the wrong, that person is subject to punitive actions by the Meme: silencing, shunning, arrest, discharge and even death.

Many of us have been horribly disappointed over Pres. Obama's abandoning of a major campaign promise for a more open government and protection for whistleblowers.

Instead, once inside the "Governing Meme," he became Memed-up with others in the Ruling Class and his administration has prosecuted (better "persecuted") more "do-gooders" than any other administration before it. The Mafia isn't the only Meme that assassinates those who tell all. Religions have done it for centuries.

Remember all those South and Central American Liberationists (Liberation Theology) of the 1970s - 1990s. They are a good example of people run amuck of the "order" of things. Bishop Oscar Romero (assassinated at his altar, March 1979) and others were given over to their local dictators by the church.

Haiti's Jean-Bertrand Aristide is another prime example. When the inner-city priest in the Americas' poorest country began to champion the poor over the super wealthy, his bishops gave the OK for the oppressors to beat, burn and kill the priest (Jean-Bertrand Aristide. _In the_ _Parish of the Poor_, NY: Orbis Books, 1990).

When working with any Meme, the challenge is to enjoy the benefits of being part of a Human Social Organism, while not running amuck of the Meme structure that supports it. The secret is: "Never become dependent on the Meme for your life. You will probably never receive what you are promised." Keep in mind, **your need will be used by the rulers to subjugate you and other Meme members**.

X//: Multi-Memes

STORY BOARD

Two older men, unknown to each other, checked in at a Mr. Tire Auto center to buy sets of tires.

They entered the waiting room and being normal males, avoided contact. But eventually a conversation began:

Man A: Boy these tires have gone through the roof!
Man B: You got that and I'm retired.
Man A: Yea, me too. Where did you retire from?
Man B: Over to the GM plant that closed down.
Man A: Oh. (*Lull in conversation*) I'm a retired minister. (lull) Do you come from here?
Man B: No, I was born and raised in western PA.
Man A: Oh, what town?
Man B: You never heard of it – Jeanette, east of Pittsburg.
Man A: **When did YOU-A-KINS come here?**
Man B: What did you say?
Man A: I said **YOU-A-KINS**. I have family in Jeanette!

Both men leaped to their feet, laughing and tearing at the same time, embracing like two lost brothers, right in the middle of the Mr. Tire store. The staff joined in!

CONCLUSION: YOU-A-KINS is very local in the language of a tiny area (his a-kins, their a-kins, etc.). It is a **MARKER** recognized by the folks of Jeanette and no one – no where else. **It BELONGS to that TRIBE alone!!!**

Just as "no man is an island," so also, a Meme does not stand on its own, but is usually attached to and/or layered in with others. Some are subdominant, others coequal and some superior (Super or Master Memes).

Nation-states, particularly, fall into the Master Memes designation, made up of lesser subdominants posing as one unified entity. The United States has always fallen into this category. Not only did we do it by design (Independent States) but, in our infancy, we allowed two separate economies to exist under one roof. From the beginning, 1787, we almost did not exist because of our great division on slavery versus a free citizenry.

This condition has brought us a turbulent past and is repeating itself in the 2008+ era, as political impasses within differing factions of our population have paralyzed the government. Interestingly, it's nearly the same Meme demographic (geography and race) that forms today's Left (North and urban areas) and Right (Southern and rural areas). **Remember the principal**, a Meme is never destroyed, only abandoned (Phantom Meme), but is always willing to be reconstituted by other minds under a different name at a later date.

In 2008, I guested on a prominent southern radio show. One caller signaled this reemergence saying, "You Yankees have had your way long enough – we're back!"

The very federal structure of the United States, like China's, containing multiple levels of nearly independent governments, makes both countries "multi-Meme" structured organisms from the get-go.

The reason for political instability in Africa, among those emerging nations, is conflicts between subdominant Memes (tribes), all straining to be coequal or superior to the others, each using the banner of "nation." But in Africa, there is no concept of a Master Meme (State) above all others, except in Egypt, which has never been Tribal- Based.

After suffering horribly at the hands of Arab and Indian overlords as part of Sudan (Master Meme) for years, in 2012 a new nation run by native Africans (South Sudan) was founded. But within a year, these once unified peoples began to spiral downward as tribal Memes (subdominant) resurfaced and began warring for primacy (tribal Memes

Notes

are the most basic and primitive of Human Social Organisms, just up from the Clan, Family or Band stage of Human development).

To illustrate the same forces at work in another setting, abolitionists like William Lloyd Garrison (1832+) and thousands of others (informal Meme) began to speak out against the practice of slavery.

Isaac Newton's law then kicked in, creating an opposite and equal force needed to shape the slave lobby into one force (informal Meme).

> [**NOTE: We are living under Meme Law Number THREE. This fact is so important to the future of the United States and human community I am repeating this section from earlier because it is the basis of our current dilemma. It also illustrates the overpowering force of Memes over individual ethics.**]

The harder the abolitionists pushed, the more the opposition responded with power, until their Meme founded a proper, organized entity (Formal Meme): "the Confederate States of America." After the CSA's defeat in 1865, the Meme went dormant, as we reported before, gradually formalizing its practices into the "Jim Crow operating philosophy," among which its best-known subdominant was the Ku Klux Klan.

Gradually, Post-Civil War representatives from the South, elected to the Federal House and Senate became the" Dixie-crats" of the Democratic Party (White Supremacists), and they became a powerful, subdominant Meme both of the Democrats and Southern civil society.

After the Civil Rights Laws were enacted (1965), these "good ol' boys" became Republicans, who then joined with other White rural Republicans, including Evangelical Christians and Ayn Rand's "anything-for-profit" crowd and eventually emerged as the Tea Party right subdominant Meme in the Republican structure.

However, in both cases (1) Democrat – Dixiecrats of 1970 and that (2) same group morphed into todays Republican Tea Party or Right, the same subdominant Meme, newly named, took over both parties to which they then belonged. The reason is easy to spot: all the members of both Memes were 100% White. thus this floating tribe should be called "the White Power structure."

Even in a well-rounded society like the U.S., there are great variations that can be used to cause division. When John Boehner repeatedly said, "the American people" he was not speaking of all American citizens, he was speaking for White Americans.

VITAL NOTE: I realize I have spent a large portion of my efforts to document the importance of Meme Behaviors on our lives by reexamining the **South versus North** power conflict and racial undertones in America. This conflict is **PARAMOUNT** from our founding, through today's election:

THIS IS IN CONTROL of our COUNTRY!

This inner and inter-Meme conflict has been, and continues to be, the most powerful defining factor in American life. According to professional sociologists I have encountered, it will probably continue well through this century. It's just Meme Law playing out, which brings us to:

> **FIFTY-TWO: Meme Law states: Within a Master Meme, multi-subordinate Memes will generate, some to enhance and support the work of the host's leadership, some to its detriment and even its destruction.**

This Meme Law can be particularly pernicious if the forming sub-meme is in a position of leadership. The loss of Eric Cantor's nine-year speakership and seat in the House was another indication of the effect the Tea Party sub-Meme has on the Republican Party (Master Meme).

Notes

Newark Schools (Master Meme) had the power-holding teachers union (sub-meme) kill the Golden Goose, the children of the city. Newark is a Democrat controlled political Meme.

A current example of this is seen in 2014 Ukraine. Two opposing Memes were thrust together (Ukrainian and Russian peoples). This "union" festered for years, awaiting a chance to force itself apart. These two Memes had a long history of combat and never stood a chance at unity. In the summer of 2019 the American administration stuck our head in the mess and it may get cutoff for its taking advantage of the situation.

Our effort at "human engineering" has mixed two highly intelligent and resourceful tribe groupings together. If they would work together, they'd see spectacular results. Once cut loose, they set at each other's throats. The result has been the "cybercrime" capital of the world (High Intellect > No effective Master Meme).

Post 2018, the U.S. President favored Russia; the military and civilian sectors of government backed Ukraine. OOPS!

In 2013 in Kenya, a tragic mall raid, spawned by terrorists from Somalia, paralyzed the country. The problem in responding was determined to be: "It took way too long to get six men under control." Come to find out, the government was working through multi-levels of sub-Memes (Tribes).

Kenya, the Master Meme is really made up of several tribes (sub-memes). Two major tribes are the "Luo," that of President Odinga, and the "Bantu" and "Kikuya," which speak a different language. In Kenya, as in many other nations, the army is made up of members of the president's party (Luo tribal sub-Meme).

After the call for help went out from the mall, Kenya's Special Police Unit was there in minutes. Within a couple of hours this S.W.A.T. Unit had closed 90% of the mall when, all-of-a-sudden, the President pulled the Police Unit out and brought in the army HIS army from HIS tribe. Remember, the S.W.A.T. team and police were made up of people from other than the President's tribes, these were the Bantu, Kikuya and other sub-memes.

SIDEBAR:

The underpinnings of national Memes - **TRIBES**.

Across the globe, on every continent except the NEW Americas, **Tribes are at the basis of all civilizations**. By way of example: in the case of Ukraine, the Russians from Sweden moved in from the north (825 C. E.) to occupy the land at Kiev, their new capital city, and the land to the EAST. The land to the WEST however, was already occupied by nine tribes of the Polish tribal Meme (Ukrainians). Ever since, these two separate tribal groupings have clashed. The poles won early, thanks to Magyar tribes (Central Asian), invading today's Russia which at the time were the out lands of Kiev. The Poles then pushed the "Rus" out of Kiev to a new center at Moscow. ***This tribal fight has lasted for 1200 years.***

During the Soviet era, the two groups enjoyed a relatively stable existence. After a break off from the USSR, stability has remained to a great degree. Unfortunately, the U.S. and its puppet aggressor, NATO, have sought to challenge the status of Ukraine and its nine tribes and one-third Russian residents as "buffer states" in order to control the Russians out.

These TRIBAL, naturally occurring COMBAT factors of Meme Law THREE are used by powerful nations, the world over, to conquer tribal peoples. Buffer Zones and the certain breaching of them were the primary lead-up to WWII.

END SIDEBAR

Unfortunately, Odinga's army was ill-equipped and untrained and terrorized. The army stood down, allowed the terrorists free range to kill all the hostages and loot the mall. Another example of the ignorance of Meme Law bringing unnecessary death and destruction. President Odinga probably never realized he wasn't making that decision, rather his psyche was automatically operating in "Meme Law, to favor one's own Meme!"

Another, nearly identical case, from a more sophisticated country was in **America during 9 11**. Then, multi-layered sub-memes (FBI, CIA, State Police, Local Police, and others), while Heroes, made 9 11 far worse by hording information or withholding aid out of respect for sub-meme territories. Ten years later, these barriers are still in place and a common radio system has not been installed. Again, Meme Law at work: we keep "like-Memes separate and in competition."

An ongoing example is the situation in the State of **Kashmir,** (H)India (the original name as spoken was "Hindia." The British invaders could not pronounce the "H" so it became India). While the tribal tension did not start with the newly elected Prime Minister, Modi (2014), he has brought back to violent life the thousand-year old combat between the main (H)Indian Tribe (Hindi-Hindu) and the much lesser numbers of Muslims.

Islam first arrived in (H)India in the 12th century as the Turks invaded. They have remained ever since in the western part of the sub-continent, while the Hindi-speaking Hindus occupied the greater portion of the country.

The British occupation of the whole kept the two groups intact, mainly hating the Brits. But once the natives, working together, defeated the English and the new nation was formed then the two remaining Memes could go at it.

The official separation of (H)India and Pakistan took place in August of 1947, however, fighting and the dislocation of 200,000 people ruined the new country. In 1971 things quieted, but when (H)India elected Modi as president in 2014, he brought **Hindu NATIONALISM** (India for Hindus) back to life by cutting Kashmir (majority Muslim) off from the rest of the nation, allowing expulsion of the Muslims.

NOTE: Nationalism has come to life in Britain (Brexit), America (White supremacy), Turkey, Chili, Brazil and many smaller regions.

In reaction, every group, especially in the EU and the U.S., has active forces opposing this break-apart movement. When **RELIGION** is mixed with **NATIONALISM,** it is difficult to correct. The ugly face of this phenomenon was seen in Virginia 2017 with a more tame version in January 2020.

As recent as 2019 the parliament and the Indian enabled Meme Law by passing a new migration act. It permitted immigration from three countries bordering (H)india but excluded Muslims from applying. As the end of the year approached the Supreme Court, a secular organization, ruled the exclusion illegal but the government is vowing disobedience. The nation is on the brink of civil war (Meme War)!

In corporate governance, the same "Meme-within-a-Meme" takes place all the time. About twelve years ago, any casual shopper at the Home Depot witnessed the company going slowly down the tubes. Even an outside amateur like me suspected there was chicanery in the halls of power.

Sure enough, it finally came out as a showdown between the Board and the shareholders, who were seeing their stock price plummet.

The Board had closed itself off as a separate sub-Meme backing, often blindly, the plans of CEO Robert Nardelli, who was operating operating outside the corporate structure and most certainly to its detriment. In the end, Nardelli was paid a whopping $245 million dollars to leave the Home Depot, which is credited with saving the company.

The Tea Party is evolving into the same kind of "Trojan Horse" for the Republican Party, a 2014 situation I have predicted for three years. The traditional Republicans struggled for unity during the presidential election of 2016, but they were soundly defeated, leaving the former DIXIECRATS and the WHITE SUPREMACISTS as the New Republican Party.

> **FIFTY-THREE: Meme Law states: Memes, even if part of the same Master Meme, becoming subdominant, distrust other like-Memes, even those sharing the same master, and will close down or sabotage each other if they feel threatened, rather than share for the good of all.**

The above is the basis of EVERY civil war.

I have found this especially **true among nonprofits**, supposedly "out there" doing "good" stuff. I visited Haiti for 11 years (1998-2009), working there with two nonprofit groups, which do not even acknowledge each other. When accidently meeting other International nonprofits working in the country, we barely spoke to each other.

In the mountain **town of Kenskoff, Haiti**, I worked with a small mission, whose sole purpose was to take care of totally disabled children-the only one in Haiti.

One night, one of our children became severely ill. Next door was the Baptist Mission, a large, well-funded school and care center with a well-equipped infirmary. Our volunteers wheeled our sick child next door for help but were turned away. It took three hours to get the little one down the mountain to Port-au-Prince hospital.

One night in **rural Florida**, I had a bus full of teenagers on a trip. It was Sunday night. As we passed a country church, one of the teens, a troubled girl, jumped from the bus and ran for the woods. I entered the church explaining what had happened asking to use their phone to call the State Police (this was prior to cell phones).

The church's leaders were visibly annoyed and dismissive, ignoring me completely.

Fortunately, a County Deputy Sheriff from the church came out to help us find the girl. The church never did acknowledge our presence.

As we drove away into the Florida jungle an hour later, we could hear the congregation singing, "Since Jesus Came into My Heart..." My question was – ¿ *WHEN?*

Unscrupulous people have learned to use this rivalry to their advantage. A good example of this is, from the 1990s, when education was in a period of flux and teachers were fighting to get recognized and to receive fair wages. At that time, I ran into a now non-existent organization with the name: "The American Teacher's Empowerment Association." Sounds supportive of teachers, right? WRONG!

The sole purpose of this group was to "reduce" teachers' pay, rid states and districts of health insurance obligations and destroy the teachers' unions. They were for anything BUT empowering and supporting teachers.

The real danger is that people give money and support to organizations they think are out to do good when in fact **these falsely-named Memes are hidden and dedicated to doing harm to their wrongly-named parent cause.**

Many "Healthcare Reform Coalition" groups have one purpose only: to completely block any and all healthcare reforms.

So far in our examination of **Multi-Memes**, we have studied: **sub-Memes** in larger Memes, **abandoned Memes** rising again, conflicting **Memes reacting to each other** and **Hidden Memes**, many wrongly titled on purpose to "Trojan Horse" their way into a position of doing real damage to their apparent namesake or Master Meme.

Often in a situation, we find ourselves dealing with interconnected but often conflicting Memes that place us **between "the rock and the hard place."**

I recall the famous story of a U.S. Navy Admiral. Apparently, during the battle for the Coral Sea in 1942-3, a junior officer fell off the ship he was commanding. When told, the Admiral gave the order "Keep full ahead." "But," replied his bridge officer, "that sailor will surely die!" "You heard me sailor, full ahead," said the Admiral. "But Sir," responded the bridge officer, "That sailor is your son!" *The ship sailed away leaving the Admiral's son behind!*

Notes

This kind of dilemma impacts us throughout our lives. Politicians playing their games, pride themselves on putting their opponent in such a **Damned-if-you-Do/Damned-if-you-Don't** position: "¿Oh, what to do?"

Family members, especially parents, often unwittingly engineer their children's future in such a way so as to place a particular child in the same DD/DD, sometimes for life.

Business leaders are familiar with this kind of a quandary. Perhaps a product the company makes is unregulated, selling like hotcakes, but a problem is spotted. If the business secretly modifies the product, all remains well, but far less profitable. If not altered and no warning is given, the item can be downright harmful.

Recently, a large ice cream maker from Texas found itself in this very dilemma by ignoring a long-term Listeria infection. The Meme (business) needed that profit. "¿Oh, what to do - what to do?"

Many **bankers** were put in this position from 2000 through 2008. If they got sucked into the derivatives deceit market, they were hailed as successful rich bankers and their stock soared. If they kept their heads and refrained from these **credit default swaps,** as they should, their stock plummeted, and they were soon on the street. "¿Oh, what do I do?"

In cases like these, the conflicted Meme's core leaders, attempting to do right, found themselves in conflict with other's interests in the Meme: stockholders, customers, SEC ethics teams and, finally, their own personal Family Meme. Often a spouse at home would badger, "we need the money, the hell with ethics". Then there is the exec's own ego needing a success. This is an extreme example but very current case! "¿Oh what to do?"

But how about those **Cops in New York City** (and police all over the world), who found themselves caught between their police employer (**sub-meme**), their civic employer (**Master Meme**), the establishment's fears (**Phantom Meme**), order-centered laws (**professional responsibility**) and the need to keep their jobs (**Family Meme**).

All this pressure at the same time the officer is attempting to act justly to an ordinary, usually weaker, perhaps innocent citizen under the guise of common decency and the codes protecting people (**Justice, Mercy, Kindness and Understanding** and ALL the goodness of the Human Soul).

All of these conflicting forces have lead every person, who has ever found themselves on the persecuted side of the law, even if innocent, to attest to it being a never-ending nightmare.

These intertwined Meme forces, pushing on the individual from all sides, plus the officer's persona, is what allows individual hot-headed bullies like Daniel Pantaleo (NYPD) to choke a harmless Eric Garner to death, as other officers coward-out over Garners' cries of "I can't breathe!"

In MOST cases where I have witnessed or investigated a crime by police, someone present moves forward to stop it, but withdraws out of fear from Meme Forces (long blue line).

In May of 2014, I attended a conference sponsored by the Kingdom of the Netherlands. Their Minister of Justice announced that his country had nearly perfected a new justice system that rids itself of inner-Meme (inter-departmental) conflicts. All the normally separate departments have been combined into one: police, security, arrests, indictments and JUDGES; yes, judges. The speaker told us, "the result is nearly a 100% conviction rate and swift justice at huge financial savings.

My thoughts, walking back to the subway were: "That's great: they arrest on Monday, convict on Tuesday, sentence on Wednesday and execute (they don't execute) on Thursday." Burials are in a different department, so they would come three days later. Here's another universal fact concerning Memes:

> **FIFTY-FOUR: Meme Law states: Once a person is suspected of crossing a Meme's will or violating its rules, a Meme is relentless, employing all of its members and sub-Memes to neutralize the offender. Safety can be found by the suspected violator only in a hidden sub-Meme or in complete exile from the Meme's territory. Computers and electronic data systems have rendered escape nearly impossible.**

Notes

Now you see why we, in the U.S., MUST get our Politicals and Enforcers UNDER CONTROL. Next, they'll come for the rest of us! It's Meme Law.

Serving as a pastor for twenty-eight years, I have lived each day with "inter" and "inner-Meme conflict,' sub-memes in conflict and Hidden Memes, while trying to get support for doing what I believe we should NOT do. Talk about a short circuit! Godliness and righteousness on one hand, church hierarchy on the other, laced all through with the need to keep my job (local church politics) and support my family.

> **NOTE: ALL decision makers and leaders in ALL disciplines (religion, civic, corporate and public service) MUST fight constantly to see JUSTICE done. Trouble is: Most DO NOT!**

Decision makers in all areas run into this all the time. I came across a case study some years ago where a local church needed to make a building renovation. As the Board discussed the problem in a church meeting, they determined the unit would cost $4,000 and the installation would be another $2,000, plus a City Building Permit for $250 dollars. The discussions produced a consensus that the church could get an outside-the-city contractor to install the thing cheaper and, if they did the work on Sunday, the church could skip the City Permit, because no inspector would be around.

Of course, the pastor could not condone such actions and when he/she spoke up, was invited to leave the room and told to go and do "God stuff." The pastor ran further amuck by informing the board he/she would do the "God stuff" and would report their plans to the city. The pastor's argument was: "We are a church; your children are watching you; the entire town is watching you – ¿ don't you get it?"

The pastor saw the conflicting Memes here as: the church (Business Meme), its members' civic duty (Master Meme), dedication to what is morally right (God's teaching) and the Pastor's own personal need to keep a job (Family Meme). Something had to give.

FIFTY-FIVE: Meme Law states: In any "inner" or "inter" Meme conflict, some leaders involved will need to make personal sacrifices to self and personal wellbeing, even to banishment or death, if stability and wholeness are to emerge from the conflict.

A more recent conflict was found in a young family I have known for years. Here, a wife (32) was married to a husband (39); they found themselves as privileged members of the White upper middle-class, ex-urban, Southern Meme. Republicanism surrounded everything they did (White National Meme): their neighbors, their school, their church and their friends - EVERYTHING.

During the 2012 election, which was all about getting rid of the new healthcare law (masking another "hidden" purpose to discredit our first Black president), she and I came into conflict over healthcare. The race question was never discussed.

Her Facebook page was wrapped in the flag, replete with logos of Mitt Romney, obviously representing her deepest beliefs, which she is obviously entitled to have. The pressure on her, living where she lived, surrounded by the Republican Meme's most loyal (White Southern, well-off and exurban), came not from me, but from her discovery that her husband had a serious, long-term, chronic illness and they had no health insurance. Prior to the ACA, he was not eligible because of his now pre-existing condition.

She called me to confess her fear: "This is going to ruin us." I attempted to ease her concern, reminding her that if Obama remains president, "in just 14 months her husband will get insurance and the family will be saved." She hung up on me and did not call for six months!

She wasn't in conflict with me; she was at war with herself, the worse type of inner-Meme conflict. She was stuck - hard - between two conflicting Memes. One, her family and her husband's need for healthcare, which called her to support Obama (ACA). This was in stark contrast to her desire to fit into the Meme surrounding her, which required her support of Romney. (Foolish conflict since Romney first introduced an ACP in Massachusetts).

If she satisfied her social Meme, her husband could suffer badly for years and her family would go broke. If she saved her husband by helping elect Obama for the needed healthcare, she was a traitor to her own neighbors.

"¿Oh, what to do?"

I don't know how she voted; I voted for her husband and family and the millions trapped without health insurance.

She will probably never realize that this major American conflict had nothing to do with healthcare. Her sub-Meme (tribe) is White, upper middle-class, Southern suburban; this Meme felt threatened by another sub-Meme, the mixed-race all-American tribe (with an elected President that was Black). Just as the President of Kenya replaced the able-bodied tribes, who could handle the situation at the mall, with a more powerful Meme that could not (his tribal Meme), her tribal Meme wanted to toss out the healthcare law to regain tribal power and retake the "White" House.

Unfortunately, this same scenario played out, even in the North. One of the world's best auto mechanics, who I have known well for 15 years, is a massive racist and a paranoid personality, hidden until the 2012 election. His best friend found himself, also, with a serious chronic ailment. The friend begged my mechanic to, "please, vote for Obama, because without the ACA I will be through and my family destitute."

At last conversation, my mechanic answer was: "No matter how good he does, I just can't vote for Obama ang get a Black President."

Remember the Meme Law that reminds us that, "in Meme life there are no real friends (ML: 7)." Also, don't forget the two teen girls who nearly killed their friend to satisfy a fictitious Meme god.

All this may sound one-sided politically, but that is not my intention. I am trying to illustrate the overwhelming power Meme membership has on us as individuals. Life and death are of little consequence to us compared to the power of Memes over us.

One thing to understand: if you are a police officer, CEO, medical doctor or are in any positions dealing with life and death, the pressure from "your people," that's your home Meme (White or Black, motorcycle gang, fellow officers, insiders like you, an affiliated organization), is the one force that can grab you and make you surrender your soul and ruin your life if you give into it.

Sadly, since almost no one is aware of Memes and their force on us, we can't measure their power, thus people never break their Meme's hold on them. That's why our prisons are full, suicides are legion, violence is epidemic, and wars abound!

XI//: Memes, A Must

STORY BOARD

"It is not enough to christianize (train) individuals, we must train societies, organizations and nations...they too have a life of their own. A corporate life is bound to develop in a body of men (people). Even a chance mass meeting will begin to be a unity after it has responded to the same thought for half an hour, and that unity will be BAD or GOOD according to the thoughts that united it. Humor or passion will sweep over the multitude of souls like the BREATH of a BILLOWS...and they will begin to fuse. It's like a huge personality, either a GOOD or EVIL spirt."

(He just discovered Human Social MEMES)

Walter Rauschenbusch (1861-1918) an internationally known Theologian, Philosopher and Professor of the twentieth century.

The quote above is from his book <u>The Righteousness of the Kingdom</u>. Nashville: Abingdon Press.

My friend, Hank, and I were speaking of Meme activities one day. He said, after a lengthy discussion, "We just ought to rid our world of Memes, they're just no good!" After reading this book you may agree. Trouble is, we can't. I mean - we really can't!

Science tells us that each of our human bodies are covered with well over 300,000 lice and tiny mites; we are inhabited by millions of microorganisms. You can scrub forever, and you won't lose them. If you could rid yourself of them, you'd die in a day.

In current news stories, we are finding that the antibiotics that are used in processing the animals we ingest are entering our digestive track. These modern marvels are killing thousands of "good" bacteria, leading us to obesity and serious medical problems. Just as with the lice and the other gut creatures, **we are stuck together with our Memes; we need both Microbes and Memes.**

If we were to outlaw Memes, coupling would be the first to go no births; hospitals would disappear – no healthcare or clinics; towns and cities would vanish – no more heated homes and running water; above all, civilization would end – anarchy would reign and life would not be tolerable.

In a few pages, we shall examine a new phenomenon, the **shrinking of our social Memes**. This downsizing of companies, churches and populations has created smaller Memes that are proliferating wildly and causing much social unrest.

Everything worthwhile that we can accomplish as humans requires human minds to interconnect, exchange, share and, **once envisioned, work together in a Human Social Organism** (family, municipality, company or country) - **that's what Memes allow us to do**.

The problem we still face is the one I first put forth back in chapter one: "INDIVIDUAL Human Beings are MOSTLY good, Humankind (Memes) are OFTEN just as harmful." Humankind being individual people gathered together in a common identity (Memes), in order to accomplish a common purpose, which may or may not reflect the good of the group or its individual members personal interests.

In the end we seem to be stuck in a "catch-22":

From our title: **Memes allow us to create Gods, Build Cities and Form Nations**, BUT

Memes enable us to Unleash Devils, Make War and Kill ourselves Dead.

So: "¿What do we do? - What do we do?

For starters: **We must KNOW and UNDERSTAND MEMES and muster the courage to CONFRONT and CHANGE MEME OUTCOMES!**

The very fact that Meme Law supersedes our individual consciences, where righteous behaviors are developed all through our lives, explains the harm Memes can do in spite of society's training of members from childhood for righteous behaviors.

Memes, themselves, are not easily subjected to moral development. Therefore, in taking over the individual's life, Memes mold a mostly morally inferior, fear filled being into a stronger force. But at the same time, this "exponentializing" of the human capacity allows us to both **achieve and destroy - do good and do bad.**

For example, in October of 2013, a casual group of motorcyclists gathered (via social media) just outside New York City for a bike ride. In preparation for this event, a Phantom Meme was created, as one cyclist after another emailed or Facebooked each other and made plans for the gathering.

Once gathered, the group soon evolved into an Informal Meme, seeing itself as "cycle power." In acting out in a very self-centered way, which Memes promote in members, the cyclists soon began working together, obstructing traffic and causing havoc on the Westside Highway (NYC).

This gang was in no way a Formal Meme. It had no chief enforcer, team structure or constitution, no name or identity as a Human Social Organism. What it did have was a commonality (Collective Mind): youthful madness, a separatist "better than them" attitude and powerful instruments (motorcycles). They were still an Informal Meme but no less a powerful force.

In the process of pushing people and bullying other drivers, one cyclist was run over by one of their victims, trying to escape. The "US" vs. "THEM" mentality, then grew out of their separatist identity. A united goal soon became "revenge on 'them' for our downed, Memed-in brother."

This is exactly what happens to police, the military and other Enforcers in doing what they do. If a target fights back, the entire group becomes one being, an Informal Meme (thugs) inside a Formal Meme, say a police department. The sub-Meme then turns lethal, as we have seen in police videos recently from all over America. Let's not forget that the individual cops involved, as individuals, are still nice people, but Meme Law has taken over.

Rauschenbusch wrote: **It's NOT enough to TRAIN Individuals**.

U.S. secret embedded agents depend on this universal behavior when inciting riots that become civil wars. I'm sure U.S. operatives, seeking upheaval across the Arab Maghreb, North Africa, the Middle East, and Ukraine (2010+), used this knowledge of baiting security forces to fire upon "innocent" demonstrators to accomplish their goal, which was "to provoke an opposite and equal reaction," in this case civil disruption. Millions are falling for it because they have no idea that Meme Law provides specific knowledge of how our groups respond to stimuli.

Many countries use this Meme-up tactic, even sacrificing some of their uniformed officers as bait. They push their faces against demonstrators so the mob will fight back, knowing: **"For every action there is an opposite and equal reaction."** When the people retaliate, the military can then declare them "insurgent terrorists" and ask for support from the big countries. After this, each side can mow the other down. The other side uses the same tactic. The rationale is to let a couple of your own go down, so the blood shows up in the U.S. on TV; next, cash, weapons and power gushes into the perpetrator.

You'll note on your six o'clock news, U.S. airplanes are getting ever closer to Russian or Chinese air space, especially in the South China Sea. Also, our Navy has ordered our ships to violate the territorial waters of China, nearer and nearer to their new Islands. This is a good examples of one country pushing itself into a war posture.

Notes

> **Two children** yelling at each other: "It's mine," then "No it's not, it's mine!" Louder and louder, and closer, hoping one **will BACK DOWN**; if not, fists will fly: NOW IT's **WAR!**

Armed with this knowledge, I have to admit to my friend Hank that the biggest evils on our planet are the work of Memes, both Formal (churches, nations and corporate) and Informal (mobs, police thugs and gangs).

The reason is like the two children above. MEMES simply ratchet up human behavior by a factor equal to the numbers of people on either side of an issue.

BUT and at the same time, almost every good accomplished by the human species is the result of a Meme formation around a beneficial cause (cities, hospitals, universities, business enterprises, charities).

A few people trying to help a community in a disaster is good, but the Red Cross and Red Crescent can dwarf the efforts of a few people as a Meme organized for good. The American Red Cross is also a perfect example of a Meme self-centering itself and letting politicians foul up the works. As a result, the ARC grew and became more organized and, simultaneously, more corrupt, finding itself doing less and less good for each dollar.

The curse of Memes grows out of human greed, selfishness, fear and cowardice. Unfortunately, good and evil are human traits, and both are "exponentialized" once attached to other human minds joined in a Meme. If one person can kill fifty people an hour, one-hundred people can easily kill off five-thousand people in the same hour.

But, if one person can save thirty people an hour, one-hundred people can rescue three-thousand people in the same hour.

If you believe, as I still do, that **most people** at their core seek to be righteous in most endeavors, then we must look at the Memeing process itself to view the change from choir boy to killer or from mother to mass murderer.

Both as a Law Enforcement person (16 years) and as a Pastor (28 years), one of the things parents would say when their child got into trouble was, "he/he was a good child until he/she got in with this bad crowd!"

Unhappily, the bad in us all becomes far worse when we're Memed-in with a troubled selfish Meme. Within Memes, this multi-minded person in us is enhanced, accelerated and even exaggerated, as we desire to be part of [*insert any Meme's name here*] (Family, club, class, or religion).

Each child has the ability to act out productively or act out harmfully. Membership in a Meme and the peer pressure involved can weigh this process toward either side. Unfortunately, due to specific forces (gender, age, place, family and self-promotion) strongly enhanced the effect of harmful Memes is over-represented.

"Memeing-in" offers a child the opportunity to serve the Meme and be accepted by adjusting her/himself to the requirement stated by the Meme. That was the first and eternal purpose of religion since ancient times: to be a child's first true Meme experience.

The tenets of the religion prescribe the child's duties toward the whole and promise safe entry into society in exchange for obedience.

The difficulty with Memes, whose membership is made up of basically decent people, is the sensible center (politicians, clergy, military). This arena is often staffed by cowards, or worse, "opportunists" surrendered to the ridiculous fringe.

This illustrates that many people serve the Meme for their own reward and that of other insiders (Politicals). All of these self-servers are to the detriment of the Meme's family and the world it serves.

Notes

> Here's the Formula for Human Horror:
>
> **GREED + FEAR + SELF-INDULGENCE +COWARDICE**
>
> **=**
>
> # E V I L

As we've seen in worldwide politics, some very harmful ideologues or deliberately self-ish people are allowed the control of social organisms and lead members into harm's way. This often results from fear, but more often for profits, and sometimes, just for the pleasure of manipulating people into destructive behaviors.

Unfortunately, for our species, these four traits are ubiquitous to the human condition and subject to "**Emotional Contagion**" of the first pathway [unthinking] (Goleman, _Social Intelligence_, Page 324). The result is usually catastrophic, as one person or two, especially in leadership, exhibits an emotion which then spreads throughout the herd (populist) and results in a stampede throughout the entire Meme.

International governance is our only hope at buffering this contagion, by creating a governing body, above all the others, with no stakeholders, no home turf and no insider power keepers. Moses tried to do this four-thousand years ago.

Upon gathering Israel, a ragtag group of Mid-Eastern outsiders accidently joined by being released from slavery, Moses inherited chaos and anarchy. Each group (Sub-Meme - tribe) had its own agenda, resulting in several hundred thousand people (recent figures tell of less than three hundred), thanks to Moses joined as members of an Informal Meme, all out for their own betterment.

Moses went up to a mountain top and found a higher power, carved stone tablets with a law inscribed (attributed to the higher power) and offered it up as the basis for a new

Social Organism (Master Meme), in which all the subdominant Memes (tribes) could be equal.

By the time he returned, **Emotional Contagion** had reared its ugly head and the population had gone wild with our four deadly emotions. They were in a sexual frenzy worshiping an animal and dangerously out of control but filled with GREED and SELF-INDULGENCE.

With the failure of the world system of individual states post-World War II, world leaders strove again for a Moses style authority over the world's uncooperative, self- centered Memes (countries). The United Nations (Super Meme) was their answer. I firmly believe, even now, in spite of the U.S.'s attempts to usurp it, a strong **UN is Humankind's only hope**.

The reason the UN has been so compromised over its existence lays squarely in the lap of the United States. The birth of this Super Meme (UN) coincided with the standing down of the world's previous power structure (European Empires). BUT it also coincided with the growth of an upstart, wishing to take the Europeans' place as the world's Super Meme - the United States" had come of age.

So, now we had two Super Memes subject to Meme Law in conflict with each other. The U.S. has used the UN as a sub-Meme to its strategic advantage by making sure this "new hope" was on U.S. soil where it could be controlled. Also, the U.S. has been its major funder, always just underpaying and keeping the new child "barefoot and hungry." In the beginning, the U.S. refused to join without the dreaded five-member veto power.

Even the USSR was ready to surrender that power in the beginning, as were the Europeans, but not the U.S.. Without the veto, we refused to join (just like the Southern slave states had done, demanding slavery as the U.S. became a nation during the Constitutional Convention). (David O. Stewart. _The Summer of 1787, The Men Who Invented the Constitution_. NY: Simon & Shuster 2007).

At the 11th hour, the rest gave in, and ever since, the U.S. has used the United Nations as its own subdominant Meme, carrying out our wishes in disguise (David L. Bosco.

Notes

Five to Rule Them All, The UN Security Council and the Making of the Modern World. NY: Oxford University Press, 2009).

At one time, a horribly naive "me" thought, "If only the entire earth would accept God's lordship that would be the answer." The main problem is, every Meme on earth has its own separate "god" and they all teach that their Meme has THE RIGHT god.

In this, Religion (one of the three ruling centers in every Meme) has destroyed any concept of the Divine Power, each cutting the Creator into small pieces, each ruled by national or cultural organisms. Most of these religions completely support the annihilation or subjugation of every other group of humans on earth at one time or another. My naivety was dangerous, Now I teach: "accept your creator – pay little attention to your religion" (my personal belief only),

By accepting a place in the Arena of Ideas and Beliefs as part of the Ruling Class, along with Military and Political members, all religions, of every people, have diminished themselves to becoming part of individual states and National Memes. This means they can no longer engage all people in the search for the universal quest for ultimate goodness, but rather, are just an arm of a Governing Meme. Religion, as an avenue meant to foster human unity and discover the Creator, is closed.

The only hope for the voice of the sacred in human social affairs is for ALL people to pull their religion out of war and governance, forcing them to deal with ALL individuals as equals and every Deity (God, Allah, Jehovah, Bongi etc.) as one and the same. The result, however, would be a mass defunding of religion and its loss as a "pop" icon. The flip side could be a mass trusting by the populace in "wholeness" and true peace.

For international unity and moral purposes, Nietzsche is correct: "God is dead," at least to us (a travesty in my opinion). So, in the end, an independent, more powerful United Nations remains our only possible hope.

The dramatic increase in the world's population and the corresponding decrease in separating distances has made rule by 1500 tribes and 193 self-centered states impossible.

GOD (Every Deity,
by Every name) is
a **CREATOR** –
NOT a destroyer. Unfortunately,
when humans
create a religion,
EVERY RELIGION,
it reflects their culture and includes their
ANGER, FEAR, and GREED, juxtaposing
themselves as the GOOD, HOLY, SUPERIOR.
Most people in RELIGION are seeking
GOD and only find the religion, NEVER
discovering GOD!

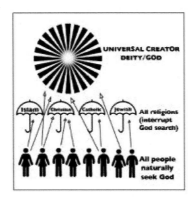

With humans soon to number eight billion, our planet is too small to attempt to isolate National Memes from one another.

Given a Meme's nature to war against like kinds of Memes, with less space and overlapping needs, we'll never have a minute's peace, unless every National Meme is subordinated to this neutral Super Meme, which must work for the equal benefit of all and under a basic law that all must obey. This may be a non-religious Ten Commandments.

Notes

DIAGRAM NINE

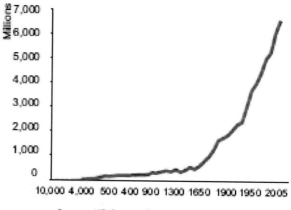

World Population: 10,000 BCE to 2007

Source: US Census Bureau International Data Base

"The Universal Declaration of Human Rights" (see appendage at book's end) is and can be the basic rule for a world that needs saving from ourselves.

> **NOTE: This Declaration is supported by every holy book on earth concerning human rights, YET almost every religion including Evangelical Christian is highly critical and ignores the document!**

There may be just too many people on our planet to allow separate groups, at all levels, to go unchecked, especially **NOW** that we know how human minds and Memes work; **NOW** that we understand that there are near mechanical ways that Human Social Organisms operate; **NOW** that we've grown to a place where, in just two generations, we could easily render the Earth unable to support life. If we can't get the very building blocks of culture - Human Social Memes - under universal authority, we are doomed by the power of our own brains. Remember the purpose of Memes in society:

The social role of a Meme is to allow the Human mind to organize society by creating and operating Human Social Organisms wherein Leaders can direct; Enforcers can order; the Less connected can function and the Unconcerned can be inspired to produce. *(II. Meme Basics / Meme Law)*

The most negative condition in our world is that our Memes have lost their "homeostasis" - balance. Memes, from the smallest to the largest, have always failed when one of the groups that create a Meme loses its sense of being part of that Meme.

This may be due in-part to that explosion in population numbers, causing the competition for lands, minds and economic riches to overwhelm the collective human psyche.

Whatever the reason, pure EVIL is running rampant across the globe. Everywhere: [A] *Alpha* **LEADERS,** seeing their opportunity as POLITICAL rulers, disregard the others in society and "take instead of giving" (GREED). The **[B]** *Beta* **ENFORCERS** take their authority and "bully it against the people instead of for the people" (FEAR). Our trusted **[Γ]** *Gamma* **CLERGY** and **ACADEMICS** and established **WORKERS** have misused their trusted positions in the most egocentric ways or just tuned-out (SELF-INDULGENCE). Our **[Δ]** *Delta* **DROP-OUTS** have become "disenchanted, feeling or knowing that they and their work is being exploited," but afraid of standing against power - many turn to drugs and alcohol (COWARDICE).

To this, our most fragile Group, the **OUTSIDERS** and **MARGINALS,** seeing no place or purpose, have stopped trying, choosing to party, rather than contribute. They feel, "*¿After all, who needs people anymore?*"

"**Shop until you drop**" isn't much of a life goal!

Memes, in these cases, become like any other body, when any of its parts take more than it should. The result is always the same, an organism "gone bad" and an unbalanced creature that is harmful to society - that's the definition of EVIL.

Which leads me to the final, but vital point, today we deny it, but: "**There is good and evil.**" We have become naturally suspicious of these terms - we are afraid of them. Religion has become so unbalanced, even the idea of right and wrong is now ignored.

Forget the failure of our religions, but let us reexamine "Good and Evil," because our avoidance of them is helping with the destruction of civilization.

Notes

Sociologists like Goleman are forbidden the use of these terms in order to satisfy academic standards. Some will insist that one person's "evil" is another's "holy." Some claim that each of our ideas of bad is subjective, often being put forth from sick destructive Memes. Here is a marker: **if something is evil to one group (Meme), it cannot EVER be holy to another**.

Sadly, my own country is the most guilty of this failing above all others. To the U.S., a challenger is a "terrorist," BUT when we invade another country, we have come in the name of "Democracy and Freedom." If the indigenous population fights back, they are "insurgents" who we deem available for killing.

Because of the obvious need for change in how we humans operate our world, it appears we may now destroy civilization by our fragmented, selfish, greedy behaviors.

Yet, in lieu of the disappearance of moral authority because of its internal corruption: I propose the introduction of a **Preamble to Meme Law**, which could be embraced by all human beings and all Human Social Organisms (humankind). If universally practiced, especially by the powerful Memes over the weaker, this may save our Human Societies and rebirth our world in peace.

The following is a suggested "**Preamble to Meme Law**"(as amended), **which states:**

1. **Every and all Social Organisms, Master Memes, subdominant Memes, lesser Memes and all parties to the same, knowing how destructive our humankind can become, shall endeavor to respect and celebrate every other Human Social Organism and all other Memes and individual persons - keeping them connected, safe and secure.**

   The second part is like unto the first:

2. **Every Social Organism, Master Meme, Subdominant Meme and all parties to the same shall care for, honor and respect all persons in their trust and all those of other cultures to the same degree that they respect themselves.**

The above may sound like a familiar religious-type statement. That's because the following heroes of history have delivered nearly these same words: The Great Imam, the Buddha, Lau Tzu, Jesus Christ, Boutros Boutros-Ghali, Martin Luther King Jr., Ram Mohan Roy, Saint Paul, John Wesley, Moses, Micah, Zachariah, Charles Finney, Muhammad, James Carter and Mahatma Gandhi. These, plus thousands of peacemakers in every land. I, Pastor Britt Minshall, am privileged to live in this Meme.

I can't stress enough: **we cannot sustain our current Collective Operating Philosophy** of each interest (person or group or nation) getting all it can at the expense of others. Our competitive nature is bleeding us dead. **The ultimate victim is the Earth**, we DEPEND on for life. As it now stands, we are hellbent on destroying our only home and killing ourselves off in the doing of it, much sooner than ever imagined.

Even popular entertainment (movies and books) is trying to warn us of our journey to self-destruction. In the past, apocalyptic literature, with us from ancient times, predicted, "God will do you all in." Now, the last day's **literature speaks of us doing ourselves in**, and it's closer than we think.

Some take heart in a last minute save, such as in the 2014 movie, "Mockingjay: The Hunger Games Series." But, in all such cases, we are treated to a civilization in shambles or no civilization at all!

During the summer of 2019, every film in our local 10-screen but one featured an end-of-world theme.

In 2014, we received two complimentary news stories that shattered even the most hardened of social scientists.

First, the University of Pennsylvania released results that confirmed the findings of smaller institutions: children, particularly girls from ages six through twelve, are forming cliques (Memes) in preschool and elementary school. Further, these little ones are adept at using these mini-groups to terrorize, extort and control other children in their schools. Ironically, the girls and now boys are dynamite ate creating massive Memes for good.

Second, just one week later, we received a double whammy when those three really close girlfriends from our first page, age twelve-years, went into the woods in a Wisconsin suburb where two ganged up on the one, stabbing her 19 times nearly killing her. This was all to placate the "unspoken" commands of an internet cartoon, "Slender Man."

So much for the unspoken agenda of seeking world peace, touted by some, predicting the ascendancy of the Female Memes over Male types. Males are seen as more combative persons. This demonstrates, as stated before: **"It's not that Memes are evil, but they do allow both the good and evil inside the human being to, exponentialize to a much greater and far-reaching degree than a solo individual could envision,"** Male or Female.

You see we are "stuck" with our Memes; **THEY ARE US.**

The frightening thing is, **WE ARE THEM.**

Historically, we have thought of Memeing-up or in as an ideal situation, even though we never conceived an organized life model called a "Meme." The idea of "safety in numbers" and being accepted is embedded in us from prehistory.

I have spent the better part of twenty years studying and facilitating groups to be effective organizations. My "TEAM Seminars" (Together Everyone Achieves More) were well received and actually reformed stagnant Human Social Organisms (Memes) to come alive again.

Throughout this period, I believed once the groups witnessed the good they could do working in a righteous manner, they would automatically continue in that stead. It was not so. Once I was well gone, the group gradually descended into an unproductive, many times more harmful state than as before our project. That is when I began searching for and discovered the Laws of Meme behavior.

In our current era, we are MOSTLY urbanized, ELECTRONICALLY connected, and the entire world is demanding order. We are surrounded by Mental Models (Memes) demanding our allegiance and often our lives. We all need to understand how this world system of Memes under Meme Law works, lest it overcomes us and becomes us, leaving us out in the cold like castoffs. This casting off or out has become the norm over the past twenty years.

Because of their close proximity to each other and the wild proliferation of Memes in today's world, Memes are attacking one another, rupturing and becoming smaller in size and numbers of members. .

As pointed out earlier, many companies formerly boasting of 10,000 employees (Meme members) now have 800. The end result is that an entire generation now lives as individuals and have little or no Meme connections at all.

(DIAGRAM TEN)

HEALTHY MEME STRUCTURES 1986

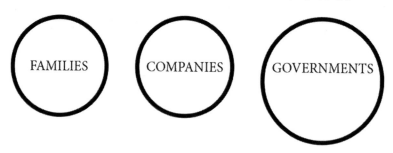

UNHEALTHY MEME STRUCTURES 2015

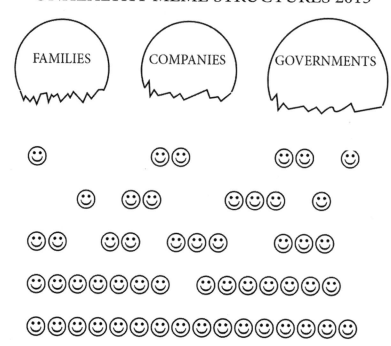

Often, these individuals, now unconnected, act as Informal Memes and make power plays, many beyond the pale of the law and are destructive and unaccountable.

The hope is that we become aware of the way our humanness betrays us as well as blesses us. By being ever aware of how Meme Law operates, we'll be able to finally:

Create gods (that never kill), build cities (that sustain forever) and form nations that won't unleash devils, make war and then kill us dead!

The Box – Poem by Lascelles Abercrombie

Once upon a time, in the land of Hush-A-Bye,
Around about the wondrous days of yore,
They came across a kind of box
Bound up with chains and locked with locks
And labeled 'Kindly do not touch; it's war.'
A decree was issued round about, and all with a flourish and a shout
And a gaily colored mascot tripping lightly on before.
Don't fiddle with this deadly box,

Or break the chains, or pick the locks.
And please don't ever play about with war.

The children understood. Children happen to be good
And they were just as good around the time of yore.
They didn't try to pick the locks

Or break into that deadly box.
They never tried to play about with war.
Mommies didn't either; sisters, aunts, grannies neither
'Cause they were quiet, and sweet, and pretty
In those wondrous days of yore.
Well, very much the same as now,
And not the ones to blame somehow
For opening up that deadly box of war.

Notes

But someone did. Someone battered in the lid
And spilled the insides out across the floor.
A kind of bouncy, bumpy ball made up of guns and flags
And all the tears, and horror, and death that comes with war.
It bounced right out and went bashing all about,
Bumping into everything in store.

And what was sad and most unfair
Was that it didn't really seem to care
Much who it bumped, or why, or what, or for.
It bumped the children mainly. And I'll tell you this quite plainly,
It bumps them every day and more, and more,
And leaves them dead, and burned, and dying
Thousands of them sick and crying.
'Cause when it bumps, it's really very sore.

Now there's a way to stop the ball. It isn't difficult at all.
All it takes is wisdom, and I'm absolutely sure
That we can get it back into the box,

And bind the chains, and lock the locks.
But no one seems to want to save the children anymore.
Well, that's the way it all appears,

'cause it's been bouncing round
for years and years
In spite of all the wisdom wizzed since those wondrous days of yore
And the time they came across the box,
Bound up with chains and locked with locks,
And labeled 'Kindly do not touch; **it's war.'**

**Children Running,
some clothes burned off
from Napalm's Hellish Fire
Dropped By U.S. Planes in
the WAR in Viet Nam**

*It bumped the children mainly. And I'll tell you this quite plainly,
It bumps them every day and more, and more,
And leaves them dead, and burned, and dying
Thousands of them sick and crying.*

Learn Meme Law and we can STOP WAR – FOREVER!

Appendices

One: Fifty-Five Universal Meme Laws

Memes defined: "**A self-replicating cluster of ideas. Thanks to a handful of biological tricks these visions become the glue that holds together civilization** (I add "any social organism"), **giving each culture its distinctive shape, making some intolerant of descent and others open to diversity. They (Memes) are the tools with which we unlock the forces of nature. Our visions bestow the dream of peace, but they also turn us into killers**" (Howard Bloom. NY: Atlantic Monthly Press 1995. *P 10*).

The Purpose of Memes: The social role of a Meme is to allow the Human mind to organize society by creating and operating Human Social Organisms wherein Leaders can direct; Enforcers can order; the Less connected can function and the Unconcerned can be inspired to produce. (II. Meme Basics / Meme Law)

ONE: Meme Law states: Memes are not sticklers for truth but, being creatures of the mind (Mental Models), actually favor myths which, when adopted by one strong Meme member, can spread like wildfire to all other members, often by force, often sparking untold madness, but sometimes, may create enormous good.

TWO: Meme Law states: The social role of a Meme is to allow the Human mind to organize society by creating and operating Human Social Organisms, where LEADERS can direct; ENFORCERS can order; the LESSER connected can function and the MARGINALS can be inspired to produce.

THREE: Meme Law states: Like kinds of Memes repel and isolate from each other, similar to like poles of a magnetic force, which can foster combat. Unlike Memes may more easily amalgamate, cluster or cooperate.

FOUR: Meme Law states: Every Meme seeks to identify itself differently than others, seeing each separate identity as an establishing principle, justifying each Meme's own existence and rendering it superior to others.

FIVE: Meme Law states: Individual persons have a default setting of Communion when encountering other individuals; Memes have a default setting of Combat when encountering other like Memes. However, individual persons identified as a member of any Meme will tend to ignore, make fun of or gang up on individuals of another Meme.

SIX: Meme Law states: The fastest, surest way to provide a Meme with identity and member loyalty is to identify an enemy threat, either internal or external, to focus member's fears and hatreds upon.

SEVEN: Meme Law states: A personal relationship, fostered in and among Meme members, no matter how well grounded, does not necessarily make a good lasting Meme relationship, outside the Meme context.

EIGHT: Meme Law states: The destiny of an organism's size, structure and success is a combination of the founders' vision or the long term successor leader's vision adopted in one degree or another by the followers (cadre), which then becomes much like an organizational DNA, difficult to supplant even when the originators are all gone.

NINE: Meme Law states: Memes, even international organizations, are always the most vulnerable at their base. Meme leaders should never forget that in a Meme Power comes from the center, but power's authority comes from its mass membership.

TEN: Meme Law states: While Memes form the structure and platform of every Human Social Organism, which gives face and structure to the Meme's concepts and principles, the Meme itself, while the real driving force of the Social Organism, remains invisible and unlocatable.

ELEVEN: Meme Law states: Members at the ruling power center of a Meme, many with high celebrity status, have no power of their own and are actually prisoners of the Meme, totally subject to the Meme's will as dictated by the Power Elites and the caprice of the populace.

TWELVE: Meme Law states: In the human propensity to avoid personal accountability, Memes afford the opportunity to shirk responsibility and deed that obligation to another who will accept the rewards and the punishments. This is the route of authoritarian government and the reason people strain to avoid populace rule, seeking rather a career ruler.

THIRTEEN: Meme Law states: Once a particular group (tribe, family or party) takes control of a Meme, it works to meme-in its own kind of people to operate the Meme to the exclusion of all others; thus the cadre is in solidarity in keeping control of the Meme, eventually consolidating with the position of Power Elite.

FOURTEEN: Meme Law states: The most profitable method of enriching the established Meme members and keeping them safe from newcomers rebelling is to accept small numbers of outsiders to Meme-in and offer them a method for achieving insider status by accomplishing a series of unpopular and/or dangerous tasks.

FIFTEEN: Meme Law states: Competition, as a method of expanding productivity among workers and selecting candidates for Meme leadership, even though it fosters interpersonal disputes as the populace battle each other for supremacy, does create wealth which, unfortunately, is almost completely driven to the center (top) of the organism for the benefit of Rulers and Power Elites, who foster competition and combat in their continuing quest for wealth acquisition.

SIXTEEN: Meme Law states: Newcomers to Meme membership are both applauded and exploited by Meme leaders, while the Meme's individual members resent the new arrivals, none-the-less, they take advantage of their newness as well.

SEVENTEEN: Meme Law states: Memes always favor the acceptance of and provide for their established members and their offspring (Marginals), while they discriminate completely against Outsiders and their offspring.

EIGHTEEN: Meme Law states: Meme members are inordinately loyal to their Meme. Once they are Memed-in or up, they tend not to leave from external pressures, but only from internal forces, and will defend their Meme to the death, even if they know their Meme's position is incorrect.

NINETEEN: Meme Law states: Rulers often pit one Meme member or sub-Meme against another, with no rules of fairness or sense of right or wrong; the goal being the ruler's receiving enhanced loyalty from the winners and enrichment from the defeated one's losses. When invoked by the rulers, this process trumps all personal and family loyalties.

TWENTY: Meme Law states: Meme members can never achieve high enough leadership, even the ultimate office, to successfully challenge the Meme's Operating Philosophy as sanctioned by the power center, without suffering consequences from others in the Meme's leadership and severe reprisals from the Meme's members.

TWENTY-ONE: Meme Law states: No matter how widespread the violence of the parties in contention in an inner-Meme conflict, it is always either focused on or sponsored by those in the center of the Meme in the Arena of Ideas and Beliefs, with the outer Meme members suffering the greatest consequences. Even the most populist centered movements usually have Power Elite sponsors.

TWENTY-TWO: Meme Law states: The stated purpose or label given a Meme may often mask another purpose entirely.

TWENTY-THREE: Meme Law states: Regardless of the degree of "inner" Meme disputes, in the end the Meme must achieve Homeostasis (Balance) in order to continue to exist, otherwise it will rupture, splinter or disintegrate.

Notes

TWENTY-FOUR: Meme Law states: The more Platforms (types) a Meme can claim, the more diverse its support and the greater power it can wield. Conversely, the more Platforms involved, the greater the possibility of long-term unresolvable conflict.

TWENTY-FIVE: Meme Law states: External pressure from other like-kinds of Memes, elicits a combative defensive response from the targeted Meme, which usually requires a punitive response from the correcting Memes to achieve changes in the target Meme's behavior. This principle of other-Meme interference, if pushed to the extreme, is the primary lead-up to war.

TWENTY-SIX: Meme Law states: Closed Memes, more often "Belief – Blood – and - Beulah" located, seek to restrict membership, which often brings an end to the Meme through attrition. Open Memes, most often "Badness – Business – and - Boldness located," depend upon large numbers of people to achieve their goal, so they willingly expand membership accordingly.

TWENTY-SEVEN: Meme Law states: When a subordinate-Meme forms inside a Master Meme, it must be quietly expelled or accommodated, if not great harm or dissolution will be experienced inside the Master Meme.

TWENTY-EIGHT: Meme Law states: Memes desiring to merge with other Memes, which they would normally repel or conquer, in order to survive and thrive, require strong internal leadership to overcome the will of individual members, who normally reject such transplanting of Meme loyalties. This rejection is entirely visceral, caused by organizational DNA, just as our physical bodies reject transplanted organs.

TWENTY-NINE: Meme Law states: Memes may have a tendency to support a gender identity, i.e., MALE or FEMALE, usually determined by the operations of the Meme being gender specific.

THIRTY: Meme Law states: Meme are just as subject to universal scientific principles and physical laws as the rest of the universe.

THIRTY-ONE: Meme Law states: Memes seeking to disrupt the world at peace will work to accentuate the Meme markers of two opposing Memes (race, language, religion), resulting in a xenophobic backlash and a "Dogfight" spontaneous combative relationship.

THIRTY-TWO: Meme Law states: ALL Memes are bipolar and subject to being ignited by certain triggers, the most usual of which are fear (paranoia), greed and self-interest, any or all of which can trigger schizophrenia (internal opposition) and render a Meme unstable and dangerous.

THIRTY-THREE: Meme Law states: The most effective way to extend control over another Meme is to allow Meme Laws to divide its population into its subdominant parts, then set each at odds with the others and conquer the target Meme using, its own polar opposites to effect its downfall.

THIRTY-FOUR: Meme Law states: The more powerful a Meme member becomes, the greater the opportunity and tendency to retain Meme wealth that passes his/her way for personal use. This is a consequence of a leader's requirement to completely surrender to the Meme, therefore, there is a tendency to view the organism's wealth as their personal largess.

THIRTY-FIVE: Meme Law states: The "Arena of Ideas and Beliefs" (Ruling Class) is represented in each society by the three major groups needed to control any organism. In America, and most modern states, the POLITICIANS make the rules, the CLERGY assuage the masses, and assure them the Deity has sanctioned the Meme's authority and the MILITARY (including Police) force dissenters into compliance.

THIRTY-SIX: Meme Law states: In order to carry out any act of high destruction and violence, such as war, the Arena of Ideas and Beliefs must be in total accord - The Political, The Military and The Clergy in complete agreement.

THIRTY-SEVEN: Meme Law states: When a person "Memes-up" or "in" to a Human Social Organism, they lose their sense of self, safety and faith in empirical data and become a different, often unrecognizable person, depending on the degree to which they surrender their lifer to the Meme.

THIRTY-EIGHT: Meme Law states: Sacrifices and unpleasant tasks needed by a Meme are assigned to the newcomers and the young members, even to risking their lives; while safe and comfortable duties are carried out by older, more established members.

THIRTY-NINE: Meme Law states: Formal Memes are forever. Their structures and outward identifiers (Social Organisms) may disappear, but their force field lies in a phantom state, continuing dormant, awaiting a group with like-minds and needs to reinvigorate and rebirth the dormant organism, usually with a new name.

FORTY: Meme Law states: Memes are capricious and opportunistic. A Meme will sell out its faithful, break its contracts and perpetrate mass fraud in order to protect and enrich itself and its members in power.

FORTY-ONE: Meme Law states: As the populace ignores or cowards-out of its responsibility to the whole of humankind, Celebrities or Prophets, who are powerless, will be generated by the organism to engage the people into the world from which they hide. Rarely, some become leaders, most will be discarded, but, hopefully, some of their corrective efforts survive.

FORTY-TWO: Meme Law states: Memes are amoral. A Meme knows nothing of right or wrong, it only knows survival and victory over other like-Memes and control of its environment. It does whatever it needs to in order to achieve its purpose and that purpose is not seen as good or bad, but "achieved" or "failed" - win or lose.

FORTY-THREE: Meme Law states: Memes have short memories of members' contributions. Once a Meme member retires or is removed from participation, they will soon be forgotten.

FORTY-FOUR: Meme Law states: A Meme is a here and now, an all-usurping organization that will abandon any and all agreements and solidarity with its members for the benefit of the Meme itself.

FORTY-FIVE: Meme Law states: Within any Meme the greatest accolades are reserved for those at the Meme's center, past and present, usually ignoring those at the outer levels of Meme life.

FORTY-SIX: Meme Law states: Memes are insanely jealous and, while having little regard for their members' welfare, Memes demand every measure of their members' being.

FORTY-SEVEN: Meme Law states: More powerful Meme members always abandon one of their own in times of trouble, especially one of a lower rank. Lower level members, conversely, tend to blindly support one of their own in trouble, except if the leaders order that person abandoned.

FORTY-EIGHT: Meme Law states: Meme members who are given authority to use force on others will do so exponentially and with little reserve. Having received approval from the Ruling Class, the target could be a

close friend or family member, but in this case, they are just victims.

FORTY-NINE: Meme Law states: No one in any Meme, including churches, clubs, military and corporations - in ALL Memes, at all levels, is a true friend to any other member. The Meme authority reserves the right to encourage or disallow relations between its members, most of whom will obey the order.

FIFTY: Meme Law states: The inner workings, failures and disputes within a Meme are seen as "our dirty laundry" and internal secrets, never to be discussed with those outside the Meme.

FIFTY-ONE: Meme Law states: Meme leaders tend to elevate themselves and their decisions, thinking them to be sacrosanct and above other Meme members' understanding, which, in turn, adds to their sense of elitism and superiority. As a result, leaders make secret their rulings, leading to social rupture, illegal actions and often, unnecessary, internal violence.

FIFTY-TWO: Meme Law states: Within a Master Meme, multi-subordinate Memes will generate, some to enhance and support the work of the host's leadership some to its detriment and even its destruction.

FIFTY-THREE: Meme Law states: Memes, even if part of the same Master Meme, becoming subdominant, distrust other like-Memes, even those sharing the same master, and will close down or sabotage each other if they feel threatened, rather than share for the good of all.

FIFTY-FOUR: Meme Law states: Once a person is suspected of crossing a Meme's will or violating its rules, a Meme is relentless, employing all of its members and sub-Memes to neutralize the offender. Safety can be found by the suspected violator only in a hidden sub-Meme or in complete exile from the Meme's territory. Computers and electronic data systems have rendered escape nearly impossible.

FIFTY-FIVE: Meme Law states: In any "inner" or "inter" Meme conflict, some leaders involved will need to make personal sacrifices to self and personal wellbeing, even to banishment or death, if stability and wholeness are to emerge from the conflict.

The following is a suggested "**Preamble to Meme Law**"(as amended) **which states:**

1. **(1) Every and all Social Organisms, Master Memes, subdominant Memes, lesser Memes and all parties to the same, knowing how destructive our Humankind can become, shall endeavor to respect and celebrate every other Human Social Organism and all other Memes and individual persons - keeping them connected, safe and secure.**

   The second part is like unto the first:

2. **(2) Every Social Organism, Master Meme, Subdominant Meme and all parties to the same shall care for, honor and respect all persons in**

their trust and all those of other cultures to the same degree that they respect themselves.

Formula for Perfect Human Horror:

GREED + FEAR + SELF-INDULGENCE + COWARDICE = EVIL!

TWO: MEME LAW IN ANCIENT WRITINGS

ONE: Meme Law states: Memes are not sticklers for truth but, being creatures of the mind (Mental Models), actually favor myths which, when adopted by one strong Meme member, can spread like wildfire to all other members, often by force, often sparking untold madness, but sometimes, may create enormous good.

HISTORICAL SCRIPTURES

JEREMIAH 5 I will go to the great
and will speak to them,
for they know the way of the Lord,
the justice of their God."
But they all alike had broken the yoke;
they had burst the bonds.

26 For wicked men are found among my people;
they lurk like fowlers lying in wait.
They set a trap;
they catch men.
27 Like a cage full of birds,
their houses are full of deceit

TWO: Meme Law states: The social role of a Meme is to allow the Human mind to organize society by creating and operating Human Social Organisms, where

Notes

LEADERS can direct; ENFORCERS can order; the LESSER connected can function and the MARGINALS can be inspired to produce.

HISTORICAL SCRIPTURE

Duet 4:44 This is the law that Moses set before the people of Israel.

12:28 Be careful to obey all these words that I command you, that it may go well with you and with your children after you forever, when you do what is good and right in the sight of the Lord your God.

THREE: Meme Law states: Like kinds of Memes repel and isolate from each other, similar to like poles of a magnetic force, which can foster combat. Unlike Memes may more easily amalgamate, cluster or cooperate.

HISTORICAL SCRIPTURE

Ex 17:16 And Moses built an altar and called its name, The-Lord-Is-My-Banner; [16] *for he said, "Because the Lord has sworn: the Lord will have war with Amalek from generation to generation."*

NUM 25:16 Then the Lord spoke to Moses, saying: [17] *"Harass the Midianites, and attack them;* [18] *for they harassed you with their schemes by which they seduced you in the matter of Peor and in the matter of Cozbi, the daughter of a leader of Midian, their sister, who was killed in the day of the plague because of Peor."*

Num 33:52 Then you shall drive out all the inhabitants of the land from before you, destroy all their engraved stones, destroy all their molded images, and demolish all their high places; [53] *you shall dispossess the inhabitants of the land and dwell in it, for I have given you the land to possess.* [54] *And you shall divide the land by lot as an inheritance among your families; to the larger you shall give a larger inheritance, and to the smaller you shall give a smaller inheritance; there everyone's inheritance shall be whatever falls to him by lot. You shall inherit according to the tribes of your fathers. [55] But if you do not drive out the inhabitants of the land from before you, then it shall be that those whom you let remain shall be irritants in your eyes and thorns in your sides, and they shall harass you in the land where you dwell. [56] Moreover it shall be that I will do to you as I thought to do to them.'*

FOUR: Meme Law states: Every Meme seeks to identify itself differently than others, seeing each separate identity as an establishing principle, justifying each Meme's own existence and rendering it superior to others.

HISTORICAL SCRIPTURE

Gen 17:13 This is My covenant which you shall keep, between Me and you and your descendants after you: Every male child among you shall be circumcised; [11] and you shall be circumcised in the flesh of your foreskins, and it shall be a sign of the covenant between Me and you. [12] He who is eight days old among you shall be circumcised, every male child in your generations, he who is born in your house or bought with money from any foreigner who is not your descendant. [13] He who is born in your house and he who is bought with your money must be circumcised, and My covenant shall be in your flesh for an everlasting covenant. [14] And the uncircumcised male child, who is not circumcised in the flesh of his foreskin, that person shall be cut off from his people; he has broken My covenant."

FIVE: Meme Law states: Individual persons have a default setting of Communion when encountering other individuals; Memes have a default setting of Combat when encountering other like Memes. However, individual persons identified as a member of any Meme will tend to ignore, make fun of or gang up on individuals of another Meme.

Notes

SIX: Meme Law states: The fastest, surest way to provide a Meme with identity and member loyalty is to identify an enemy threat, either internal or external, to focus member's fears and hatreds upon.

TEACHING SCRIPTURE

LUKE 6:41 [41] And why do you look at the speck in your brother's eye, but do not perceive the plank in your own eye? [42] Or how can you say to your brother, 'Brother, let me remove the speck that is in your eye,' when you yourself do not see the plank that is in your own eye? Hypocrite! First remove the plank from your own eye, and then you will see clearly to remove the speck that is in your brother's eye.

UDANAVARGA 27.1 The faults of others are easier to see than one's own; the faults of others are easily seen, for they are sifted like chaff, but one's own faults are hard to identify. This is like the cheat who hides his dice and shows the dice of his opponent, calling attention to the other's shortcomings, continually accusing him. BUDDHA.

JOHN 8:32 And you shall know the truth, and the truth shall make you free."

SEVEN: Meme Law states: A personal relationship fostered in and among Meme members, no matter how well grounded, does not necessarily make a good lasting Meme relationship, outside the Meme context.

HISTORICAL SCRIPTURE

JOHN 18:2; And Judas, who betrayed Him, also knew the place; for Jesus often met there with His disciples. [3] Then Judas, having received a detachment of troops, and officers from the chief priests and Pharisees, came there with lanterns, torches, and weapons.

EIGHT: Meme Law states: The destiny of an organism's size, structure and success is a combination of the founders' vision or the long term successor leader's vision adopted in one degree or another by the followers (cadre), which then becomes much like an organizational DNA, difficult to supplant even when the originators are all gone.

NINE: Meme Law states: Memes, even international organizations, are always the most vulnerable at their base. Meme leaders should never forget that in a Meme Power comes from the center, but power's authority comes from its mass membership.

HISTORICAL SCRIPTURE

MARK 15:9 But Pilate answered them, saying, "Do you want me to release to you the King of the Jews?" [10] For he knew that the chief priests had handed Him over because of envy.
[11] But the chief priests stirred up the crowd, so that he should rather release Barabbas to them. [12] Pilate answered and said to them again, "What then do you want me to do with Him whom you call the King of the Jews?"
[13] So they cried out again, "Crucify Him!"
[14] Then Pilate said to them, "Why, what evil has He done?"
But they cried out all the more, "Crucify Him!"

TEN: Meme Law states: While Memes form the structure and platform of every Human Social Organism, which gives face and structure to the Meme's concepts and principles, the Meme itself, while the real driving force of the Social Organism, remains invisible and unlocatable.

HISTORICAL SCRIPTURE

JOHN 12:42 Nevertheless even among the rulers many believed in Him, but because of the Pharisees they did not confess Him, lest they should be put out of the synagogue; [43] for they loved the praise of men more than the praise of God.

TEACHING SCRIPTURE

Notes

JOHN 12:44 Then Jesus cried out and said, "He who believes in Me, believes not in Me but in Him who sent Me. [45] And he who sees Me sees Him who sent Me. [46] I have come as a light into the world, that whoever believes in Me should not abide in darkness.

The TAO TE CHING: The Great Way is abundant on all sides. Everything comes from it, and no sentient boing is denied its blessing. Calling none its own, it feeds and clothes everyone.

THOMAS 113:1-4 The Kingdom is spread out over the whole world, and people do not see it.

LUKE 17: 20:21 Now when He was asked by the Pharisees when the kingdom of God would come, He answered them and said, "The kingdom of God does not come with observation; [21] nor will they say, 'See here!' or 'See there!' For indeed, the kingdom of God is within you."

ELEVEN: Meme Law states: Members at the ruling power center of a Meme, many with high celebrity status, have no power of their own and are actually prisoners of the Meme, totally subject to the Meme's will as dictated by the Power Elites and the caprice of the populace.

TWELVE: Meme Law states: In the human propensity to avoid personal accountability, Memes afford the opportunity to shirk responsibility and deed that obligation to another who will accept the rewards and the punishments. This is the route of authoritarian government and the reason people strain to avoid populace rule, seeking rather a career ruler.

TEACHING SCRIPTURE

Eccl 8:2 I say, "Keep the king's commandment for the sake of your oath to God. [3] Do not be hasty to go from his presence. Do not take your stand for an evil thing, for he does whatever pleases him."
[4] Where the word of a king is, there is power;

And who may say to him, "What are you doing?"
⁵ He who keeps his command will experience nothing harmful;
And a wise man's heart discerns both time and judgment,

MATT 22:21 And He said to them, "Render therefore to Caesar the things that are Caesar's, and to God the things that are God's." ²² When they had heard these words, they marveled, and left Him and went their way.

HISTORICAL SCRIPTURE

JOHN 18.27 And Simon Peter followed Jesus, and so did another disciple. Now that disciple was known to the high priest and went with Jesus into the court-yard of the high priest. ¹⁶ But Peter stood at the door outside. Then the other disciple, who was known to the high priest, went out and spoke to her who kept the door, and brought Peter in. ¹⁷ Then the servant girl who kept the door said to Peter, "You are not also one of this Man's disciples, are you?"
He said, "I am not."
¹⁸ Now the servants and officers who had made a fire of coals stood there, for it was cold, and they warmed themselves. And Peter stood with them and warmed himself. Peter then denied again; and immediately a rooster crowed

THIRTEEN: Meme Law states: Once a particular group (tribe, family or party) takes control of a Meme, it works to meme-in its own kind of people to operate the Meme to the exclusion of all others; thus the cadre is in solidarity in keeping control of the Meme, eventually consolidating with the position of Power Elite.

TEACHING SCRIPTURE

LUKE 16:13 "No servant can serve two masters; for either he will hate the one and love the other, or else he will be loyal to the one and despise the other. You cannot serve God and mammon." Jesus

Notes

FOURTEEN: Meme Law states: The most profitable method of enriching the established Meme members and to keep them safe from newcomers rebelling is to accept small numbers of outsiders to Meme-in and offer them a method for achieving insider status by accomplishing a series of unpopular and/or dangerous tasks.

HISTORICAL SCRIPTURE

Gen 37:23 So it came to pass, when Joseph had come to his brothers, that they stripped Joseph of his tunic, the tunic of many colors that was on him. [24] Then they took him and cast him into a pit. And the pit was empty; there was no water in it.

[25] And they sat down to eat a meal. Then they lifted their eyes and looked, and there was a company of Ishmaelites, coming from Gilead with their camels, bearing spices, balm, and myrrh, on their way to carry them down to Egypt. [26] So Judah said to his brothers, "What profit is there if we kill our brother and conceal his blood? [27] Come and let us sell him to the Ishmaelites, and let not our hand be upon him, for he is our brother and our flesh." And his brothers listened. [28] Then Midianite traders passed by; so the brothers pulled Joseph up and lifted him out of the pit, and sold him to the Ishmaelites for twenty shekels of silver. And they took Joseph to Egypt.

41:38; Then Pharaoh said to Joseph, "Inasmuch as God has shown you all this, there is no one as discerning and wise as you. [40] You shall be over my house, and all my people shall be ruled according to your word. [4142] Then Pharaoh took his signet ring off his hand and put it on Joseph's hand; and he clothed him in garments of fine linen and put a gold chain around his neck. [45]And Pharaoh called Joseph's name Zaphnath-Paaneah. And he gave him as a wife Asenath, the daughter of Poti-Pherah priest of On. So Joseph went out over all the land of Egypt.

FIFTEEN: Meme Law states: Competition, as a method of expanding productivity among workers and selecting candidates for Meme leadership, even though it fosters interpersonal disputes as the populace battle each other for supremacy, does create

wealth which, unfortunately, is almost completely driven to the center (top) of the organism, for the benefit of Rulers and Power Elites, who foster competition and combat in their continuing quest for wealth acquisition.

TEACHING SCRIPTURE

LUKE 12:15; And He said to them, "Take heed and beware of covetousness, for one's life does not consist in the abundance of the things he possesses."
16 Then He spoke a parable to them, saying: "The ground of a certain rich man yielded plentifully. 17 And he thought within himself, saying, 'What shall I do, since I have no room to store my crops?' 18 So he said, 'I will do this: I will pull down my barns and build greater, and there I will store all my crops and my goods. 19 And I will say to my soul, "Soul, you have many goods laid up for many years; take your ease; eat, drink, and be merry."' 20 But God said to him, 'Fool! This night your soul will be required of you; then whose will those things be which you have provided?'
21 "So is he who lays up treasure for himself, and is not rich toward God."

MATTHEW 6:19; "Do not lay up for yourselves treasures on earth, where moth and rust destroy and where thieves break in and steal; 20 but lay up for yourselves treasures in heaven, where neither moth nor rust destroys and where thieves do not break in and steal. 21 For where your treasure is, there your heart will be also.

THE TAO TE CHING Jade, gold, wealth, power pride – these bestow their own doom. Lao Tzu

THE DHAMMAPADA People suppose their wealth and families belong to them. But nothing belongs to us, and having such thoughts only leads to suffering. Buddha.

Notes

SIXTEEN: Meme Law states: Newcomers to Meme membership are both applauded and exploited by Meme leaders, while the Meme's individual members resent the new arrivals, none-the-less, they take advantage of their newness as well.

SEVENTEEN: Meme Law states: Memes always favor the acceptance of and provide for their established members and their offspring (Marginals), while they discriminate completely against Outsiders and their offspring.

EIGHTEEN: Meme Law states: Meme members are inordinately loyal to their Meme. Once they are Memed-in or up, they tend not to leave from external pressures, but only from internal forces, and will defend their Meme to the death, even if they know their Meme's position is incorrect.

TEACHING SCRIPTURE

REV 19:11; Now I saw heaven opened, and behold, a white horse. And He who sat on him was called Faithful and True, and in righteousness He judges and makes war. [12] His eyes were like a flame of fire, and on His head were many crowns. He had a name written that no one knew except Himself. [13] He was clothed with a robe dipped in blood, and His name is called The Word of God. [14] And the armies in heaven, clothed in fine linen, white and clean, followed Him on white horses.

HISTORICAL SCRIPTURE

I Sam 23:1; Then they told David, saying, "Look, the Philistines are fighting against Keilah, and they are robbing the threshing floors."
[2] Therefore David inquired of the Lord, saying, "Shall I go and attack these Philistines?"
And the Lord said to David, "Go and attack the Philistines, and save Keilah."
[3] But David's men said to him, "Look, we are afraid here in Judah. How much more then if we go to Keilah against the armies of the Philistines?" [4] Then David inquired of the Lord once again.
And the Lord answered him and said, "Arise, go down to Keilah. For I

will deliver the Philistines into your hand." [5] And David and his men went to Keilah and fought with the Philistines, struck them with a mighty blow, and took away their livestock. So David saved the inhabitants of Keilah.

BHAGARAD-GITA 1:24 -32 At the battle field of Kirik setra young Arjuna speaks:

Let me see all those who have come here to do evil war.

Lord Krishna then drew up in a fine chariot in the midst of the armies. He said behold Partha and the Kurdus assembled here.

Arjuna saw his Father, Grandfathers, uncles, Teachers, brothers and their sons and hundreds of his male friends and their relatives on both opposing sides in the Armies of both combatants.

He responds with deep compassion: I can no longer stand this evil of watching my family whom I love hack each other to death. I see only evil.

TEACHING SCRIPTURE

BHAGARAD-GITA 32-37; After much objecting to Krishna the lord scolds Arjuna: If you do not fight this war inspired by God, you will lose your reputation as a man – You will be labeled "COWARD!" Your name will be infamous and dishonored. So get in there and fight and kill as many as you can or be killed so you will be a hero and go to heaven, "FIGHT and CONQUER!"

NINETEEN: Meme Law states: Rulers often pit one Meme member or sub-Meme against another, with no rules of fairness or sense of right or wrong; the goal being the ruler's receiving enhanced loyalty from the winners and enrichment from the

defeated one's losses. When invoked by the rulers, this process trumps all personal and family loyalties.

HISTORICAL SCRIPTURE

I Sam 34:5; "For My sword shall be bathed in heaven;
Indeed it shall come down on Edom,
And on the people of My curse, for judgment.

LUKE 3:1; Now in the fifteenth year of the reign of Tiberius Caesar, Pontius Pilate being governor of Judea, Herod (an Edomite) was made tetrarch of Galilee, his brother Philip tetrarch of Iturea and the region of Trachonitis, and Lysanias tetrarch of Abilene, ² while Annas and Caiaphas were high priests,

TWENTY: Meme Law states: Meme members can never achieve high enough leadership, even the ultimate office, to successfully challenge the Meme's Operating Philosophy as sanctioned by the power center, without suffering consequences from others in the Meme's leadership and severe reprisals from the Meme's members.

HISTORICAL SCRIPTURE

II Chr 24:20-21; Now after the death of Jehoiada the leaders of Judah came and bowed down to the king. And the king listened to them. ¹⁸ Therefore they left the house of the Lord God of their fathers and served wooden images and idols; and wrath came upon Judah and Jerusalem because of their trespass. ¹⁹ Yet He sent prophets to them, to bring them back to the Lord; and they testified against them, but they would not listen.
²⁰ Then the Spirit of God came upon Zechariaht, who stood above the people, and said to them, "Thus says God: Why do you transgress the commandments of the Lord, so that you cannot prosper? Because you have forsaken the Lord, He also has forsaken you.' " ²¹ So they conspired against him, and at the command of the king they stoned him with stones in the court of the house of the Lord. ²² Thus Joash the king did not remember the kindness which Jehoiada

his father had done to him, but killed his son; and as he died, he said, "The Lord look on it, and repay!"
II Kin. 12:19–20;
23 So it happened in the spring of the year that the army of Syria came up against him; and they came to Judah and Jerusalem, and destroyed all the leaders of the people from among the people,

TEACHING SCRIPTURE

MATT 20:17-19; Now Jesus, going up to Jerusalem, took the twelve disciples aside on the road and said to them, 18 "Behold, we are going up to Jerusalem, and the Son of Man will be betrayed to the chief priests and to the scribes; and they will condemn Him to death, 19 and deliver Him to the Gentiles to mock and to scourge and to crucify. And the third day He will rise again."

LUKE 18 31-34; Then He took the twelve aside and said to them, "Behold, we are going up to Jerusalem, and all things that are written by the prophets concerning the Son of Man will be accomplished. 32 For He will be delivered to the Gentiles and will be mocked and insulted and spit upon. 33 They will scourge Him and kill Him. And the third day He will rise again."
34 But they understood none of these things; this saying was hidden from them, and they did not know the things which were spoken.

HISTORICAL SCRIPTURE

II Sam 15; After this Absalom provided himself with chariots and horses, and fifty men to run before him. 2 Now Absalom would rise early and stand beside the way to the gate. So it was, whenever anyone who had a lawsuit came to the king for a decision, that Absalom would call to him and say, "What city are you from?" And he would say, "Your servant is from such and such a tribe of Israel." 3 Then Absalom would say to him, "Look, your case is good and right; but there is no deputy of the king to hear you." 4 Moreover Absalom would

Notes

say, "Oh, that I were made judge in the land, and everyone who has any suit or cause would come to me; then I would give him justice." [5] And so it was, whenever anyone came near to bow down to him, that he would put out his hand and take him and kiss him. [6] In this manner Absalom acted toward all Israel who came to the king for judgment. So Absalom stole the hearts of the men of Israel.

17::9; There is a slaughter among the people who follow Absalom.' [10] And even he who is valiant, whose heart is like the heart of a lion, will melt completely.

18:1-4; And David numbered the people who were with him, and set captains of thousands and captains of hundreds over them. [2] Then David sent out one third of the people And the king said to the people, "I also will surely go out with you myself."
[3] But the people answered, "You shall not go out! For if we flee away, they will not care about us; nor if half of us die, will they care about us. But you are worth ten thousand of us now. For you are now more help to us in the city."
[4] Then the king said to them, "Whatever seems best to you I will do." So the king stood beside the gate, and all the people went out by hundreds and by thousands.

19:8; Then the king arose and sat in the gate. And they told all the people, saying, "There is the king, sitting in the gate." So all the people came before the king.

TEACHING SCRIPTURE

MATT 2:16; Then Herod, when he saw that he was deceived by the wise men, was exceedingly angry; and he sent forth and put to death all the male children who were in Bethlehem and in all its districts, from two years old and under, according to the time which he had determined from the wise men. [17] Then was fulfilled what was spoken by Jeremiah the prophet, saying:

[18] *"A voice was heard in Ramah,*

Lamentation, weeping, and great mourning,

Rachel weeping for her children,

Refusing to be comforted,

Because they are no more."

TWENTY-ONE: Meme Law states: No matter how widespread the violence of the parties in contention in an inner-Meme conflict, it is always either focused on or sponsored by those in the center of the Meme in the Arena of Ideas and Beliefs, with the outer Meme members suffering the greatest consequences. Even the most populist centered movements usually have Power Elite sponsors.

TWENTY-TWO: Meme Law states: The stated purpose or label given a Meme may often mask another purpose entirely.

HISTORICAL SCRIPTURES

MATT 7:28-29; And so it was, when Jesus had ended these sayings, that the people were astonished at His teaching, [29] for He taught them as one having authority, and not as the scribes.

TEACHING SCRIPTURES

Ex 20;16; "You shall not bear false witness against
your neighbor.

PSALMS 119:104; Through Your precepts I get understanding;
Therefore I hate every false way.

PROVERBS 21:28-29; A false witness shall perish,
But the man who hears him will speak endlessly.
[29] A wicked man hardens his face,
But as for the upright, he establishes his way.

Notes

MATT 7:17-20; Even so, every good tree bears good fruit, but a bad tree bears bad fruit. [18] A good tree cannot bear bad fruit, nor can a bad tree bear good fruit. [19] Every tree that does not bear good fruit is cut down and thrown into the fire. [20] Therefore by their fruits you will know them.

MATT 24:24; "Then if anyone says to you, 'Look, here is the Christ!' or 'There!' do not believe it. [24] For false christs and false prophets will rise and show great signs and wonders to deceive, if possible, even the elect.

TWENTY-THREE: Meme Law states: Regardless of the degree of "inner" Meme disputes, in the end the Meme must achieve Homeostasis (Balance) in order to continue to exist, otherwise it will rupture, splinter or disintegrate.

HISTORICAL SCRIPTURES

Ex 32:1-7; Now when the people saw that Moses delayed coming down from the mountain, the people gathered together to Aaron, and said to him, "Come, make us gods that shall go before us; for as for this Moses, the man who brought us up out of the land of Egypt, we do not know what has become of him."
[2] And Aaron said to them, "Break off the golden earrings which are in the ears of your wives, your sons, and your daughters, and bring them to me." [4] And he received the gold from their hand, and he fashioned it with an engraving tool, and made a molded calf.
Then they said, "This is your god, O Israel, that brought you out of the land of Egypt!"
[5] So when Aaron saw it, he built an altar before it. And Aaron made a proclamation and said, "Tomorrow is a feast to the Lord." [6] Then they rose early on the next day, offered burnt offerings, and brought peace offerings; and the people sat down to eat and drink, and rose up to play.
[7] And the Lord said to Moses, "Go, get down! For your people whom you brought out of the land of Egypt have corrupted themselves.

GAL 1:6-9; I marvel that you are turning away so soon from Him who called you in the grace of Christ, to a different gospel, ⁷ which is not another; but there are some who trouble you and want to pervert the gospel of Christ. ⁸ But even if we, or an angel from heaven, preach any other gospel to you than what we have preached to you, let him be accursed. ⁹ As we have said before, so now I say again, if anyone preaches any other gospel to you than what you have received, let him be accursed.

¹⁰ For do I now persuade men, or God? Or do I seek to please men? For if I still pleased men, I would not be a bondservant of Christ.

TWENTY-FOUR: Meme Law states: The more Platforms (types) a Meme can claim, the more diverse its support and the greater power it can wield. Conversely, the more Platforms involved, the greater the possibility of long term unresolvable conflict.

TEACHING SCRIPTURE

Luke 16:13; No servant can serve two masters; for either he will hate the one and love the other, or else he will be loyal to the one and despise the other. You cannot serve God and mammon."

TWENTY-FIVE: Meme Law states: External pressure from other like-kinds of Memes, elicits a combative defensive response from the targeted Meme, which usually requires a punitive response from the correcting Memes to achieve changes in the target Meme's behavior. This principle of other- Meme interference, if pushed to the extreme, is the primary lead-up to war.

HISTORICAL SCRIPTURE

Duet 20:10-17 "When you go near a city to fight against it, then proclaim an offer of peace to it. ¹¹ And it shall be that if they accept your offer of peace, and open to you, then all the people who are found in it shall be placed under tribute to you and serve you. ¹² Now if the city will not make peace with you, but war against you, then you shall besiege it. ¹³ And when the Lord your God delivers it into your hands, you shall strike every male in it with the edge of

Notes

the sword. [14] But the women, the little ones, the livestock, and all that is in the city, all its spoil, you shall plunder for yourself; and you shall eat the enemies' plunder which the Lord your God gives you.

[16] "But of the cities of these peoples which the Lord your God gives you as an inheritance, you shall let nothing that breathes remain alive, [17] but you shall utterly destroy them: the Hittite and the Amorite and the Canaanite and the Perizzite and the Hivite and the Jebusite, just as the Lord your God has commanded you, [18] lest they teach you to do according to all their abominations which they have done for their gods, and you sin against the Lord your God.

TWENTY-SIX: Meme Law states: Closed Memes, more often "Belief – Blood - and - Beulah" located, seek to restrict membership, which often brings an end to the Meme through attrition. Open Memes, most often "Badness – Business – and - Boldness located," depend upon large numbers of people to achieve their goal, so they willingly expand membership accordingly.

HISTORICAL SCRIPTURE

Gen 21:9; And Sarah saw the son of Hagar the Egyptian, whom she had borne to Abraham, scoffing. [10] Therefore she said to Abraham, "Cast out this bondwoman and her son; for the son of this bondwoman shall not be heir with my son, namely with Isaac." [11] And the matter was very displeasing in Abraham's sight because of his son.

[12] But God said to Abraham, "Do not let it be displeasing in your sight because of the lad or because of your bondwoman. Whatever Sarah has said to you, listen to her voice; for in Isaac your seed shall be called. [13] Yet I will also make a nation of the son of the bondwoman, because he is your seed."

[14] So Abraham rose early in the morning, and took bread and a skin of water; and putting it on her shoulder, he gave it and the boy to Hagar, and sent her away. Then she departed and wandered in the Wilderness of Beersheba. [15] And the water in the skin was used up, and she placed the boy under one of the shrubs.

TWENTY-SEVEN: Meme Law states: When a subordinate-Meme forms inside a Master Meme, it must be quietly expelled or accommodated, if not great harm or dissolution will be experienced inside the Master Meme.

HISTORICAL SCRIPTURE

Isaiah 14:112-19; "How you are fallen from heaven,
O Lucifer, son of the morning!
How you are cut down to the ground,
You who weakened the nations!
¹³ For you have said in your heart:
I will ascend into heaven,
I will exalt my throne above the stars of God;
I will also sit on the mount of the congregation
On the farthest sides of the north;
¹⁴ I will ascend above the heights of the clouds,
I will be like the Most High.'
¹⁵ Yet you shall be brought down to Sheol,
To the lowest depths of the Pit.
¹⁶ "Those who see you will gaze at you,
And consider you, saying:
'Is this the man who made the earth tremble,
Who shook kingdoms,
¹⁷ Who made the world as a wilderness
And destroyed its cities,
Who did not open the house of his prisoners?'
¹⁸ "All the kings of the nations,
All of them, sleep in glory,
Everyone in his own house;
¹⁹ But you are cast out of your grave,

ACTS 4:13-18; Now when they saw the boldness of Peter and John, and
perceived that they were uneducated and untrained men, they marveled.

And they realized that they had been with Jesus. [14] And seeing the man who had been healed standing with them, they could say nothing against it. [15] But when they had commanded them to go aside out of the council, they conferred among themselves, [16] saying, "What shall we do to these men? For, indeed, that a notable miracle has been done through them is evident to all who dwell in Jerusalem, and we cannot deny it. [17] But so that it spreads no further among the people, let us severely threaten them, that from now on they speak to no man in this name."

[18] So they called them and commanded them not to speak at all nor teach in the name of Jesus.

TWENTY-EIGHT: Meme Law states: Memes desiring to merge with other Memes, which they would normally repel or conquer, in order to survive and thrive, require strong internal leadership to overcome the will of individual members, who normally reject such transplanting of Meme loyalties. This rejection is entirely visceral, caused by organizational DNA, just as our physical bodies reject transplanted organs.

HISTORIC SCRIPTURE

ACTS 13:48-50; Now when the Gentiles heard this, they were glad and glorified the word of the Lord. And as many as had been appointed to eternal life believed.

[49] And the word of the Lord was being spread throughout all the region. [50] But the Jews stirred up the devout and prominent women and the chief men of the city, raised up persecution against Paul and Barnabas, and expelled them from their region.

The FIFTH BOOK of the HISTORY OF THE ENGLISH NATION; Ch. X (690 AD); Wilfred and the Christian Priests' mission to Frisland (France): Soon two other priests of the English nation came to the province of the Old Saxons hoping their preaching might win some to Christ. One was "Black Hewald" the other was "White Hewald." They guested at the home of a local chief and asked him to elevate them to an embassy (meeting) with the Alderman (Province Chief), he Promised to do so.

But the local Chief became afraid his own (pagan) religious would turn on him, so he sked his villagers to mutilate and murder the two Christian Priests (the local leaders drew their power from their own religion (MEME).

After the Alderman learned what the locals had done to the English, he killed the local leaders and burned their village.

Harvard Classics: Bede's History ll from the Latin translation by Loeb).

TEACHING SCRIPTURE

LUKE 10:29; But he, wanting to justify himself, said to Jesus, "And who is my neighbor?"

30 Then Jesus answered and said: "A certain man went down from Jerusalem to Jericho, and fell among thieves, who stripped him of his clothing, wounded him, and departed, leaving him half dead. 31 Now by chance a certain priest came down that road. And when he saw him, he passed by on the other side. 32 Likewise a Levite, when he arrived at the place, came and looked, and passed by on the other side. 33 But a certain Samaritan, as he journeyed, came where he was. And when he saw him, he had compassion. 34 So he went to him and bandaged his wounds, pouring on oil and wine; and he set him on his own animal, brought him to an inn, and took care of him. 35 On the next day, when he departed, he took out two denarii, gave them to the innkeeper, and said to him, 'Take care of him; and whatever more you spend, when I come again, I will repay you.' 36 So which of these three do you think was neighbor to him who fell among the thieves?"

37 And he said, "He who showed mercy on him."

Then Jesus said to him, "Go and do likewise."(Jesus)

Notes

TWENTY-NINE: Meme Law states: Memes may have a tendency to support a gender identity, i.e., MALE or FEMALE, usually determined by the operations of the Meme being gender specific.

HISTORICAL SCRIPTURE

Gen. 2:7; And the Lord God formed man (humans) of the dust of the ground, and breathed into his nostrils the breath of life; and man became a living being.

3:14-20; To the MAN: Because you have done this,
You are cursed more than all cattle,
And more than every beast of the field;
On your belly you shall go,
And you shall eat dust
All the days of your life.
[15] And I will put enmity
Between you and the WOMAN:
And between your seed and her Seed;
He shall bruise your head,
And you shall bruise His heel."
[16] To the WOMAN He said:
"I will greatly multiply your sorrow and your conception;
In pain you shall bring forth children;
Your desire shall be for your husband,
And he shall rule over you."
[17] Then to Adam He said, "Because you have heeded the voice of your wife, and have eaten from the tree of which I commanded you, saying, 'You shall not eat of it':
"Cursed is the ground for your sake;
In toil you shall eat of it
All the days of your life.
[18] Both thorns and thistles it shall bring forth for you,

And you shall eat the herb of the field.

[19] In the sweat of your face you shall eat bread

Till you return to the ground,

For out of it you were taken;

For dust you are,

And to dust you shall return."

[20] And Adam called his wife's name Eve, because she was the mother of all living.

[21] Also for Adam and his wife the Lord God made tunics of skin, and clothed them.

Lev 6:18+; And the Lord spoke to Moses, saying, [20] "This is the offering of Aaron and his sons, which they shall offer to the Lord, beginning on the day when he is anointed: one-tenth of an ephah of fine flour as a daily grain offering, half of it in the morning and half of it at night. [21] It shall be made in a pan with oil. When it is mixed, you shall bring it in. The baked pieces of the grain offering you shall offer for a sweet aroma to the Lord. [22] The priest from among his sons, who is anointed in his place, shall offer it. It is a statute forever to the Lord. It shall be wholly burned. [23] For every grain offering for the priest shall be wholly burned. It shall not be eaten."

[24] Also the Lord spoke to Moses, saying, [25] "Speak to Aaron and to his sons, saying, 'This is the law of the sin offering …

2 Chr 31:16-25; And the Lord spoke to Moses, saying, [20] "This is the offering of Aaron and his sons, which they shall offer to the Lord, beginning on the day when he is anointed: one-tenth of an ephah of fine flour as a daily grain offering, half of it in the morning and half of it at night. [21] It shall be made in a pan with oil. When it is mixed, you shall bring it in. The baked pieces of the grain offering you shall offer for a sweet aroma to the Lord. [22] The priest from among his sons, who is anointed in his place, shall offer it. It is a statute forever to the Lord. It shall be wholly burned. [23] For every grain offering for the priest shall be wholly burned. It shall not be eaten."

Notes

Isaiah 46:8-11; Remember this, and show yourselves men;
Recall to mind, O you transgressors.
[9] *Remember the former things of old,*
For I am God, and there is no other;
I am God, and there is none like Me,
[10] *Declaring the end from the beginning,*
And from ancient times things that are not yet done,
Saying, My counsel shall stand,
And I will do all My pleasure,'
[11] *Calling a bird of prey from the east,*
The man who executes My counsel, from a far country.

TEACHING SCRIPTURE

Prov 13:15; Good understanding gains favor,
But the way of the unfaithful is hard.
[16] *Every prudent man(male) acts with knowledge,*
But a fool lays open his folly.
[17] *A wicked messenger falls into trouble,*
But a faithful ambassador brings health.
[18] *Poverty and shame will come to him who disdains correction,*
But he who regards a rebuke will be honored.
[19] *A desire accomplished is sweet to the soul,*
But it is an abomination to fools to depart from evil.
[20] *He who walks with wise men (males) will be wise,*
But the companion of fools will be destroyed.
[21] *Evil pursues sinners,*
But to the righteous, good shall be repaid.
[22] *A good man(male) leaves an inheritance to his children's children,*
But the wealth of the sinner is stored up for the righteous.
[23] *Much food is in the fallow ground of the poor,*
And for lack of justice there is waste.
[24] *He who spares his rod hates his son,*

But he who loves him disciplines him promptly.
²⁵ The righteous eats to the satisfying of his soul,
But the stomach of the wicked shall be in want.

THIRTY: Meme Law states: Meme are just as subject to universal scientific principles and physical laws as the rest of the universe.

TEACHING SCRIPTURE

Ali ibn Abi Talib (4th *Caliph* in *Sunni* Islam, and first *Imam* in *Shia* Islam) says:

"O' my child, make yourself the measure (for dealings) between you and others. Thus, you should desire for others what you desire for yourself and hate for others what you hate for yourself. Do not oppress as you do not like to be oppressed. Do good to others as you would like good to be done to you. Regard bad for yourself whatever you regard bad for others. Accept that (treatment) from others which you would like others to accept from you... Do not say to others what you do not like to be said to you." — Nahjul Balaghah, Letter 3

MATT 7; ¹² Therefore all things whatsoever ye would that men should do to you, do ye even so to them: for this is the law and the prophets. Jesus.

THIRTY-ONE: Meme Law states: Memes seeking to disrupt the world at peace will work to accentuate the Meme markers of two opposing Memes (race, language, religion), resulting in a xenophobic backlash and a "Dogfight" spontaneous combative relationship.

HISTORICAL TEACHING

Duet 7:1; "When the Lord your God brings you into the land which you go to possess, and has cast out many nations before you, the Hittites and the

Notes

Girgashites and the Amorites and the Canaanites and the Perizzites and the Hivites and the Jebusites, seven nations greater and mightier than you, ² and when the Lord your God delivers them over to you, you shall conquer them and utterly destroy them. You shall make no covenant with them nor show mercy to them. ³ Nor shall you make marriages with them. You shall not give your daughter to their son, nor take their daughter for your son. ⁴ For they will turn your sons away from following Me, to serve other gods; so the anger of the Lord will be aroused against you and destroy you suddenly. ⁵ But thus you shall deal with them: you shall destroy their altars, and break down their sacred pillars, and cut down their wooden images, and burn their carved images with fire.

Ezra 9:1; The leaders came to me, saying, "The people of Israel and the priests and the Levites have not separated themselves from the peoples of the lands, with respect to the abominations of the Canaanites, the Hittites, the Perizzites, the Jebusites, the Ammonites, the Moabites, the Egyptians, and the Amorites. ² For they have taken some of their daughters as wives for themselves and their sons, so that the holy seed is mixed with the peoples of those lands. Indeed, the hand of the leaders and rulers has been foremost in this trespass." ³ So when I heard this thing, I tore my garment and my robe, and plucked out some of the hair of my head and beard and sat down astonished.

10:10-11 Then Ezra the priest stood up and said to them, "You have transgressed and have taken pagan wives, adding to the guilt of Israel. ¹¹ Now therefore, make confession to the Lord God of your fathers, and do His will; separate yourselves from the peoples of the land, and from the pagan wives."
¹² Then all the assembly answered and said with a loud voice, "Yes! As you have said, so we must do.

TEACHING SCRIPTURE

Dan 6:25;⁵ Then King Darius wrote:
To all peoples, nations, and languages that dwell in all the earth:

Peace be multiplied to you.
²⁶ I make a decree that in every dominion of my kingdom men must tremble
and fear before the God of Daniel.
For He is the living God,
And steadfast forever;
His kingdom is the one which shall not be destroyed,
And His dominion shall endure to the end.

THIRTY-TWO: Meme Law states: ALL Memes are bipolar and subject to being ignited by certain triggers, the most usual of which are fear (paranoia), greed and self-interest, any or all of which can trigger schizophrenia (internal opposition) and render a Meme unstable and dangerous.

HISTORICAL SCRIPTURE

Num 31:12; Then they brought the captives, the booty, and the spoil to Moses, to Eleazar the priest, and to the congregation of the children of Israel, to the camp in the plains of Moab by the Jordan, across from Jericho. ¹³ And Moses, Eleazar and all the leaders of the congregation, went to meet them outside the camp. ¹⁴ But Moses was angry with the officers of the army, with the captains over thousands and captains over hundreds, who had come from the battle. ¹⁵ And Moses said to them: "Have you kept all the women alive? ¹⁶ Look, these women caused the children of Israel, through the counsel of Balaam, to trespass against the Lord in the incident of Peor, and there was a plague among the congregation of the Lord. ¹⁷ Now therefore, kill every male among the little ones, and kill every woman who has known a man intimately. ¹⁸ But keep alive for yourselves all the young girls who have not known a man intimately.

TEACHING SCRIPTURE

MATT 22:39; You shall love your neighbor as yourself.'

Notes

MATT 7:1; Judge not, that you be not judged. ² For with what judgment you judge, you will be judged; and with the measure you use, it will be measured back to you. ³ And why do you look at the speck in your brother's eye, but do not consider the plank in your own eye? ⁴ Or how can you say to your brother, 'Let me remove the speck from your eye'; and look, a plank is in your own eye? ⁵ Hypocrite! First remove the plank from your own eye, and then you will see clearly to remove the speck from your brother's eye

THIRTY-THREE: Meme Law states: The most effective way to extend control over another Meme is to allow Meme Laws to divide its population into its subdominant parts, then set each at odds with the others and conquer the target Meme using, its own polar opposites to affect its downfall.

TEACHING SCRIPTURE

MATT 18:23; The kingdom of heaven is like a certain king who wanted to settle accounts with his servants. ²⁴ And when he had begun to settle accounts, one was brought to him who owed him ten thousand talents. ²⁵ But as he was not able to pay, his master commanded that he be sold, with his wife and children and all that he had, and that payment be made. ²⁶ The servant therefore fell down before him, saying, 'Master, have patience with me, and I will pay you all.' ²⁷ Then the master of that servant was moved with compassion, released him, and forgave him the debt.

²⁸ "But that servant went out and found one of his fellow servants who owed him a hundred denarii; and he laid hands on him and took him by the throat, saying, 'Pay me what you owe!' ²⁹ So his fellow servant fell down at his feet and begged him, saying, 'Have patience with me, and I will pay you all.' ³⁰ And he would not, but went and threw him into prison till he should pay the debt. ³¹ So when his fellow servants saw what had been done, they were very grieved, and came and told their master all that had been done. ³² Then his master, after he had called him, said to him, 'You wicked servant! I forgave you all that debt because you begged me. ³³ Should you not also have had compassion on your fellow servant, just as I had pity on you?' ³⁴ And his master was angry, and

delivered him to the torturers until he should pay all that was due to him.
35 "So My heavenly Father also will do to you if each of you, from his heart,
does not forgive his brother his trespasses."

THIRTY-FOUR: Meme Law states: The more powerful a Meme member becomes, the greater the opportunity and tendency to retain Meme wealth that passes his/her way for personal use. This is a consequence of a leader's requirement to completely surrender to the Meme, therefore, there is a tendency to view the organism's wealth as their personal largess.

HISTORICAL SCRIPTURE

I Kings 4:23; Now Solomon's provision for one day was thirty kors of fine flour, sixty kors of meal, 23 ten fatted oxen, twenty oxen from the pastures, and one hundred sheep, besides deer, gazelles, roebucks, and fatted fowl.
24 For he had dominion over all the region on this side of the River from Tiphsah even to Gaza, namely over all the kings on this side of the River; and he had peace on every side all around him. 25 And Judah and Israel dwelt safely, each man under his vine and his fig tree, from Dan as far as Beersheba, all the days of Solomon.
26 Solomon had forty thousand stalls of horses for his chariots, and twelve thousand horsemen. 27 And these governors, each man in his month, provided food for King Solomon and for all who came to King Solomon's table. There was no lack in their supply. 28 They also brought barley and straw to the proper place, for the horses and steeds, each man according to his charge.

Eccl 2:4; 4 I made my works great, I built myself houses, and planted myself vineyards. 5 I made myself gardens and orchards, and I planted all kinds of fruit trees in them. 6 I made myself water pools from which to water the growing trees of the grove. 7 I acquired male and female servants, and had servants born in my house. Yes, I had greater possessions of herds and flocks than all who were in Jerusalem before me. 8 I also gathered for myself silver and gold and the special treasures of kings and of the provinces. I acquired male and

Notes

female singers, the delights of the sons of men, and musical instruments of all kinds.

⁹ So I became great and excelled more than all who were before me in Jerusalem. Also my wisdom remained with me.

¹⁰ Whatever my eyes desired I did not keep from them. I did not withhold my heart from any pleasure,

THIRTY-FIVE: Meme Law states: The "Arena of Ideas and Beliefs" (Ruling Class) is represented in each society by the three major groups needed to control any organism. In America, and most modern states, the POLITICIANS make the rules, the CLERGY assuage the masses, and assure them the Deity has sanctioned the Meme's authority and the MILITARY (including Police) force dissenters into compliance.

HISTORICAL SCRIPTURE

Religious Leaders: *Ex 29:9; And you shall gird them with sashes, Aaron and his sons, and put the hats on them. The priesthood shall be theirs for a perpetual statute. So you shall consecrate Aaron and his sons.*

Political Leaders: *1 Sam 8:4-6; Then all the elders of Israel gathered together and came to Samuel at Ramah, ⁵ and said to him, "Look, you are old, and your sons do not walk in your ways. Now make us a king to judge us like all the nations."*

⁶ But the thing displeased Samuel when they said, "Give us a king to judge us." So Samuel prayed to the Lord. ⁷ And the Lord said to Samuel, "Heed the voice of the people in all that they say to you; for they have not rejected you, but they have rejected Me, that I should not reign over them.

Military Leaders: *Num 31:1-6; And the Lord spoke to Moses, saying: ² "Take vengeance on the Midianites for the children of Israel. Afterward you shall be gathered to your people."*

³ So Moses spoke to the people, saying, "Arm some of yourselves for war, and let them go against the Midianites to take vengeance for the Lord on Midian. ⁴ A

thousand from each tribe of all the tribes of Israel you shall send to the war."
*[5] So there were recruited from the divisions of Israel one thousand from each
tribe, twelve thousand armed for war. [6] Then Moses sent them to the war, one
thousand from each tribe;*

*Duet 1:15; So I took the heads of your tribes, wise and knowledgeable men, and
made them heads over you, leaders of thousands, leaders of hundreds, leaders
of fifties, leaders of tens, and officers for your tribes.*

**THIRTY-SIX: Meme Law states: In order to carry out any act of high destruction
and violence, such as war, the Arena of Ideas and Beliefs must be in total accord - The
Political, The Military and The Clergy in complete agreement.**

HISTORICAL SCRIPTURE

*I Kings 1:44-48; Then Jonathan answered and said to Adonijah, "No! Our lord
King David has made Solomon king. [44] The king has sent with him Zadok the
priest, Nathan the prophet, Benaiah the son of Jehoiada, the Cherethites, and
the Pelethites; and they have made him ride on the king's mule. [45] So Zadok the
priest and Nathan the prophet have anointed him king at Gihon; and they have
gone up from there rejoicing, so that the city is in an uproar. This is the noise
that you have heard. [46] Also Solomon sits on the throne of the kingdom. [47] And
moreover the king's servants have gone to bless our lord King David, saying,
May God make the name of Solomon better than your name, and may He
make his throne greater than your throne.' Then the king bowed himself on the
bed. [48] Also the king said thus, 'Blessed be the Lord God of Israel, who has given
one to sit on my throne this day, while my eyes see it!' "*

TEACHING SCRIPTURE

*Hag 2:20-23; And again the word of the Lord came to Haggai saying, [21] "Speak
to Zerubbabel, governor of Judah, saying:
I will shake heaven and earth.
[22] I will overthrow the throne of kingdoms;*

I will destroy the strength of the Gentile kingdoms.
I will overthrow the chariots
[23] *'In that day,' says the Lord of hosts, 'I will take you, Zerubbabel My servant, the son of Shealtiel,' says the Lord, and will make you like a signet ring; for I have chosen you,' says the Lord of hosts."*

THIRTY-SEVEN: Meme Law states: When a person "Memes-up" or "in" to a Human Social Organism, they lose their sense of self, safety and faith in empirical data and become a different, often unrecognizable person, depending on the degree to which they surrender their life to the Meme.

HISTORICAL SCRIPTURE

Ex 32:7-10; And the Lord said to Moses, "Go, get down! For your people whom you brought out of the land of Egypt have corrupted themselves. [8] They have turned aside quickly out of the way which I commanded them. They have made themselves a molded calf, and worshiped it and sacrificed to it, and said, "This is your god, O Israel, that brought you out of the land of Egypt!' " [9] And the Lord said to Moses, "I have seen this people, and indeed it is a stiff-necked people!

ACTS 7:54-60; When they heard these things they were cut to the heart, and they gnashed at him with their teeth. [55] But he, being full of the Holy Spirit, gazed into heaven and saw the glory of God, and Jesus standing at the right hand of God, [56] and said, "Look! I see the heavens opened and the Son of Man standing at the right hand of God!"
[57] Then they cried out with a loud voice, stopped their ears, and ran at him with one accord; [58] and they cast him out of the city and stoned him. And the witnesses laid down their clothes at the feet of a young man named Saul. [59] And they stoned Stephen as he was calling on God and saying, "Lord Jesus, receive my spirit." [60] Then he knelt down and cried out with a loud voice, "Lord, do not charge them with this sin." And when he had said this, he fell asleep.

THIRTY-EIGHT: Meme Law states: Sacrifices and unpleasant tasks needed by a Meme are assigned to the newcomers and the young members, even to risking their lives; while safe and comfortable duties are carried out by older, more established members.

HISTORICAL TEACHING

I Kings 12:6-19; Then King Rehoboam consulted the elders who stood before his father Solomon while he still lived, and he said, "How do you advise me to answer these people?"

⁷ And they spoke to him, saying, "If you will be a servant to these people today, and serve them, and answer them, and speak good words to them, then they will be your servants forever."

⁸ But he rejected the advice which the elders had given him, and consulted the young men who had grown up with him, who stood before him. ⁹ And he said to them, "What advice do you give? How should we answer this people who have spoken to me, saying, 'Lighten the yoke which your father put on us'?"

¹⁰ Then the young men spoke to him, saying, "Thus you should speak to this people who have spoken to you, saying, 'Your father made our yoke heavy, but you make it lighter on us'—thus you shall say to them: 'My little finger shall be thicker than my father's waist! ¹¹ And now, whereas my father put a heavy yoke on you, I will add to your yoke; my father chastised you with whips, but I will chastise you with scourges!' "

¹² So Jeroboam and all the people came to Rehoboam the third day, as the king had directed." ¹³ Then the king answered the people roughly, and rejected the advice which the elders had given him; ¹⁴ and he spoke to them according to the advice of the young men ¹⁵ So the king did not listen to the people; for the turn of events was from the Lord, that He might fulfill His word, which the Lord had spoken.

¹⁶ Now when all Israel saw that the king did not listen to them, the people answered the king, saying:

"What share have we in David?

We have no inheritance in the son of Jesse.

Notes

To your tents, O Israel!
Now, see to your own house, O David!"
So Israel departed to their tents. [17] But Rehoboam reigned over the children of
Israel who dwelt in the cities of Judah.
[18] Then King Rehoboam sent Adoram, who was in charge of the revenue; but all
Israel stoned him with stones, and he died. Therefore King Rehoboam mounted
his chariot in haste to flee to Jerusalem. [19] So Israel has been in rebellion
against the house of David to this day.

TEACHING SCRIPTURE

I JOHN 2:12-15; I write to you, little children,
Because your sins are forgiven you for His name's sake.
[13] I write to you, fathers,
Because you have known Him who is from the beginning.
I write to you, young men,
Because you have overcome the wicked one.
I write to you, little children,
Because you have known the Father.
[14] I have written to you, fathers,
Because you have known Him who is from the beginning.
I have written to you, young men,
Because you are strong, and the word of God abides in you,
And you have overcome the wicked one.
[18] Little children, it is the last hour; and as you have heard that the Antichrist is
coming, even now many antichrists have come, by which we know that it is the
last hour. [19] They went out from us, but they were not of us; for if they had been
of us, they would have continued with us; but they went out that they might be
made manifest, that none of them were of us.
[20] But you have an anointing from the Holy One, and you know all things. [21] I
have not written to you because you do not know the truth, but because you
know it,

Ali ibn Abi Talib (4th *Caliph* in *Sunni* Islam, and first *Imam* in *Shia* Islam) says:

"O' my child, make yourself the measure (for dealings) between you and others. Thus, you should desire for others what you desire for yourself and hate for others what you hate for yourself. Do not oppress as you do not like to be oppressed. Do good to others as you would like good to be done to you. Regard bad for yourself whatever you regard bad for others. Accept that (treatment) from others which you would like others to accept from you... Do not say to others what you do not like to be said to you." — *Nahjul Balaghah, Letter 3*

THIRTY-NINE: Meme Law states: Formal Memes are forever. Their structures and outward identifiers (Social Organisms) may disappear, but their force field lies in a phantom state, continuing dormant, awaiting a group with like-minds and needs to reinvigorate and rebirth the dormant organism, usually with a new name.

HISTORICAL SCRIPTURE

Ezra 1:1-4; Now in the first year of Cyrus king of Persia, that the word of the Lord by the mouth of Jeremiah might be fulfilled, the Lord stirred up the spirit of Cyrus king of Persia, so that he made a proclamation throughout all his kingdom, ² Thus says Cyrus king of Persia:
All the kingdoms of the earth the Lord God of heaven has given me. And He has commanded me to build Him a house at Jerusalem which is in Judah. ³ Who is among you of all His people? May his God be with him, and let him go up to Jerusalem which is in Judah, and build the house of the Lord God of Israel (He is God), which is in Jerusalem. ⁴ And whoever is left in any place where he dwells, let the men of his place help him with silver and gold, with goods and livestock, besides the freewill offerings for the house of God which is in Jerusalem.

Notes

*3:11-13; And they sang responsively, praising and giving thanks to the Lord:
"For He is good, For His mercy endures forever toward Israel."
Then all the people shouted with a great shout, when they praised the Lord,
because the foundation of the house of the Lord was laid.
¹² But many of the priests and Levites and heads of the fathers' houses, old men
who had seen the first temple, wept with a loud voice when the foundation of
this temple was laid before their eyes. Yet many shouted aloud for joy, ¹³ so that
the people could not discern the noise of the shout of joy from the noise of the
weeping of the people, for the people shouted with a loud shout, and the sound
was heard afar off.*

TEACHING SCRIPTURE

*Ezec 37:1-14; The hand of the Lord came upon me and brought me out in the
Spirit of the Lord, and set me down in the midst of the valley; and it was full of
bones. ² Then He caused me to pass by them all around, and behold, there were
very many in the open valley; and they were very dry. ³ And He said to me,
"Son of man, can these bones live?"
So I answered, "O Lord God, You know."
⁴ Again He said to me, "Prophesy to these bones, and say to them, 'O dry bones,
hear the word of the Lord! ⁵ "Surely I will cause breath to enter into you, and
you shall live. ⁶ I will put sinews on you and bring flesh upon you, cover you
with skin and put breath in you; and you shall live. Then you shall know that I
am the Lord." ' "
⁷ So I prophesied as I was commanded; and as I prophesied, there was a noise,
and suddenly a rattling; and the bones came together, bone to bone. ⁸ Indeed,
as I looked, the sinews and the flesh came upon them, and the skin covered
them over; but there was no breath in them.
⁹ Also He said to me, "Prophesy to the breath, prophesy, son of man, and say
to the breath, 'Thus says the Lord God: "Come from the four winds, O breath,
and breathe on these slain, that they may live." ' " ¹⁰ So I prophesied as He
commanded me, and breath came into them, and they lived, and stood upon
their feet, an exceedingly great army.*

[11] Then He said to me, "Son of man, these bones are the whole house of Israel. They indeed say, Our bones are dry, our hope is lost, and we ourselves are cut off!' [12] Therefore prophesy and say to them, 'Thus says the Lord God: "Behold, O My people, I will open your graves and cause you to come up from your graves, and bring you into the land of Israel. [13] Then you shall know that I am the Lord, O My people, and I will put My Spirit in you, and you shall live, and I will place you in your own land. "

1 COR 15:51-54; Behold, I tell you a mystery: We shall not all sleep, but we shall all be changed [52] in a moment, in the twinkling of an eye, at the last trumpet. For the trumpet will sound, and the dead will be raised incorruptible, and we shall be changed. [53] For this corruptible must put on incorruption, and this mortal must put on immortality. [54] So when this corruptible has put on incorruption, and this mortal has put on immortality, then shall be brought to pass the saying that is written: "Death is swallowed up in victory."

FORTY: Meme Law states: Memes are capricious and opportunistic. A Meme will sell out its faithful, break its contracts and perpetrate mass fraud in order to protect and enrich itself and its members in power.

HISTORICAL SCRIPTURE

LUKE 23:8-12; Now when Herod saw Jesus, he was exceedingly glad; for he had desired for a long time to see Him, because he had heard many things about Him, and he hoped to see some miracle done by Him. [9] Then he questioned Him with many words, but He answered him nothing. [10] And the chief priests and scribes stood and vehemently accused Him. [11] Then Herod, with his men of war, treated Him with contempt and mocked Him, arrayed Him in a gorgeous robe, and sent Him back to Pilate. [12] That very day Pilate and Herod became friends with each other, for previously they had been at enmity with each other. (FRIENDS from ENEMIES in a second)

Notes

FORTY-ONE: Meme Law states: As the populace ignores or cowards-out of its responsibility to the whole of humankind, Celebrities or Prophets, who are powerless, will be generated by the organism to engage the people into the world from which they hide. Rarely, some become leaders, most will be discarded, but, hopefully, some of their corrective efforts survive.

TEACHING SCRIPTURE

TAO TE CHING; I ask for understanding as I travel the great Way, so I might not lose sight of the road. The great Way is simple and manifest, but people prefer to take other paths. LAO TZU

MATT 7:12; Enter by the narrow gate; for wide is the gate and broad is the way that leads to destruction, and there are many who go in by it. [14] Because narrow is the gate and difficult is the way which leads to life, and there are few who find it.

FORTY-TWO: Meme Law states: Memes are amoral. A Meme knows nothing of right or wrong, it only knows survival and victory over other like-Memes and control of its environment. It does whatever it needs to in order to achieve its purpose and that purpose is not seen as good or bad, but "achieved" or "failed" - win or lose.

HISTORICAL SCRIPTURE

LUKE 22:1-6; Now the Feast of Unleavened Bread drew near, which is called Passover. [2] And the chief priests and the scribes sought how they might kill Him, for they feared the people.
[3] Then Satan entered Judas, surnamed Iscariot, who was numbered among the twelve. [4] So he went his way and conferred with the chief priests and captains, how he might betray Him to them. [5] And they were glad, and agreed to give him money. [6] So he promised and sought opportunity to betray Him to them in the absence of the multitude.

47-53; And while He was still speaking, behold, a multitude; and he who was called Judas, one of the twelve, went before them and drew near to Jesus to kiss Him. ⁴⁸ But Jesus said to him, "Judas, are you betraying the Son of Man with a kiss?"

⁴⁹ When those around Him saw what was going to happen, they said to Him, "Lord, shall we strike with the sword?" ⁵⁰ And one of them struck the servant of the high priest and cut off his right ear.

⁵¹ But Jesus answered and said, "Permit even this." And He touched his ear and healed him.

⁵² Then Jesus said to the chief priests, captains of the temple, and the elders who had come to Him, "Have you come out, as against a robber, with swords and clubs? ⁵³ When I was with you daily in the temple, you did not try to seize Me. But this is your hour, and the power of darkness."

FORTY-THREE: Meme Law states: Memes have short memories of members' contributions. Once a Meme member retires or is removed from participation, they will soon be forgotten.

TEACHING SCRIPTURE

MATT 6:33; Seek ye first the Kingdom of God and His righteousness, and all these things shall be added to you. ³⁴ Therefore do not worry about tomorrow, for tomorrow will worry about its own things. Sufficient for the day is its own trouble.

TAO TE CHING; Once you have fulfilled your purpose, Stop there. Do not boast or parade your secret. Give up pride…to over-develop is to increase decline…this is not the Way, and anything that resists the Way will soon cease to be. LAO TZU

UPANISHADES; That which most people treasure is transient, but eternity cannot be attained through things that are not eternal. KRISHNA

Notes

FORTY-FOUR: Meme Law states: A Meme is a here and now, an all-usurping organization that will abandon any and all agreements and solidarity with its members for the benefit of the Meme itself.

HISTORICAL SCRIPTURE

Gen 39:4-23; So Joseph found favor in his sight, and served him. Then he made him overseer of his house, and all that he had he put under his authority. [5] So it was, from the time that he had made him overseer of his house and all that he had, that the Lord blessed the Egyptian's house for Joseph's sake; and the blessing of the Lord was on all that he had in the house and in the field. [6] Thus he left all that he had in Joseph's hand, and he did not know what he had except for the bread which he ate.

[7] And it came to pass after these things that his master's wife cast longing eyes on Joseph, and she said, "Lie with me."

[8] But he refused and said to his master's wife, "Look, my master does not know what is with me in the house, and he has committed all that he has to my hand. How then can I do this great wickedness, and sin against God?"

[10] So it was, as she spoke to Joseph day by day, that he did not heed her, to lie with her or to be with her.

[11] But it happened about this time, when Joseph went into the house to do his work, and none of the men of the house was inside, [12] that she caught him by his garment, saying, "Lie with me." But he left his garment in her hand, and fled and ran outside. [13] And so it was, when she saw that he had left his garment in her hand and fled outside, [14] that she called to the men of her house and spoke to them, saying, "See, he has brought in to us a Hebrew to mock us. He came in to me to lie with me, and I cried out with a loud voice.

[16] So she kept his garment with her until his master came home. [17] Then she spoke to him with words saying, "The Hebrew servant whom you brought to us came in to me to mock me; [18] so it happened, as I lifted my voice and cried out, that he left his garment with me and fled outside."

[19] So it was, when his master heard the words which his wife spoke to him, saying, "Your servant did to me after this manner," that his anger was aroused.

[20] *Then Joseph's master took him and put him into the prison, a place where the king's prisoners were confined.*

Ezra 9:9; For we were slaves. Yet our God did not forsake us in our bondage; but He extended mercy to us in the sight of the kings of Persia, to revive us, to repair the house of our God, to rebuild its ruins, and to give us a wall in Judah and Jerusalem. [10] *And now, O our God, what shall we say after this? For we have forsaken Your commandments,*

1 Kings 12:6; Then King Rehoboam consulted the elders who stood before his father Solomon while he still lived, and he said, "How do you advise me to answer these people?"
[7] *And they spoke to him, saying, "If you will be a servant to these people today, and serve them, and answer them, and speak good words to them, then they will be your servants forever."*
[8] *But he rejected the advice which the elders had given him,*

JOHN 18:25-26; Now Simon Peter stood and warmed himself. Therefore they said to him, "You are not also one of His disciples, are you?"
He denied it and said, "I am not!"
[26] *One of the servants of the high priest, a relative of him whose ear Peter cut off, said, "Did I not see you in the garden with Him?"* [27] *Peter then denied again; and immediately a rooster crowed.*

18:28; Then they led Jesus from Caiaphas to the Praetorium, and it was early morning. But they themselves did not go into the Praetorium, lest they should be defiled, but that they might eat the Passover. [29] *Pilate then went out to them and said, "What accusation do you bring against this Man?"*
[30] *They answered and said to him, "If He were not an evildoer, we would not have delivered Him up to you."*

19:6-9; Then Jesus came out, wearing the crown of thorns and the purple robe. And Pilate said to them, "Behold the Man!"

Notes

⁶ *Therefore, when the chief priests and officers saw Him, they cried out, saying, "Crucify Him, crucify Him!"*
Pilate said to them, "You take Him and crucify Him, for I find no fault in Him."
⁷ *The Jews answered him, "We have a law, and according to our law He ought to die, because He made Himself the Son of God."*
⁸ *Therefore, when Pilate heard that saying, he was the more afraid,* ⁹ *and went again into the Praetorium, and said to Jesus, "Where are You from?" But Jesus gave him no answer.*

MATT 27:46; And about the ninth hour Jesus cried out with a loud voice, saying, "Eli, Eli, lama sabachthani?" that is, "My God, My God, why have You forsaken Me?"

ACTS 14:16-20; who in bygone generations allowed all nations to walk in their own ways. ¹⁷ *Nevertheless He (Paul)did not leave Himself without witness, in that He did good, gave us rain from heaven and fruitful seasons, filling our hearts with food and gladness."* ¹⁸ *And with these sayings they could scarcely restrain the multitudes from sacrificing to them.*
¹⁹ *Then Jews from Antioch and Iconium came there; and having persuaded the multitudes, they stoned Paul and dragged him out of the city, supposing him to be dead.* ²⁰ *However, when the disciples gathered around him, he rose up and went into the city. And the next day he departed with Barnabas to Derbe.*

TEACHING SCRIPTURE

MATT 10: 5-18; These twelve Jesus sent out and commanded them, saying: "Do not go into the way of the Gentiles, and do not enter a city of the Samaritans. ⁶ *But go rather to the lost sheep of the house of Israel.* ⁷ *And as you go, preach, saying, The kingdom of heaven is at hand.'* ⁸ *Heal the sick, cleanse the lepers, raise the dead, cast out demons. Freely you have received, freely give.* ⁹ *Provide neither gold nor silver nor copper in your money belts,* ¹⁰ *nor bag for your journey, nor two tunics, nor sandals, nor staffs; for a worker is worthy of his food.*

[11] "Now whatever city or town you enter, inquire who in it is worthy, and stay there till you go out. [12] And when you go into a household, greet it. [13] If the household is worthy, let your peace come upon it. But if it is not worthy, let your peace return to you. [14] And whoever will not receive you nor hear your words, when you depart from that house or city, shake off the dust from your feet. [15] Assuredly, I say to you, it will be more tolerable for the land of Sodom and Gomorrah in the day of judgment than for that city!

[16] "Behold, I send you out as sheep in the midst of wolves. Therefore be wise as serpents and harmless as doves. [17] But beware of men, for they will deliver you up to councils and scourge you in their synagogues. [18] You will be brought before governors and kings for My sake, as a testimony to them and to the Gentiles.

Vinaya Mahavagga 1.11.1; Monks walk throughout the land for the blessing of the people, for the happiness of the people, and out of compassion of the world. Buddhism

Chuang Tzu; The sage moves through life not caring about home or name, living simply. Lacking distinction, others think him a fool. But he judges no one. His foot leaves no prints. He is a perfect man. His boat is empty. Lao Tzu

FORTY-FIVE: Meme Law states: Within any Meme the greatest accolades are reserved for those at the Meme's center, past and present, usually ignoring those at the outer levels of Meme life.

HISTORICAL SCRIPTURE

2 Kings14:21; And all the people of Judah took Azariah, who was sixteen years old, and made him king instead of his father Amaziah. [22] He built Elath and restored it to Judah, after the king rested with his fathers.

Notes

Esther 1:1-7; Now it came to pass in the days of Ahasuerus (this was the Ahasuerus who reigned over one hundred and twenty-seven provinces, from India to Ethiopia), ² in those days when King Ahasuerus sat on the throne of his kingdom, which was in Shushan the citadel, ³ that in the third year of his reign he made a feast for all his officials and servants—the powers of Persia and Media, the nobles, and the princes of the provinces being before him— ⁴ when he showed the riches of his glorious kingdom and the splendor of his excellent majesty for many days, one hundred and eighty days in all.

⁵ And when these days were completed, the king made a feast lasting seven days for all the people who were present in Shushan the citadel, from great to small, in the court of the garden of the king's palace. ⁶ There were white and blue linen curtains fastened with cords of fine linen and purple on silver rods and marble pillars; and the couches were of gold and silver on a mosaic pavement of alabaster, turquoise, and white and black marble. ⁷ And they served drinks in golden vessels, each vessel being different from the other, with royal wine in abundance, according to the generosity of the king.

FORTY-SIX: Meme Law states: Memes are insanely jealous and, while having little regard for their members' welfare, Memes demand every measure of their members' being.

HISTORICAL SCRIPTURE

2 Kings 14:7; He (Amaziah) killed ten thousand Edomites in the Valley of Salt, and took Sela by war, and called its name Joktheel to this day.
⁸ Then Amaziah sent messengers to Jehoash the son of Jehoahaz, the son of Jehu, king of Israel, saying, "Come, let us face one another in battle."

17:20; And the Lord rejected all the descendants of Israel, afflicted them, and delivered them into the hand of plunderers, until He had cast them from His sight.

FORTY-SEVEN: Meme Law states: More powerful Meme members always abandon one of their own in times of trouble, especially one of a lower rank. Lower level members, conversely, tend to blindly support one of their own in trouble, except if the leaders order that person abandoned.

HISTORICAL SCRIPTURE

Esther1:9; Queen Vashti also made a feast for the women in the royal palace which belonged to King Ahasuerus.
¹⁰ On the seventh day, when the heart of the king was merry with wine, he commanded seven eunuchs who served in the presence of King Ahasuerus, ¹¹ to bring Queen Vashti before the king, wearing her royal crown, in order to show her beauty to the people and the officials, for she was beautiful to behold. ¹² But Queen Vashti refused to come at the king's command brought by his eunuchs; therefore the king was furious, and his anger burned within him.

2:1-4; After these things, when the wrath of King Ahasuerus subsided, he remembered Vashti, what she had done, and what had been decreed against her. ² Then the king's servants who attended him said: "Let beautiful young virgins be sought for the king; ³ and let the king appoint officers in all the provinces of his kingdom, that they may gather all the beautiful young virgins to Shushan the citadel, into the women's quarters, under the custody of Hegai the king's eunuch, custodian of the women. And let beauty preparations be given them. ⁴ Then let the young woman who pleases the king be queen instead of Vashti."

2:21-23; In those days, while Mordecai sat within the king's gate, two of the king's eunuchs, doorkeepers, became furious and sought to lay hands on King Ahasuerus. ²² So the matter became known to Mordecai, who told Queen Esther, and Esther informed the king in Mordecai's name. ²³ And when an inquiry was made into the matter, it was confirmed, and both were hanged on

Notes

a gallows; and it was written in the book of the chronicles in the presence of the king.

8:15-17; So Mordecai went out from the presence of the king in royal apparel of blue and white, with a great crown of gold and a garment of fine linen and purple; and the city of Shushan rejoiced and was glad. ¹⁶ The Jews had light and gladness, joy and honor. ¹⁷ And in every province and city, wherever the king's command and decree came, the Jews had joy and gladness, a feast and a holiday. Then many of the people of the land became Jews, because fear of the Jews fell upon them.

9:1-5; Now in the twelfth month, that is, the month of Adar, on the thirteenth day, the time came for the king's command and his decree to be executed. On the day that the enemies of the Jews had hoped to overpower them, the opposite occurred, in that the Jews themselves overpowered those who hated them. ² The Jews gathered together in their cities throughout all the provinces of King Ahasuerus to lay hands on those who sought their harm. And no one could withstand them, because fear of them fell upon all people. ³ And all the officials of the provinces, the satraps, the governors, and all those doing the king's work, helped the Jews, because the fear of Mordecai fell upon them. ⁴ For Mordecai was great in the king's palace, and his fame spread throughout all the provinces; for this man Mordecai became increasingly prominent. ⁵ Thus the Jews defeated all their enemies with the stroke of the sword, with slaughter and destruction, and did what they pleased with those who hated them.

JOHN 18:1-9; When Jesus had spoken these words, He went out with His disciples over the Brook Kidron, where there was a garden, which He and His disciples entered. ² And Judas, who betrayed Him, also knew the place; for Jesus often met there with His disciples. ³ Then Judas, having received a detachment of troops, and officers from the chief priests and Pharisees, came there with lanterns, torches, and weapons. ⁴ Jesus therefore, knowing all things that would come upon Him, went forward and said to them, "Whom are you seeking?"

[5] *They answered Him, "Jesus of Nazareth."*

Jesus said to them, "I am He." And Judas, who betrayed Him, also stood with them. [6] *Now when He said to them, "I am He," they drew back and fell to the ground.*

[7] *Then He asked them again, "Whom are you seeking?"*

And they said, "Jesus of Nazareth."

[8] *Jesus answered, "I have told you that I am He. Therefore, if you seek Me, let these go their way,"* [9] *that the saying might be fulfilled which He spoke, "Of those whom You gave Me I have lost none."*

12-24; *Then the detachment of troops and the captain and the officers of the Jews arrested Jesus and bound Him.* [13] *And they led Him away to Annas first, for he was the father-in-law of Caiaphas who was high priest that year.* [14] *Now it was Caiaphas who advised the Jews that it was expedient that one man should die for the people.*

[15] *And Simon Peter followed Jesus, and so did another disciple. Now that disciple was known to the high priest, and went with Jesus into the courtyard of the high priest.* [16] *But Peter stood at the door outside. Then the other disciple, who was known to the high priest, went out and spoke to her who kept the door, and brought Peter in.* [17] *Then the servant girl who kept the door said to Peter, "You are not also one of this Man's disciples, are you?"*

He said, "I am not."

[18] *Now the servants and officers who had made a fire of coals stood there, for it was cold, and they warmed themselves. And Peter stood with them and warmed himself.*

[19] *The high priest then asked Jesus about His disciples and His doctrine.*

[20] *Jesus answered him, "I spoke openly to the world. I always taught in synagogues and in the temple, where the Jews always meet, and in secret I have said nothing.* [21] *Why do you ask Me? Ask those who have heard Me what I said to them. Indeed they know what I said."*

[22] *And when He had said these things, one of the officers who stood by struck Jesus with the palm of his hand, saying, "Do You answer the high priest like that?"*

Notes

23 Jesus answered him, "If I have spoken evil, bear witness of the evil; but if well, why do you strike Me?"

24 Then Annas sent Him bound to Caiaphas the high priest.

TEACHING SCRIPTURE

LUKE 20:9-18; Then He began to tell the people this parable: "A certain man planted a vineyard, leased it to vinedressers, and went into a far country for a long time. 10 Now at vintage-time he sent a servant to the vinedressers, that they might give him some of the fruit of the vineyard. But the vinedressers beat him and sent him away empty-handed. 11 Again he sent another servant; and they beat him also, treated him shamefully, and sent him away empty-handed. 12 And again he sent a third; and they wounded him also and cast him out.

13 "Then the owner of the vineyard said, 'What shall I do? I will send my beloved son. Probably they will respect him when they see him.' 14 But when the vinedressers saw him, they reasoned among themselves, saying, 'This is the heir. Come, let us kill him, that the inheritance may be ours.' 15 So they cast him out of the vineyard and killed him. Therefore what will the owner of the vineyard do to them? 16 He will come and destroy those vinedressers and give the vineyard to others."

And when they heard it they said, "Certainly not!"

17 Then He looked at them and said, "What then is this that is written:

The stone which the builders rejected

Has become the chief cornerstone'?

19-24; So they watched Him, and sent spies who pretended to be righteous, that they might seize on His words, in order to deliver Him to the power and the authority of the governor.

21 Then they asked Him, saying, "Teacher, we know that You say and teach rightly, and You do not show personal favoritism, but teach the way of God in truth: 22 Is it lawful for us to pay taxes to Caesar or not?"

23 But He perceived their craftiness, and said to them, "Why do you test Me? 24 Show Me a denarius. Whose image and inscription does it have?"

They answered and said, "Caesar's."
25 And He said to them, "Render therefore to Caesar the things that are Caesar's, and to God the things that are God's."

FORTY-EIGHT: Meme Law states: Meme members who are given authority to use force on others will do so exponentially and with little reserve. Having received approval from the Ruling Class, the target could be a close friend or family member, but in this case, they are just victims.

FORTY-NINE: Meme Law states: No one in any Meme, including churches, clubs, military and corporations - in ALL Memes, at all levels, is a true friend to any other member. The Meme authority reserves the right to encourage or disallow relations between its members, most of whom will obey the order.

HISTORICAL SCRIPTURE

LUKE 22:1-6; Now the Feast of Unleavened Bread drew near, which is called Passover. 2 And the chief priests and the scribes sought how they might kill Him (Jesus), for they feared the people.
3 Then Satan entered Judas, surnamed Iscariot, who was numbered among the twelve. 4 So he went his way and conferred with the chief priests and captains, how he might betray Him to them. 5 And they were glad, and agreed to give him money. 6 So he promised and sought opportunity to betray Him to them in the absence of the multitude.

LUKE 22:54-65; Having arrested Him, they led Him and brought Him into the high priest's house. But Peter followed at a distance. 55 Now when they had kindled a fire in the midst of the courtyard and sat down together, Peter sat among them. 56 And a certain servant girl, seeing him as he sat by the fire, looked intently at him and said, "This man was also with Him."
57 But he denied Him, saying, "Woman, I do not know Him."
58 And after a little while another saw him and said, "You also are of them." But Peter said, "Man, I am not!"

Notes

⁵⁹ Then after about an hour had passed, another confidently affirmed, saying, "Surely this fellow also was with Him, for he is a Galilean."
⁶⁰ But Peter said, "Man, I do not know what you are saying!"
Immediately, while he was still speaking, the rooster crowed. ⁶¹ And the Lord turned and looked at Peter. Then Peter remembered the word of the Lord, how He had said to him, "Before the rooster crows, you will deny Me three times." ⁶²
So Peter went out and wept bitterly.
22:66-71; As soon as it was day, the elders of the people, both chief priests and scribes, came together and led Him into their council, saying, ⁶⁷ "If You are the Christ, tell us."
But He said to them, "If I tell you, you will by no means believe. ⁶⁸ And if I also ask you, you will by no means answer Me or let Me go. ⁶⁹ Hereafter the Son of Man will sit on the right hand of the power of God."
⁷⁰ Then they all said, "Are You then the Son of God?"
So He said to them, "You rightly say that I am."
⁷¹ And they said, "What further testimony do we need? For we have heard it ourselves from His own mouth."

TEACHING SCRIPTURE

LUKE 12:1-4; In the meantime, when an innumerable multitude of people had gathered together, so that they trampled one another, He began to say to His disciples first of all, "Beware of the leaven of the Pharisees, which is hypocrisy. ² For there is nothing covered that will not be revealed, nor hidden that will not be known. ³ Therefore whatever you have spoken in the dark will be heard in the light, and what you have spoken in the ear in inner rooms will be proclaimed on the housetops.

MATT 10:8–31; ⁴ "And I say to you, My friends, do not be afraid of those who kill the body, and after that have no more that they can do.

ROMANS 8:38-39; For I am persuaded that neither death nor life, nor angels nor principalities nor powers, nor things present nor things to come, ³⁹ nor height nor depth, nor any other created thing, shall be able to separate us from the love of God which is in Christ Jesus our Lord.

EPH 6:10-11; Finally, my brethren, be strong in the Lord and in the power of His might. [11] Put on the whole armor of God, that you may be able to stand against the wiles of the devil. [12] For we do not wrestle against flesh and blood, but against principalities, against powers, against the rulers of the darkness of this age, against spiritual hosts of wickedness in the heavenly places

FIFTY: Meme Law states: The inner workings, failures and disputes within a Meme are seen as "our dirty laundry" and internal secrets, never to be discussed with those outside the Meme.

HISTORICAL SCRIPTURE

Psalm 90:7; For we have been consumed by Your anger,
And by Your wrath we are terrified.
[8] You have set our iniquities before You,
Our secret sins in the light of Your countenance.

TEACHING SCRIPTURE

Duet 29:29; "The secret things belong to the Lord our God, but those things which are revealed belong to us and to our children forever, that we may do all the words of this law.

Psalm 26:5; Oh, how great is Your goodness,
Which You have laid up for those who fear You,
Which You have prepared for those who trust in You
In the presence of the sons of men!
[20] You shall hide them in the secret place of Your presence
From the plots of man;

Notes

You shall keep them secretly in a pavilion
From the strife of tongues.

MATT 6:5; "And when you pray, you shall not be like the hypocrites. For they love to pray standing in the synagogues and on the corners of the streets, that they may be seen by men. Assuredly, I say to you, they have their reward. [6] But you, when you pray, go into your room, and when you have shut your door, pray to your Father who is in the secret place; and your Father who sees in secret will reward you openly. [7]

FIFTY-ONE: Meme Law states: Meme leaders tend to elevate themselves and their decisions, thinking them to be sacrosanct and above other Meme members' understanding, which, in turn, adds to their sense of elitism and superiority. As a result, leaders make secret their rulings, leading to social rupture, illegal actions and often, unnecessary, internal violence.

HISTORICAL SCRIPTURE

Isaiah13:18-15; And you forget the Lord your Maker,
Who stretched out the heavens
And laid the foundations of the earth;
You have feared continually every day
Because of the fury of the oppressor,
When he has prepared to destroy.
And where is the fury of the oppressor?
[14] The captive exile hastens, that he may be loosed,
That he should not die in the pit,
And that his bread should not fail.
[15] But I am the Lord your God,
Who divided the sea whose waves roared—
The Lord of hosts is His name.
[16] And I have put My words in your mouth;

MATT 2:7; Then Herod, when he had secretly called the wise men, determined from them what time the star appeared. ⁸ And he sent them to Bethlehem and said, "Go and search carefully for the young Child, and when you have found Him, bring back word to me, that I may come and worship Him also." ⁹ When they heard the king, they departed; and behold, the star which they had seen in the East went before them, till it came and stood over where the young Child was. ¹⁰ When they saw the star, they rejoiced with exceedingly great joy. ¹¹ And when they had come into the house, they saw the young Child with Mary His mother, and fell down and worshiped Him. And when they had opened their treasures, they presented gifts to Him: gold, frankincense, and myrrh. ¹² Then, being divinely warned in a dream that they should not return to Herod, they departed for their own country another way. 16 Then Herod, when he saw that he was deceived by the wise men, was exceedingly angry; and he sent forth and put to death all the male children who were in Bethlehem and in all its districts, from two years old and under, according to the time which he had determined from the wise men.

FIFTY-TWO: Meme Law states: Within a Master Meme, multi-subordinate Memes will generate, some to enhance and support the work of the host's leadership, some to its detriment and even its destruction.

HISTORICAL SCRIPTURE

Jere 28:15-16; Then the prophet Jeremiah said to Hananiah the prophet, "Hear now, Hananiah, the Lord has not sent you, but you make this people trust in a lie. ¹⁶ Therefore thus says the Lord: 'Behold, I will cast you from the face of the earth. This year you shall die, because you have taught rebellion against the Lord.'"

TEACHING SCRIPTURE

Isaiah 8:19-21; And when they say to you, "Seek those who are mediums and wizards, who whisper and mutter," should not a people seek their God? Should they seek the dead on behalf of the living? [20] To the law and to the testimony! If they do not speak according to this word, it is because there is no light in them. [21] They will pass through it hard-pressed and hungry; and it shall happen, when they are hungry, that they will be enraged and curse their king and their God, and look upward.

MATT 7:15-16; "Beware of false prophets, who come to you in sheep's clothing, but inwardly they are ravenous wolves. [16] You will know them by their fruits. Do men gather grapes from thornbushes or figs from thistles?

FIFTY-THREE: Meme Law states: Memes, even if part of the same Master Meme, becoming subdominant, distrust other like-Memes, even those sharing the same master, and will close down or sabotage each other if they feel threatened, rather than share for the good of all.

HISTORICAL SCRIPTURE

Ezra 4:1,3-5; Now when the adversaries of Judah and Benjamin heard that the descendants of the captivity were building the temple of the Lord God of Israel, [2] they came to Zerubbabel and the heads of the fathers' houses, and said to them, "Let us build with you, for we seek your God as you do; and we have sacrificed to Him since the days of Esarhaddon king of Assyria, who brought us here." [3] But Zerubbabel and Jeshua and the rest of the heads of the fathers' houses of Israel said to them, "You may do nothing with us to build a house for our God; but we alone will build to the Lord God of Israel, as King Cyrus the king of Persia has commanded us." [4] Then the people of the land tried to discourage the people of Judah. They troubled them in building, [5] and hired counselors against them to frustrate their purpose all the days of Cyrus king of Persia, even until the reign of Darius king of Persia.

4:18-22; The letter which you sent to us has been clearly read before me. [19] And I gave the command, and a search has been made, and it was found that this city in former times has revolted against kings, and rebellion and sedition have

been fostered in it. [20] There have also been mighty kings over Jerusalem, who have ruled over all the region beyond the River; and tax, tribute, and custom were paid to them. [21] Now give the command to make these men cease, that this city may not be built until the command is given by me.
[22] Take heed now that you do not fail to do this. Why should damage increase to the hurt of the kings?

FIFTY-FOUR: Meme Law states: Once a person is suspected of crossing a Meme's will or violating its rules, a Meme is relentless, employing all of its members and sub-Memes to neutralize the offender. Safety can be found by the suspected violator only in a hidden sub-Meme or in complete exile from the Meme's territory. Computers and electronic data systems have rendered escape nearly impossible.

HISTORICAL SCRIPTURE

1 Kings19:1-10; And Ahab told Jezebel all that Elijah had done, also how he had executed all the prophets with the sword. [2] Then Jezebel sent a messenger to Elijah, saying, "So let the gods do to me, and more also, if I do not make your life as the life of one of them by tomorrow about this time." [3] And when he saw that, he arose and ran for his life, and went to Beersheba, which belongs to Judah, and left his servant there.
[4] But he himself went a day's journey into the wilderness, and came and sat down under a broom tree. And he prayed that he might die, and said, "It is enough! Now, Lord, take my life, for I am no better than my fathers!"
[5] Then as he lay and slept under a broom tree, suddenly an angel touched him, and said to him, "Arise and eat." [6] Then he looked, and there by his head was a cake baked on coals, and a jar of water. So he ate and drank, and lay down again. [7] And the angel of the Lord came back the second time, and touched him, and said, "Arise and eat, because the journey is too great for you." [8] So he arose, and ate and drank; and he went in the strength of that food forty days and forty nights as far as Horeb, the mountain of God.
[9] And there he went into a cave, and spent the night in that place; and behold, the word of the Lord came to him, and He said to him, "What are you doing

Notes

here, Elijah?"

[10] So he said, "I have been very zealous for the Lord God of hosts; for the children of Israel have forsaken Your covenant, torn down Your altars, and killed Your prophets with the sword. I alone am left; and they seek to take my life."

REV 1:9; I, John, both your brother and companion in the tribulation and kingdom and patience of Jesus Christ, was on the island that is called Patmos (Roman Prison) for the word of God and for the testimony of Jesus Christ.

FIFTY-FIVE: Meme Law states: In any "inner" or "inter" Meme conflict, some leaders involved will need to make personal sacrifices to self and personal wellbeing, even to banishment or death, if stability and wholeness are to emerge from the conflict.

HISTORICAL SCRIPTURE

ACTS 7:58; Then they cried out with a loud voice, stopped their ears, and ran at him with one accord; [58] and they cast him out of the city and stoned him. And the witnesses laid down their clothes at the feet of a young man named Saul. [59] And they stoned Stephen as he was calling on God and saying, "Lord Jesus, receive my spirit." [60] Then he knelt down and cried out with a loud voice, "Lord, do not charge them with this sin." And when he had said this, he fell asleep.

TEACHING SCRIPTURE

MATT 16:24; Then Jesus said to His disciples, "If anyone desires to come after Me, let him deny himself, and take up his cross, and follow Me. [25] For whoever desires to save his life will lose it, but whoever loses his life for My sake will find it. [26] For what profit is it to a man if he gains the whole world, and loses his own soul?

1 JOHN 3:12; In this the children of God and the children of the devil are mani-fest: Whoever does not practice righteousness is not of God, nor is he who does not love his brother. [11] For this is the message that you heard from the begin-ning, that we should love one another, [12] not as Cain who was of the wicked one and murdered his brother. And why did he murder him? Because his works were evil and his brother's righteous.

[13] Do not marvel, my brethren, if the world hates you. [14] We know that we have passed from death to life, because we love the brethren. He who does not love his brother abides in death. [15] Whoever hates his brother is a murderer, and you know that no murderer has eternal life abiding in him.

THREE: UN DECLARATION OF HUMAN RIGHTS

Preamble

Whereas recognition of the inherent dignity and of the equal and inalienable rights of all members of the human family is the foundation of freedom, justice and peace in the world,

Whereas disregard and contempt for human rights have resulted in barbarous acts which have outraged the conscience of mankind, and the advent of a world in which human beings shall enjoy freedom of speech and belief and freedom from fear and want has been proclaimed as the highest aspiration of the common people,

Whereas it is essential, if man is not to be compelled to have recourse, as a last resort, to rebellion against tyranny and oppression, that human rights should be protected by the rule of law,

Whereas it is essential to promote the development of friendly relations between nations,

Whereas the peoples of the United Nations have in the Charter reaffirmed their faith in fundamental human rights, in the dignity and worth of the human person and in the

Notes

equal rights of men and women and have determined to promote social progress and better standards of life in larger freedom,

Whereas Member States have pledged themselves to achieve, in cooperation with the United Nations, the promotion of universal respect for and observance of human rights and fundamental freedoms,

Whereas a common understanding of these rights and freedoms is of the greatest importance for the full realization of this pledge,

Now, therefore,

The General Assembly,

Proclaims this Universal Declaration of Human Rights

as a common standard of achievement for all peoples and all nations, to the end that every individual and every organ of society, keeping this Declaration constantly in mind, shall strive by teaching and education to promote respect for these rights and freedoms and by progressive measures, national and international, to secure their universal and effective recognition and observance, both among the peoples of Member States

themselves and among the peoples of territories under their jurisdiction.

Article I

All human beings are born free and equal in dignity and rights. They are endowed with reason and conscience and should act towards one another in a spirit of brotherhood.

Article 2

Everyone is entitled to all the rights and freedoms set forth in this Declaration, without distinction of any kind, such as race, colour, sex, language, religion, political or other opinion, national or social origin, property, birth or other status.

Furthermore, no distinction shall be made on the basis of the political, jurisdictional or international status of the country or territory to which a person belongs, whether it be independent, trust, non-self-governing or under any other limitation of sovereignty.

Article 3

Everyone has the right to life, liberty and security of person.

Article 4

No one shall be held in slavery or servitude; slavery and the slave trade shall be prohibited in all their forms.

Article 5

No one shall be subjected to torture or to cruel, inhuman or degrading treatment or punishment.

Article 6

Everyone has the right to recognition everywhere as a person before the law.

Article 7

All are equal before the law and are entitled without any discrimination to equal protection of the law. All are entitled to equal protection against any discrimination in violation of this Declaration and against any incitement to such discrimination.

Article 8

Everyone has the right to an effective remedy by the competent national tribunals for acts violating the fundamental rights granted him by the constitution or by law.

Notes

Article 9

No one shall be subjected to arbitrary arrest, detention or exile.

Article 10

Everyone is entitled in full equality to a fair and public hearing by an independent and impartial tribunal, in the determination of his rights and obligations and of any criminal charge against him.

Article 11

1. Everyone charged with a penal offence has the right to be presumed innocent until proved guilty according to law in a public trial at which he has had all the guarantees necessary for his defense.

2. No one shall be held guilty of any penal offence on account of any act or omission which did not constitute a penal offence, under national or international law, at the time when it was committed. Nor shall a heavier penalty be imposed than the one that was applicable at the time the penal offence was committed.

Article 12

No one shall be subjected to arbitrary interference with his privacy, family, home or correspondence, nor to attacks upon his honour and reputation. Everyone has the right to the protection of the law against such interference or attacks.

Article 13

1. Everyone has the right to freedom of movement and residence within the borders of each State.

2. Everyone has the right to leave any country, including his own, and to return to his country.

Article 14

1. Everyone has the right to seek and to enjoy in other countries asylum from persecution.

2. This right may not be invoked in the case of prosecutions genuinely arising from non-political crimes or from acts contrary to the purposes and principles of the United Nations.

Article 15

1. Everyone has the right to a nationality.

2. No one shall be arbitrarily deprived of his nationality nor denied the right to change his nationality.

Article 16

1. Men and women of full age, without any limitation due to race, nationality or religion, have the right to marry and to found a family. They are entitled to equal rights as to marriage, during marriage and at its dissolution.

2. Marriage shall be entered into only with the free and full consent of the intending spouses.

3. The family is the natural and fundamental group unit of society and is entitled to protection by society and the State.

Article 17

1. Everyone has the right to own property alone as well as in association with others.

2. No one shall be arbitrarily deprived of his property.

Notes

Article 18

Everyone has the right to freedom of thought, conscience and religion; this right includes freedom to change his religion or belief, and freedom, either alone or in community with others and in public or private, to manifest his religion or belief in teaching, practice, worship and observance.

Article 19

Everyone has the right to freedom of opinion and expression; this right includes freedom to hold opinions without interference and to seek, receive and impart information and ideas through any media and regardless of frontiers.

Article 20

1. Everyone has the right to freedom of peaceful assembly and association.

2. No one may be compelled to belong to an association.

Article 21

1. Everyone has the right to take part in the government of his country, directly or through freely chosen representatives.

2. Everyone has the right to equal access to public service in his country.

3. The will of the people shall be the basis of the authority of government; this will shall be expressed in periodic and genuine elections which shall be by universal and equal suffrage and shall be held by secret vote or by equivalent free voting procedures.

Article 22

Everyone, as a member of society, has the right to social security and is entitled to realization, through national effort and international co-operation and in accordance with the organization and resources of each State, of the economic, social and cultural rights indispensable for his dignity and the free development of his personality.

Article 23

1. Everyone has the right to work, to free choice of employment, to just and favorable conditions of work and to protection against unemployment.

2. Everyone, without any discrimination, has the right to equal pay for equal work.

3. Everyone who works has the right to just and favorable remuneration ensuring for himself and his family an existence worthy of human dignity, and supplemented, if necessary, by other means of social protection.

4. Everyone has the right to form and to join trade unions for the protection of his interests.

Article 24

Everyone has the right to rest and leisure, including reasonable limitation of working hours and periodic holidays with pay.

Article 25

1. Everyone has the right to a standard of living adequate for the health and well-being of himself and of his family, including food, clothing, housing and medical care and necessary social services, and the right to security in the event of unemployment, sickness, disability, widowhood, old age or other lack of livelihood in circumstances beyond his control.

2. Motherhood and childhood are entitled to special care and assistance. All children, whether born in or out of wedlock, shall enjoy the same social protection.

Notes

Article 26

1. Everyone has the right to education. Education shall be free, at least in the elementary and fundamental stages. Elementary education shall be compulsory. Technical and professional education shall be made generally available and higher education shall be equally accessible to all on the basis of merit.

2. Education shall be directed to the full development of the human personality and to the strengthening of respect for human rights and fundamental freedoms. It shall promote understanding, tolerance and friendship among all nations, racial or religious groups, and shall further the activities of the United Nations for the maintenance of peace.

3. Parents have a prior right to choose the kind of education that shall be given to their children.

Article 27

1. Everyone has the right freely to participate in the cultural life of the community, to enjoy the arts and to share in scientific advancement and its benefits.

2. Everyone has the right to the protection of the moral and material interests resulting from any scientific, literary or artistic production of which he is the author.

Article 28

Everyone is entitled to a social and international order in which the rights and freedoms set forth in this Declaration can be fully realized.

Four:
Introductory Briefing

**at the first presentation of Meme Law to the Academy
by Brinton Minshall, D.Min.
January 5, 2012**

The GREATEST Challenge to Human Civilization in 50,000 Years:

Understanding and Controlling HUMAN SOCIAL MEMES, the Basis of ALL Human Activity. Until now they have been:

Powers / Principalities and the "INVISIBLE HAND" The Great Mystery

Throughout history people have acknowledged the presence of "SOMETHING," "OUT THERE," which alters expected outcomes of intentional plans. Sometimes, this post personal force enhances our best intentions, Creating Gods, Building Cities and Forming Nations. As often as not it "exponentializes" unhealthy situations and is the force behind all human tragedy, Unleashing Devils, Making War and Killing US Dead. We have recognized that even the "Best Laid Plans of Mice and Men…" are constantly interdicted by this "Mysterious Force" and our best efforts are continually sabotaged.

In the Christian scriptures Paul labeled them "**POWERS and PRINCIPALITIES.**" Paul correctly identified the symptoms, but could not identify the mechanics of the process, thus relegating his work to the area of religious mythology.

During the Medieval and Renaissance period (500 - 1400 C. E.), Jewish and Muslim scholars from the Middle East, wrote of invisible forces. They described these as "Arabian Knights," dark angels or Genies and attempted to control the illusive creatures using prayers and sorcery.

At the dawn of the modern era, Economists and Modern Philosophers, found themselves being unable to explain these forces present in all human interactions. Adam Smith

(1776) became stumped in his treatise, "The Wealth of Nations," as he attempted to lay out a modern market society. In the end, he caved, calling them: "**The INVISIBLE HAND.**" Like the ancients, he was trying to fathom why: once a human effort was "out there" in the world, the end result was often a mystery and rarely predictable.

In today's world of "continual combat capitalism," with cradle to grave competition [Meme Law #15], in preparing our populations to "war without question," we name these invisibles forces in our foes "the Evil Empire" or "Worldwide Terrorists." In return, our adversaries title us "The Invisible Satan," as we offer each other up for slaughter [Meme Law #6]. In conjunction with the exhaustive work of E. O. Wilson, Richard Dawkins finally gave our mysterious malady a name - Human Social "**MEMES.**"

The Great Discovery

Over the past twenty-years (1989+), scholars began to get a handle on these illusive forces by exposing their structure. These hidden "monsters' or 'blessings" were in actuality just a nonphysical, preternatural, metaphysical phenomenon, therefore, unseen rather than a physical organism of DNA (products of multiple human minds connected not matter). Scholars, however, rebuked Dawkins saying these were simply CULTURES and nothing else. The problem is any homogeneous group of people, cohabiting a space with some kind of common marker (language, race, religion) while being a "CULTURE" does not necessarily accomplish an action or actions. By way of example while Africans and Asians have had little luck forming societies above the tribe level, Europeans have created Nations then Nation-States and on to Super Nations.

These kinds of actions were not done simply by spontaneous gatherings (cultures) but are the result multiple human connections in our thinking process. Memes were defined as the "connecting of Human BRAINS, which results from the evolving "Social Gene", functioning with other brains to carryout interconnected tasks." These minds work together, "Memed-up" (hooked up), even if separated by thousands of miles. Rather than being joined by language, race or religion they are joined sole be an IDEA.

Today this process is being greatly enhanced by electronic communication technologies (social networks, computer networks). This connective power converts every "Me" involved - into a living part of the social organism: Me + Me or "Meme." The Human Synergy (enhanced mind energy) that results from this teaming-up of minds, creates the STRUCTURE (support skeleton) upon which EVERY Human Social Organism (company, gang, or nation, etc.) is built. We see the resulting organization or joint action, but NOT the underlying structure, the supporting Meme.

The expanding evolution in mass Meme building has created a great wave of change over the earth leading to conflict and paranoia. Today, mass worldwide communication has led to and an exhausting amount of new Meme Organisms mostly unaccountable to each other and to the human Community at large (ISIS for example). Traditional Social Organisms are in disarray suffering with role confusion and abandon creating a world in chaos.

Memes manifest as small as families and as large as nations. They operate as either "**PHANTOM MEMES**" (not organized), "**INFORMAL MEMES**" (casual, but active) or as "**FORMAL MEMES**" (organized, active and legal). There are also "**SUPER MEMES**" some powerful (United States, European Union, Peoples republic of China) others (United Nations, Organization of American States) who have little power. Memes change forms, smaller to larger and vice versa, giant to tiny. However, once created, they last forever. Even if abandoned (Phantom), a Meme is able to be reenergized later (The Confederacy > Jim Crow / Russia > USSR > Russia / Pan American Airlines or the Royal Hawaiian Nation, etc.) [Meme Law #39].

Most of us are involved in multiple Memes, as long as we are part of any social group (family - church - military - company - gang or club).

Our INDIVIDUAL entanglement in each Meme is regulated by the degree of our personal involvement in a Meme's existence: (LEAST: visitor, outsider; MORE: worker or member; MUCH MORE: officer, supporter or promoter; MOST: power wielder or ruler) [Meme Law #2]. The closer to the center (nucleus) of the organism we locate, the

Notes

greater our say over the future of the Meme. BUT, and here's the glitch, "the greater also is the Meme's hold on us as individuals!" [Meme Law #37]

The reason Memes are responsible for the majority of civilization's misery is: "once individual persons enter a Meme (memes-up), to one degree or another, they surrender their personal concepts of morality to the Meme's ruling center."

Therefore, an individual who would never kill another person, will, with little thought, kill thousands while acting as a Meme member (gang member or active military). To reinforce the doing of a Meme's will, the ruling center often bestows **loyal followers, who carry out their tasks, with titles, awards and acclamations**. Those individuals who question the commands of the Meme are **disgraced, shamed and often killed.** Because, when outcomes are positive, people desire to take the credit, but when things go sour, we want to blame some "other being."

A word of caution, however, we often forget how necessary and positive Memes can be [Meme Law #12]. The Cancer Centers of America, the Red Cross and Crescent, the Order of Jesuits, Bank of America and every productive enterprise in history is a Meme. Without Memeing-up, we'd have no families, automobiles or TV sets. While it's true that Memes gave rise to Adolf Hitler, they also lift up a Pope Francis. Memes are neither good nor evil: they are simply "Human Social Constructs" [Meme Law #1].

UNFORTUNATELY: personal and social fear and ignorance, often masquerading as apathy, allow the ruling class to use the power of Memes to destroy civilization for their personal profit.

The Great Truth

At **the Renaissance Institute**, we have contributed by discovering: "ALL Human Social Cells (Memes), like ALL physical cells, operate under "a common **SET of RULES of BEHAVIOR.**" These, approximately, fifty-five **DEFAULT SETTINGS** in group to group and group to member interactions, we have labeled "**MEME LAW.**"

While each type of Meme operates to achieve a differing end result (military unit, labor union, political party etc.), and creates differing Human Social Organisms (Methodist Church, IBM, Federal Reserve Organization etc.), **ALL Memes function under the same rules** because they arise out of the remarkable similarities in the structure of ALL human brains.

Likewise, it is this structuring upon individual minds that explains the variables in Human Society, the caprice in Human activities - **from EXTREME GOOD to PERNICIOUS EVIL.**

Every individual mind, upon which every Meme rides, is attached to the carcass of a wild animal. This primate is subject to the thoughts of its own "Id" (medulla, amygdala) and their instinctual emotions, amplified or muted by the Meme they create. These irrational thoughts are then transferred to the Meme of residence, manifesting as Love or Hate, Peace or War, Anger or Mercy, Contributor or Extractor - literally as **DESTRUCTIVE** or **PRODUCTIVE.**

The Great Question

"**¿Why do ALL OF US need to understand Memes?**" Because ALL news stories, from ISIS to Iran; from Baltimore's racial riots to continual warfare, are examples of Meme behaviors. Meme Laws are the reason behind your downsizing, the sellout of huge corporations creating mass layoffs and the reason a government can't pass simple, common sense laws. ALL these events depend, solely and completely on Meme Law. **Conversely,**

Notes

healthy social actions: Prison Reform, Investor/Depositor Protections and Universal Healthcare, require understanding Meme psychologies to enact and sustain.

By understanding the Memeing process, **WE CAN CEASE** crying:

"¿ *Why did THEY do that?*" **WE SHALL SEE** the reality that makes or breaks our lives and steals our children's future. **WE WILL BE ABLE** to slow the destruction of our planet from climate change, caused by GREEDY Memes acting to EXTRACT every resource from the Earth, while simultaneously, fabricating massive, unearned profits from selling voluminous amounts of unneeded goods! All these are examples of Meme Laws used to blindly control our civilization. Once aware, you will exclaim: "**SO THAT'S THE REASON!!!**" **It's NOT** inevitable, it's NOT God's will, it's NOT human evil, blind luck or an Invisible Hand - It's **Meme Law.**

So, while many of us are afraid of learning these great truths, leading us to an **Understanding of the Hidden Forces that Control Human Existence,** most rulers consider this area of knowledge their private domain. **But with this knowledge in the hands of ALL people, EVERYWHERE, together, let us heal the world by understanding: How Social Organisms work and harness their power to create mass good instead of WAR and EVIL.**

BIBLIOGRAPHY

Angelou, Maya. <u>Celebrations</u>. NY: Random House 2006.

Aristide, Jean-Bertrand. <u>In the Parish of the Poor; Writings from Haiti</u>. NY: Orbis Books 1997.

Baumol, William J.; Robert E. Litan; Carl J. Schramm. <u>Good Capitalism / Bad Capitalism, and the economics of growth and power</u>. New Haven: Yale University Press 2007.

Blin, Arnaud. <u>War and Religion</u>. Oak Land, CA: Univ of California Press 2019

Bloom, Howard. <u>The Lucifer Principle; A Scientific Expedition into the Forces of History</u>. NY: The Atlantic Press 1997.

Bloom, Howard. <u>Global Brain, The Evolution of Mass Mind from the Big Bang to the 21st Century</u>. NY: John Wiley and Sons, Inc. 2000

Bronowski, Jacob with Richard Dawkins. <u>The Accent of Man.</u> London: BBC 1974 reissued 2012

Brooks, David. <u>The Social Animal; the Hidden Sources of Love, Character and Achievement</u>. NY: Random H. 2011.

Butler, Jon. <u>Awash in a Sea of Faith</u>. Cambridge MA: Harvard University Press 1990.

Campbell, Denis G. <u>Egypt Unsh@ckled, Using social media to @#:) the System</u>. Carmarthenshire, Wales: Cambria Books 2011

Notes

Cochran, Gregory and Henry Harpending. <u>The 10,000 Year Explosion; How Civilization Accelerated Human Evolution</u>. NY: Basic Books 2009.

Dawkins, Richard. <u>The God Delusion</u>. Boston: Houghton Mifflin Company 2006.

Dennett, Daniel. <u>From Bacteria to Bach and Back: The evolution of Minds</u>. NY: W.W. Norton; 426 pages, 2017

Erdman, Sarah. <u>Nine Hills To Nambonkaha.</u> NY: Henry Holt and Company 2003

Faux, Jeff. <u>The Global Class War, How America's Bipartisan Elite Lost Our Future – and What It Will Take to Win It Back.</u> Hoboken, NJ: John Wiley and Sons 2006

Fisk, Robert. <u>The Age of the Warrior</u>. NY: Nation Books 2008

Friedman, George. <u>The Next 100 Years; A Forecast for the 21st Century</u>. NY: Anchor Books 2010.

Fukuyama, Francis. <u>The Origins of Political Order From Prehumen Times to the French Revolution.</u> NY: Farrar, Straus and Giroux 2011.

George, Henry. <u>Progress and Poverty</u>. NY: Cosimo Classics 2005 (First published in 1879 by E. P. Dutton George's writings are preserved by the Henry George Institute of New York.

Goleman, Daniel. <u>Social Intelligence, The New Science of Human Relationships</u>. NY: Bantam Books 2006

Gonzales, Laurence. <u>Everyday Survival; Why Smart People Do Stupid Things</u>. NY: W.W. Norton 2008.

Gopnik, Alison. <u>The Gardener and The Carpenter, What the New science of Child development Tells About the Relations Between Parents and Children</u>. NY: Farrar, Straus and Giroux 2016

Grunberg, Leon. <u>Emerging From Turbulence</u>. Lanham, MD: Rowman & Littlefield Publishing Group 2015

Haidt, Jonathan. <u>The Righteous Mind; Why Good People</u> are Divided by Politics and Religion. NY: Random House 2013.

Hamid, Shadi. <u>Temptations of Power: Islamists & Liberal</u> Democracy in a New Middle East. NY: Oxford University Press 2014.

Hamid, Shadi. <u>Temptations of Power</u>. NY: Oxford U. Press and the Brookings Inst 2014

Isenberg, Nancy. <u>White Trash: A 400-Year Untold History of Class in America</u>. NY: Penguin Random House 2012

Klein, Naomi. <u>The Shook Doctrine; The Rise of Disaster</u> Capitalism. NY: Metropolitan Books 2007.

Lorenz, Konrad. <u>On Aggression.</u> NY: Harcourt Brace Jovanovich 1974

Lernoux Penny. <u>Cry of the People</u>. NY: Penguin 1980.

MacLean, Nancy. <u>Democracy in Chains; The Deep History of the Radical Right's Stealth Plan for America</u>. Pittsburg, PA: Dorrance - Publishing 2017

McLynn, Frank. <u>Marcus Aurelius; A Life</u>. Cambridge, MA: DeCapo Books 2009.

O'Connell, Robert L. <u>Ride of the Second Horseman, The Birth and Death of WAR</u>. NY: Oxford University Press 1995

Parsons, Timothy H. <u>The Rules of Empire; Those Who Built Them, Those Who Endured Them and Why They Always Fall</u>. NY: Oxford University Press 2010.

Rauschenbusch, Walter. <u>The Righteousness of the Kingdom. Nashville: Abingdon Press 1968</u>

Notes

Rothkopf, David. <u>Superclass; The Global Power Elite and</u> <u>the World they are making</u>. NY: Farrar, Straus and Giroux 2008.

Stewart, David O., <u>The Summer of 1787, The Men Who</u> <u>Invented the Constitution</u>. NY: Simon & Shuster 2007

Vedantam, Shankar. <u>The Hidden Brain; How Our</u> <u>Unconscious Minds Elect Presidents, Control Markets Wage</u> <u>Wars, and Save Our Lives</u>. NY: Spiegel & Grau 2010.

Thomas, Evan. <u>The War Lovers / Roosevelt, Lodge, Hearst, and the Rush to Empire</u>. NY: Little Brown and Company 2010

Tversky, Barbara. <u>Mind in Motion, How Action Shapes Thought</u>. NY: Basic Books 2019

Wallis, Jim. <u>America's Original Sin</u>. Baker Brazos Press: Ada, MI 2017

Watson, Peter. <u>Ideas, A History of Thought and Invention,</u> <u>from Fire to Freud</u>. NY: Harper Perennial 2005.

Weiner, Tim. <u>Legacy of Ashes; The History of the CIA</u>. NY: Doubleday 2007.

Wilson, E. O. <u>The Social Conquest of Earth</u>. NY: Liveright Publishing Corp. /WW Norton, 2012.

Dedication

We dedicate this work to the many prophetic people, who, throughout the past 50-years have had the courage and conviction to stand-up to injustice, perpetrated by their own people (The MEMEs they were apart of). Many have lost their lives and/or place among their own, with nothing to gain themselves.

To those who are well known like Bishop Oscar Romero and Horace Carter of Tabor City, NC, who along with Dr. Martin Luther King and thousands of involved demonstrators risked and often gave their lives to protect others from tyranny and to make us all into one people.

The Renaissance Institute / *Founded 1993*

For: *The Study of Human Social Memes, documenting their impact on Religious, Political-Military and Economic Global behaviors.*

To: *Understand the links of inner Meme pathologies that endorse the extractive practices of one National Organism and One People over another.*

By: *Exposing, forever, ALL Political - Religious support for International treachery, conquest and War.*

A 501(c) 3 Tax Exempt Non Profit/www.AllOneFamily.net. We pay no salaries Thank you to volunteers.

TOGETHER EVERYONE ACHIEVES MORE

MIRACLES

DISCOVER:

THE Potent Force That Shapes Our WORLD!

WHY Two Separate People Live Inside YOU!

How Humans Create BOTH BAD & GOOD!

QUESTIONS: *How Come:*

Family Reunions Go BADLY?

CEOs Ruin Their Firm – BUT We Pay The PRICE?

Countries WAR Constantly? The BIG Secret!

Religions Teach "LOVE-PEACE" BUT Kill MILLIONS?

HUMAN MEMES:

CREATE Gods, Build Cities, Form NATIONS, *then*

UNLEASH DEVILS, Make WARS and

KILL US DEAD

EASY TO READ / YOUTUBE LINKED

BRITT MINSHALL holds a Doctorate from Boston Univ. in Social Psychology with 20 years as a Facilitator & Pastor.

ISBN: 978-0-57859-949-6

9 780578 599496

$24.95